本书提出了经济新引擎理论。这种新引擎对世界各国而言是新的经济增长极，因此应全力推动以基础设施开发建设为主体的投资新引擎、创新新引擎和规则新引擎。它有别于"贸易引擎"，将促进世界各国经济可持续增长。

New Economic Engine

—Effective Government and
Efficient Market

经济新引擎

——兼论有为政府与有效市场

陈云贤 著　　[澳] Ethan F. Chung 译

外语教学与研究出版社
FOREIGN LANGUAGE TEACHING AND RESEARCH PRESS
北京 BEIJING

图书在版编目（CIP）数据

经济新引擎：兼论有为政府与有效市场：汉英对照／陈云贤著；（澳）钟礼荣
(Ethan F. Chung) 译. −− 北京：外语教学与研究出版社，2019.10（2020.3 重印）
书名原文：New Economic Engine—Effective Government and Efficient Market
ISBN 978−7−5213−1229−4

Ⅰ. ①经… Ⅱ. ①陈… ②钟… Ⅲ. ①中国经济−社会主义市场经济−研究−
汉、英 Ⅳ. ①F123.9

中国版本图书馆 CIP 数据核字 (2019) 第 243897 号

出 版 人　徐建忠
系列策划　吴　浩
责任编辑　赵雅茹
责任校对　易　璐
装帧设计　视觉共振设计工作室
出版发行　外语教学与研究出版社
社　　址　北京市西三环北路 19 号（100089）
网　　址　http://www.fltrp.com
印　　刷　涿州市星河印刷有限公司
开　　本　650×980　1/16
印　　张　19
版　　次　2019 年 10 月第 1 版　2020 年 3 月第 2 次印刷
书　　号　ISBN 978-7-5213-1229-4
定　　价　66.00 元

购书咨询：（010）88819926　电子邮箱：club@fltrp.com
外研书店：https://waiyants.tmall.com
凡印刷、装订质量问题，请联系我社印制部
联系电话：（010）61207896　电子邮箱：zhijian@fltrp.com
凡侵权、盗版书籍线索，请联系我社法律事务部
举报电话：（010）88817519　电子邮箱：banquan@fltrp.com
物料号：312290001

记载人类文明
沟通世界文化
www.fltrp.com

"博雅双语名家名作"出版说明

　　1840 年鸦片战争以降，在深重的民族危机面前，中华民族精英"放眼看世界"，向世界寻求古老中国走向现代、走向世界的灵丹妙药，涌现出一大批中国主题的经典著述。我们今天阅读这些中文著述的时候，仍然深为字里行间所蕴藏的缜密的考据、深刻的学理、世界的视野和济世的情怀所感动，但往往会忽略：这些著述最初是用英文写就，我们耳熟能详的中文文本是原初英文文本的译本，这些英文作品在海外学术界和文化界同样享有崇高的声誉。

　　比如，林语堂的 *My Country and My People*（《吾国与吾民》）以幽默风趣的笔调和睿智流畅的语言，将中国人的道德精神、生活情趣和中国社会文化的方方面面娓娓道来，在美国引起巨大反响——林语堂也以其中国主题系列作品赢得世界文坛的尊重，并获得诺贝尔文学奖的提名。再比如，梁思成在抗战的烽火中写就的英文版《图像中国建筑史》文稿（*A Pictorial History of Chinese Architecture*），经其挚友费慰梅女士（Wilma C. Fairbank）等人多年的奔走和努力，于 1984 年由麻省理工学院出版社（MIT Press）出版，并获得美国出版联合会颁发的"专业暨学术书籍金奖"。又比如，1939 年，费孝通在伦敦政治经济学院的博士论文以 *Peasant Life in China—A Field Study of Country Life in the Yangtze Valley* 为名在英国劳特利奇书局（Routledge）出版，后以《江村经济》作为中译本书名——《江村经济》使得靠桑蚕为生的"开弦弓村"获得了世界性的声誉，成为国际社会学界研究中国农村的首选之地。

　　此外，一些中国主题的经典人文社科作品经海外汉学家和中国学者的如椽译笔，在英语世界也深受读者喜爱。比如，艾恺（Guy S. Alitto）将他1980 年用中文访问梁漱溟的《这个世界会好吗——梁漱溟晚年口述》一书译成英文（*Has Man a Future?—Dialogues with the Last Confucian*），备受海内外读者关注；

此类作品还有徐中约英译的梁启超著作《清代学术概论》（*Intellectual Trends in the Ch'ing Period*）、狄百瑞（W. T. de Bary）英译的黄宗羲著作《明夷待访录》（*Waiting for the Dawn: A Plan for the Prince*），等等。

有鉴于此，外语教学与研究出版社推出"博雅双语名家名作"系列。

博雅，乃是该系列的出版立意。博雅教育（Liberal Education）早在古希腊时代就得以提倡，旨在培养具有广博知识和优雅气质的人，提高人文素质，培养健康人格，中国儒家六艺"礼、乐、射、御、书、数"亦有此功用。

双语，乃是该系列的出版形式。英汉双语对照的形式，既同时满足了英语学习者和汉语学习者通过阅读中国主题博雅读物提高英语和汉语能力的需求，又以中英双语思维、构架和写作的形式予后世学人以启迪——维特根斯坦有云："语言的边界，乃是世界的边界"，诚哉斯言。

名家，乃是该系列的作者群体。涵盖文学、史学、哲学、政治学、经济学、考古学、人类学、建筑学等领域，皆海内外名家一时之选。

名作，乃是该系列的入选标准。系列中的各部作品都是经过时间的积淀、市场的检验和读者的鉴别而呈现的经典，正如卡尔维诺对"经典"的定义：经典并非你正在读的书，而是你正在重读的书。

胡适在《新思潮的意义》（1919 年 12 月 1 日，《新青年》第 7 卷第 1 号）一文中提出了"研究问题、输入学理、整理国故、再造文明"的范式。秉着"记载人类文明、沟通世界文化"的出版理念，我们推出"博雅双语名家名作"系列，既希望能够在中国人创作的和以中国为主题的博雅英文文献领域"整理国故"，亦希望在和平发展、改革开放的新时代为"再造文明"、为"向世界说明中国"略尽绵薄之力。

PREFACE

There are at least three main highlights in *New Economic Engine—Effective Government and Efficient Market*:

1. Breaking Through the Limitations of the Mainstream Western Economics System and the Market Theory Framework

The book is divided into nine chapters and one appendix. The first chapter looks at how Adam Smith's third book attempted to analyze the dealings of government, and explores the roles governments should play and their functions. The second chapter reveals that John Maynard Keynes did not explain why national governments should participate or even be one of the main subjects in promoting infrastructure investment and construction, but he hastily launched a series of measures of governmental intervention in effective demand. The third chapter explicitly states that "resource generation" research is virgin ground in current mainstream economic theories. The fourth chapter points out that the government is a competitor in the field of "generative resources". The fifth chapter describes government competition in its broad and narrow senses. The sixth chapter describes the three levels of efficient market. The seventh chapter describes the three levels of performance for an effective government. The eighth chapter expresses the view that there are nine modes of combinations of an effective government and efficient market. The ninth chapter proposes the need to build up the new economic engine in the field of generative resources. The appendix proposes to build up the framework of "mezzoeconomics".

In its entirety, the book breaks through the limitations of Western mainstream economics system and the market theory framework. Firstly, as to the theory of market economy, this book suggests that a mature market economy is an "effective government plus efficient market" economy. Specifically, this book analyzes the "horizontal system of market economy", that is, resource allocation, resource scarcity, resource generation, and the roles of livelihood economy, industrial economy, urban economy and others in the horizontal system of the market. It explores the "vertical system of market economy", that is, the market factor system, market organization system, market legal system, market supervision system, market environment system and market infrastructure. These six subsystems form an organic whole in

序　言

《经济新引擎——兼论有为政府与有效市场》至少有三大亮点：

一、突破了西方主流经济学体系和市场理论框架的局限

全书有九章和一个附录。第一章揭示亚当·斯密的第三本书对国家政府行为的分析，并由此探讨政府应该扮演的角色和具有的职能。第二章指出，凯恩斯没有回答国家政府为什么可以作为参与者甚至主要主体之一去推动基础设施投资建设，却匆匆忙忙推出了一系列政府干预有效需求的措施。第三章直接表明，"资源生成"研究在当今的主流经济学理论中是个空白。第四章提出，政府在"生成性资源"领域是个竞争主体。第五章论述政府竞争有广义、狭义范畴。第六章阐述了有效市场的三个层次划分。第七章提出了有为政府的三个层次的表现。第八章认为，有为政府与有效市场的结合有九种模式选择。第九章倡议，应构建生成性资源领域的"经济新引擎"。附录展开了架构"中观经济学"的设想。

通观全文，本书突破了西方主流经济学体系和市场理论框架的局限：首先，在市场经济理论方面，本书提出成熟的市场经济是"强式有为政府＋强式有效市场"的经济。具体来说，本书分析了"市场经济横向体系"，即资源配置、资源稀缺、资源生成，以及民生经济、产业经济、城市经济和各类型经济在市场横向体系中的角色、作用；探讨了"市场经济纵向体系"，即市场要素体系、市场组织体系、市场法制体系、市场监管体系、市场环境体系和市场基础设施，这六个子系统组成了市场规则在其中发挥作用，实现公

which market rules exert their effects and realize openness, fairness and justice. It analyzes the "dual competitors in the market", that is, the main competitor in industrial economy is the enterprise, the main competitor in urban economy is the government; the two competitors are distinguishable from each other, and yet interrelated, becoming the dual driving forces behind the industrial upgrading and national development across the world. It points out that both industrial and urban economic competitions must abide by the rules of the market; enterprises and governments, being the dual main competitors, must firstly abide by the rules of the market, participate in market competition, and at the same time, governments should function in a better way. It suggests that many theoretical and practical problems faced by nations in their economic development are not the problems of the market itself, but stem from defects of traditional market theory and a void of modern market theory.

Secondly, as to the economics system, the book proposes to establish a "mezzoeconomics" framework: Microeconomics takes the industrial economy as the carrier and develops a fairly complete discussion from the analysis of commodities, prices, supply and demand, competition, and equilibrium; whilst macroeconomics, under the circumstances of economic globalization, is feasible on one hand, but needs reform and innovation on the other hand. Henceforth, a mezzoeconomics system should be established, in which the effects of government competition are demonstrated in the allocation of newly generated resources, with regional economy or urban economy as its operating carrier, regional government as one of the main competitors. It has a positive effect of innovation and development on correcting the defects of the traditional economics system and filling the void left by the existing economics system.

Finally, as to economic growth across the world, this book puts forward the theory of new economic engine. This new engine is in the field of resource generation, different from industrial economy and livelihood economy. It is manifested at the current stage in the development of the urban economy, whose main content is the investment and construction of software and hardware infrastructure and the development and operation of intelligent cities (followed by the development and operation of space resources, deep-sea resources, polar economy and network economy). This new engine is a new pole of economic growth for the world. Thus, every effort should be made to promote new engines on investment, innovation and regulations with infrastructure development and construction as the main content. It is different from the "trade engine", and will promote sustainable economic growth across the world.

开、公平、公正的有机整体；分析了"市场竞争双重主体"，即产业经济竞争主体主要是企业，城市经济竞争主体主要是政府，两者相互区分，互相联系，成为各国产业提升和国家发展的双重原动力，指出产业经济竞争和城市经济竞争都需要遵循市场规则，企业和政府作为双重竞争主体，首要的仍是遵循市场规则，参与市场竞争，同时政府在其中更好地发挥作用；提出了世界各国经济发展中存在的很多理论与实践问题，不是市场本身的问题，而是源于传统市场理论的缺陷和现代市场理论的空白。

其次，在经济学体系方面，本书提出了创建中观经济学架构的设想：微观经济学以产业经济为载体，从商品、价格、供求、竞争、均衡分析入手展开的阐述较具完整性；而宏观经济学在全球经济一体化的格局中具有可行的一面，又有需要改革创新之处；因此应创立以区域经济或城市经济作为运行载体、区域政府作为竞争主体之一，并在新生成性资源配置中发挥政府竞争作用的中观经济学体系。这对纠正传统经济学体系的缺陷和填补现有经济学体系的空白，有着积极的创新发展作用。

最后，在世界各国经济增长方面，本书提出了经济新引擎理论。这种新引擎，在资源生成领域，有别于产业经济和民生经济，现阶段主要体现在以基础设施软硬件投资建设乃至智能城市开发运营为主体的城市经济发展中（接下来还会逐步体现在太空资源、深海资源以及极地经济、网络经济的开发运营中）。这种新引擎对世界各国而言是新的经济增长极，因此应全力推动以基础设施开发建设为主体的投资新引擎、创新新引擎和规则新引擎。它有别于"贸易引擎"，将促进世界各国经济可持续增长。

2. Correctly Explaining the Successful Experience of China's Reform and Opening Up over the Past 40 Years from an Economic Perspective

This book explores the dual attributes of regional governments. Regional governments, in comparison with the world or the central government, are "quasi-macro" and "quasi-micro". The "quasi-macro" attribute emphasizes "coordination"; the "quasi-micro" attribute emphasizes "interests". Such dual attributes prompt regional governments to implement policies of "general underpinning, fairness and justice, and effective promotion" in the livelihood economy, "planning and guidance, support and coordination, supervision and management" in the industrial economy, and "participation in competition, supervision in allocation" in the urban economy.

This book analyzes the dual competitions in the market. In industrial economy, there is market competition with enterprises as main competitors, and in urban economy, there is market competition with governments as main competitors. Through the buildup of the "new economic engine" mentioned above, governments continuously explore new economic growth points and promote the sustainable growth of the national economy.

This book points out that a mature market economy must be an organic integration of strong effective governments with strong efficient markets that operates in an orderly manner. In accordance with the major functions of the six subsystems of the modern market system, efficient market can be divided into three levels: "weak", "semi-strong", "strong". In accordance with whether or not there are supporting policies and measures for livelihood economy, industrial economy and urban economy, effective government can be divided into three levels: "weak", "semi-strong", "strong". The organic combinations of the two form the nine modes of "effective government plus efficient market". Among these, "strong effective government plus strong efficient market" is the targeted mode for a mature market economy. It can be said that up until the present, China's market economic mode still needs to be upgraded, whilst the US market economic mode is not yet a mature market economy.

This book puts forward the view of government foresighted leading (GFL). The premise of government foresighted leading is to rely on market rules and market mechanism. The principles of government foresighted leading are that the market decides the allocation of resources,

二、从经济学角度正确解释了中国改革开放四十年来的成功经验

第一，本书探讨了区域政府的双重属性。区域政府相对于全球或国家来说，具有"准宏观"属性和"准微观"属性。准宏观属性强调的是"协调"，准微观属性强调的是"利益"。这样的双重属性促使区域政府在民生经济中实施"基本托底、公平公正、有效提升"政策，在产业经济中实施"规划、引导，扶持、调节，监督、管理"政策，在城市经济中实施"参与竞争、调配监督"政策。

第二，本书分析了市场双重竞争行为，即在产业经济领域，存在以企业为主体的市场竞争，在城市经济领域，存在以政府为主体的市场竞争。政府通过对前文所说的"经济新引擎"的建设，不断开拓新的经济增长点，推动一国经济的可持续增长。

第三，本书指出，成熟市场经济一定是强式有为政府与强式有效市场有机结合、有序运行的经济。有效市场按现代市场体系六大子系统发挥作用的情况，分为"弱式""半强式""强式"三个层次；有为政府按国家对民生经济、产业经济和城市经济配套政策措施的有无，分为"弱式""半强式""强式"三个层面：这二者的有机结合形成"有为政府＋有效市场"的九种模式选择。其中，"强式有为政府＋强式有效市场"是成熟市场经济的目标模式。可以说，至今为止，中国的市场经济模式仍有需要提升之处；而美国的市场经济模式也还不是成熟的市场经济。

第四，本书提出了政府超前引领的观点。政府超前引领的前提是依靠市场规则和市场机制；政府超前引领的原则是市场决定资源配置，同时政府对产业经济发挥导向、调节、预警作用，对城市经

and at the same time, the government guides, adjusts, and forewarns in the industrial economy, allocates, participates in and maintains order in the urban economy, and guarantees, underpins and promotes in the livelihood economy. The measures of government foresighted leading are to use policies of planning, investment, consumption, price, taxation, interest rate, exchange rate, law, and others to innovate in value, institution, organization and technology. The purpose of government foresighted leading is to promote the structural reform on the supply side or demand side, forming the leading edge in economic growth and a path towards scientific and sustainable development. This ensures that enterprises do what they should do, and governments do what enterprises cannot do and what enterprises cannot do well; neither of them can be absent.

This book explores innovation in government competition, and points out that the government competes in nine aspects, including competitions in projects, supporting industrial chains, talent, science and technology, treasury and finance, infrastructure, imports and exports, environmental systems, policy systems, and management efficiencies. Governments in competition need to innovate constantly: "innovations in values" substantially promote resource allocation during a nation's factor-driven stage, "innovations in organizational management" have multiplier effects on resource allocation during a nation's investment-driven stage, and "innovations in institutions and technologies" have crucial effects on resource allocation during a nation's innovation-driven stage. Continuous all-round innovations throughout the process in all factors can promote scientific and sustainable development of resource allocation at various stages of development across the world.

3. Developing a New Economics System and Market Theory with China Providing Extensive Materials for Its Development (Though not Uniquely Chinese)

This book develops a mezzoeconomics system and modern market theory, which breaks away from the fields of Adam Smith's industrial economy or microeconomics, while completely differing from the theoretical nature, research focus, government behavior, and operation modes of the Keynesian government intervention theory. It can be said that this book is devoted to exploring the revolutionary innovation of market economy theory and economics system.

济发挥调配、参与、维序作用，对民生经济发挥保障、托底、提升作用；政府超前引领的手段是运用规划、投资、消费、价格、税收、利率、汇率、法律等政策，开展理念、制度、组织、技术创新；政府超前引领的目的是推动供给侧或需求侧结构性改革，形成经济增长的领先优势和科学、可持续的发展路径。这确保了企业做企业该做的事，政府做企业做不了和做不好的事，二者都不空位、虚位。

第五，本书探讨了政府竞争创新，指出政府处于九方面的竞争中，包括项目竞争、产业链配套竞争、人才科技竞争、财政金融竞争、基础设施竞争、进出口竞争、环境体系竞争、政策体系竞争和管理效率竞争。竞争中的政府需要不断创新，其中，理念创新在一国要素驱动阶段对资源配置有实质推动作用，组织管理创新在一国投资驱动阶段对资源配置具有乘数效应，制度与技术创新在一国创新驱动阶段对资源配置具有关键制胜作用，全方位、全过程、全要素的不断创新在一国发展的各阶段均能促进资源配置科学、可持续发展。

三、创建了新经济学体系和市场理论，虽无"中国"这个定语，但中国为这一理论的发展提供了广阔素材

本书创建了中观经济学体系与现代市场理论，跳出了亚当·斯密的产业经济领域或微观经济学范畴，又与凯恩斯主义政府干预理论的理论本质、研究重点、政府行为和运行模式等完全相异。可以说，本书致力于探索市场经济理论和经济学体系的颠覆性创新。

The American economist, Milton Friedman, commented that whoever accurately explained China's reform and development would win a Nobel Prize in Economics. China's economic development has become an important phenomenon in the world economy. The theoretical research and empirical analysis of China's economic development will certainly become one of the important achievements of world economic theories, which needs to be based on the exploration of China's reform and opening up, economic development and mode of operation, and also needs to learn from the practical development and research findings of the world economy. The great era has provided us with all of these.

Many people describe my life as "three-staged". Since the reform and opening up, I have spent more than 10 years in universities, more than 10 years in financial enterprises, and more than 10 years in the government; at the same time, I have studied at Harvard University, Yale University, University of Massachusetts in the US and Toronto University in Canada successively. Henceforth, this humble book of not many words, not only discusses the economic situations in countries like the United States, Britain, Germany, ROK, Singapore and organizations such as the World Bank and the International Monetary Fund; but also follows the course of my work, thought, research in practice, and distillation in analysis in the forefront of China's reform and opening up with my experience as Secretary of Shunde District Committee of the CPC, Secretary of Foshan Municipal Committee of the CPC and Mayor of Foshan City, and Vice-Governor of Guangdong Province.

The relationship between government and market is like Goldbach's conjecture in economics. From the definitions of the three types of resources in the world to the characteristics of resource allocation at various stages of economic development across the world, this book reveals the dual economic attributes of the government, and points out that there are dual competitors in the market, and that a mature market economy needs the organic combination of strong effective government and strong efficient market; that successful governments across the world cannot do without foresighted leading, and that governments need to compete in innovations and innovate in competitions. Thereby, new economic growth points and new paths to new economic engines can be found in the field of resource generation across the world. China's reform and opening up and innovative developments have provided a wide range of materials and resources for this theory; the results of this research will be integrated into world economic theories and serve the economic development and economic growth across the world.

美国经济学家米尔顿·弗里德曼说:"谁能正确解释中国改革和发展,谁就能获得诺贝尔经济学奖。"中国经济的发展成为世界经济中的重要现象,对中国经济发展的理论研究和实证分析,必将成为世界性经济理论的重要成果之一。它需立足于探索中国的改革开放、经济发展和运行模式,又需借鉴和吸收世界经济的实践发展和研究成果,伟大的时代为我们提供了这一切。

人们说我的人生是"三段式"的:改革开放以来,十多年在高校,十多年在金融企业,十多年在政府,同时又先后赴美国哈佛大学、耶鲁大学、马萨诸塞大学和加拿大多伦多大学学习。因此,字数不多的拙著,不仅探讨了美国、英国、德国、韩国、新加坡和世界银行、国际货币基金组织等经济相关情况,更是立足于自己历任顺德区委书记,佛山市市长、市委书记,广东省副省长的工作实践,总结了我在这片中国改革开放前沿热土上扎实工作、潜心思考、在实践中研思、在分析中升华的历程。

"政府与市场"关系,可谓经济学中的哥德巴赫猜想。拙著从世界各国三类资源界定,到各国经济发展不同阶段资源配置的特征,揭示出政府的双重经济属性,指出市场存在双重竞争主体,成熟市场经济需要强式有为政府与强式有效市场的有机结合,世界各国成功的政府都离不开超前引领,政府需要在创新中竞争、在竞争中创新,于是,就有了在世界各国的资源生成性领域,找到经济增长点,开拓经济新引擎之路径。中国的改革开放、创新发展为这一理论提供了广泛的素材和资源,这一研究成果又将融入于世界经济理论、服务于世界各国经济发展与经济增长过程之中。

CHAPTER 1   WHAT COULD BE THE CONTENTS OF ADAM SMITH'S THIRD BOOK?

1. The Biography of Adam Smith

Adam Smith (1723-1790), renowned English social philosopher and political economist, is the key representative figure of classical political economics.

Adam Smith's father was a customs controller in Scotland, and his mother was the daughter of a hereditary landowner. At the age of 14, Adam Smith became a student at the University of Glasgow, receiving a good education in this famous center of Enlightenment. There, Smith was moved by his mentor, Francis Hutcheson, a renowned moral philosopher, whose philosophy profoundly influenced his subsequent moral philosophy and economic views.

In 1740, Adam Smith graduated from the University of Glasgow with honors and went to Oxford to continue his education. There, he relentlessly self-educated and explored, acquiring substantial amounts of knowledge in classical and contemporary philosophy.

In 1751, aged 28, Adam Smith was appointed professor of logic at the University of Glasgow. In 1752, he turned to the field of moral philosophy to research in natural theology, ethics, jurisprudence and political economics.

In 1759, aged 36, Smith published his first work, *The Theory of Moral Sentiments*. This work laid the foundation in psychological behavior analysis for his later book, *The Wealth of Nations*.

In 1776, aged 53, Smith completed the famous *An Inquiry into the Nature and Causes of the Wealth of Nations*, which continually exerts important influence even to this day. This book looked deeply into the behavior of market economy and the complex political economics system, rendering Adam Smith a towering figure in the history of economic thoughts even to this day.

Upon completing his second masterpiece, Smith spent more than ten years exploring, thinking and investigating, and attempted to write a third book speculated to be on "the general principles of law and government". In 1790, at the age of 67 however, Smith's life, filled with honors and recognition, ended with a little pity.

壹 亚当·斯密第三本书的内容会是什么?

一、亚当·斯密简介

亚当·斯密（1723—1790），英国著名的社会哲学家和政治经济学家，古典政治经济学的代表人物。

亚当·斯密的父亲是苏格兰当地的一名海关监督，母亲则是当地一名世袭土地主的女儿。斯密十四岁进入格拉斯哥大学——在这个苏格兰著名的启蒙中心，斯密受到了良好的教育。期间，斯密的导师、著名的人性道德行为哲学家弗朗西斯·哈奇森教授的哲学思想深深地打动了斯密，并对斯密后来形成的道德哲学和经济思想产生了极为深刻的影响。

1740年，斯密以卓越的成绩从格拉斯哥大学毕业，尔后到牛津大学求学。在那里，斯密通过不断的自学探索，获取了大量的古典和当代哲学知识。

1751年，斯密时年28岁，被委任为格拉斯哥大学逻辑学教授。1752年，斯密转入道德哲学领域，从事自然神学、伦理学、法学和政治经济学的研究。

1759年，斯密时年36岁，发表了他的第一部著作《道德情操论》。这部著作也为其后完成的《国富论》奠定了心理行为分析的基础。

1776年，斯密时年53岁，完成了至今还有着重要影响的名著《国富论》。该著作对市场经济行为、对复杂的政治经济学体系作出了深刻分析，使亚当·斯密成为经济思想史的灯塔人物，并至今闪烁着光辉。

斯密在完成第二部巨著之后，花费十多年时间探索思研，曾试图撰写出第三本著作《政府与法律论》。但令人遗憾的是，1790年，时年67岁的斯密，带着一生盛誉和一点惋惜离开了人世。

In accordance with the custom at that place of his time, Smith's files and his personal possessions were destroyed rather than preserved following his passing. This rendered his unfinished third book and its core ideas a conjecture for later generations.

Adam Smith's biography described him as a man who was totally oblivious and paid little attention to all things other than those associated with learning and acquiring knowledge. He would be in a ball and might not even recognize his dance partner; he might unwittingly add butter and bread into the teapot when making tea, and complain later about the poor taste; he might be taking a morning stroll and whilst enjoying a deep breath of fresh air, fall into a bout of deep contemplation only to realize he had already ventured 15 miles away from home still dressed in his night gown. During his tenure as Commissioner of Customs, he received numerous gun salutes, and possibly in his attempt to reciprocate the gesture, performed an elaborate drill with his cane. Delivering papers and speeches in unfamiliar surrounds, Smith would initially stutter out of shyness, but once he familiarized himself with the surrounds, he would speak eloquently, fluently and uninhibitedly.[2]

During Adam Smith's era in the 18th century, Britain was experiencing a transition from workshop handicraft to mechanical industry. In the early 18th century, France and Germany remained at an infantile feudal stage dominated by cottage handicraft. Britain, on the other hand, had entered capitalist stage where workshop handicraft had developed in cities across the nation. Under the direction of a capitalist, many workers used simple tools to cooperate with due division of labor in a workshop. This is the characteristic of workshop handicraft. Such a scenario continued until 1760, when the Industrial Revolution took place and industries using machineries emerged. At that time, Britain was not only the center of world trade, but a leading industrialized country.

What can be concluded is that: (1) Adam Smith lived during the era of the onset of the British Industrial Revolution. Industrialization just commenced, though urbanization did not. It was precisely the moment at the onset of revolution. (2) Adam Smith's father was a customs controller, and his mother was the daughter of a rich landowner from a family with substantial wealth and social status. As the revolution started and unfolded, Adam Smith did not show any obvious inclination towards the pursuit of wealth, but was instead immersed in academia and learning.

根据当地当时的风俗习惯，斯密的所有文稿，包括他生平的私人物品，伴随着他的离世都被销毁一空。这使得斯密未完成的第三部著作及其核心思想，成为后人研究的一个猜想。

《亚当·斯密传》是这样描述的：亚当·斯密在对待学问以外的事情时总是心不在焉——他可能在舞会上认不出他的舞伴；沏茶时他可能会把黄油面包放进茶壶里，然后抱怨饮料的味道太差；早晨起来他在花园里散步并用力吸入新鲜空气，在一阵沉思默想之后，才发现自己穿着睡袍已经到了离家 15 英里 **1** 以外的地方了。在任海关专员时他无数次受到持枪敬礼的礼遇，可能是试图回礼，他用手杖表演了一套精心操练的动作。他在陌生的环境发表文章或演说时，刚开始会因害羞频频口吃，一旦熟悉后便恢复辩才，侃侃而谈。**2**

亚当·斯密所处的 18 世纪的英国，正值工场手工业向机器大工业过渡的时期。18 世纪前期的法国和德国，尚停留在幼稚的封建的家庭手工业阶段。但英国却已经走入资本主义阶段，工场手工业已经在国内各大城市发展起来，其特点是许多工人在一个工场劳动，在一个资本家的指挥下，使用简单的工具，分工作业。此情景一直延续到 1760 年以后发生产业革命、使用机械的大工业出现为止。当时英国不仅是世界贸易的中心国，而且是领先其他国家的工业国。

综上可知，首先，亚当·斯密所处的时代是英国工业革命刚刚开始的时代——工业化进程刚刚开始，城市化进程还未启动，这是开始变革的时代。其次，其父亲是海关监督，母亲是土地主的女儿，家庭较有地位和富裕。在这一变革过程中，亚当·斯密没有明显地去追逐财利，而是更多地沉浸在学术、学问之中。最后，亚当·

(3) Adam Smith produced only three books in his lifetime, each of which took him more than 10 years of intense research. He was already a university professor at the age of 28, and completed his first book *The Theory of Moral Sentiments* at the age of 36, investigating the social behavior and moral sentiments of people. Subsequently, Adam Smith turned his attention towards commodity pricing, supply and demand, competition, market, and the behaviors of industries, and ventured into the circle of businessmen in London; 17 years later, aged 53, he completed his second book *An Inquiry into the Nature and Causes of the Wealth of Nations*. Thereafter, not content with just enjoying the fame and fortune bestowed upon him by *The Wealth of Nations*, Adam Smith went to the customs, acknowledged then as the true source of wealth, where the import and export among nations were highly collectively reflected, and worked as a customs officer, just as his father did. There was speculation that, Adam Smith worked as a customs officer for about 14 years, during which he studied government's duties, functions, powers, laws and regulations in practice, and at the age of 67, began writing his third book, *The General Principles of Law and Government*. Regrettably, the third book was never published. But what could be postulated was that, Smith has led a life of learning and contemplating, analyzing and revealing the attributes of the behavior of individuals, industries, and states, and the principles and laws governing the market and economic bodies.

2. Analysis of the Contents of Adam Smith's Third Book

Adam Smith's academic thoughts were influenced not only by the growing and booming British industry, the theories of the physiocratic school, especially François Quesnay's and Anne Robert Jacques Turgot's, and David Hume's trade and monetary theories; but in particular, the philosophy of his mentor at the University of Glasgow, Francis Hutcheson. The philosophy proposed by Francis Hutcheson that people themselves could discover what is ethically good by discovering the actions that serve the good of humankind, had profoundly shaped Adam Smith's research on (benevolent) behavior of individuals in society, (beneficial) behavior of industries in the market, and even his later attempt to analyze the (benevolent) behavior of government.

Adam Smith's First Book, *The Theory of Moral Sentiments*

The Theory of Moral Sentiments is made up of seven parts. The first part looks at the propriety of actions. The second part discusses merits and demerits, that is, the objects of rewards and punishment. The third

斯密一生只研撰三本书，而且每本书都深入研究十几年：他28岁就已经是大学教授，36岁完成了第一部著作《道德情操论》，研究人的社会行为与道德情操。此后他转而研究商品价格、供求、竞争、市场、企业行为，并出入于伦敦的商人圈，17年后的53岁完成第二部著作《国富论》。紧接着，他没有去享受《国富论》带来的赞誉和财富的增长，而是效仿他父亲，担任海关官员——海关在当时被认为是财富的真正源泉，并高度集中地反映了国与国之间的进出口贸易情况。按时间推断，斯密在海关先后工作了约14年，亲身实践并研究国家政府的职责、职能、权力与法律规则，并在67岁左右着手撰写第三本著作《政府与法律论》。遗憾的是，这第三本书未能面世，但可以推测，亚当·斯密的一生是学习的人生，思索的人生，揭示分析个人、企业、国家行为属性的人生，揭示市场和经济主体本质规律的人生。

二、亚当·斯密的第三本书内容分析

亚当·斯密的学术思想，既受到当时英国工业蓬勃发展上升的时代影响，又受到重农学派特别是魁奈、杜尔哥以及后来休谟的贸易与货币经济学理论的影响，更受到他在格拉斯哥大学的导师弗朗西斯·哈奇森的哲学思想影响。哈奇森提出的"人们可以通过发现对人类有益的行为来认识从理论上来说什么是好的"的哲理，深深左右着亚当·斯密对社会中个人的（有益的）行为、对市场中企业的（有益的）行为，甚至后来对国家政府的（有益的）行为的探研。

亚当·斯密的第一本书《道德情操论》

《道德情操论》共分七部分：第一篇，论行为的合宜性；第二篇，

part talks about the foundation of our judgments concerning our own sentiments and conduct, and the sense of duty. The fourth part relates the effects of utility on the sentiment of approbation. The fifth part goes into the influence of custom and fashion on the sentiments of moral approbation and disapprobation. The sixth part defines character of virtue. The seventh part investigates systems of moral philosophy.

In the book, Adam Smith uses human emotions and empathies as the basic principle to decipher the roots of justice, benevolence, self-denial, and other moral sentiments, explain the nature and principles of moral evaluation and the characteristics of virtues, and introduce and evaluate other schools of thoughts on moral philosophy, revealing the foundation on which human society maintains and develops harmoniously, and some basic morals humans should adhere to.

Concepts such as "human nature", "one's own behavior", "self-preservation", "selfishness", "inner self", "impartial spectator", "self-control", "sympathy", "inner conflict", "profit seeker", "invisible hand" "empathy", "social creatures", etc., are key words in the book. Compassion, being an invisible hand, is regulating individual social behavior, promoting the organic integration of selfishness and sympathy, thereby defining the essence of human nature. Through this book, Adam Smith, for the first time, presents and demonstrates the philosophy imparted by his mentor, Francis Hutcheson, that people themselves could discover what is ethically good by discovering the actions that serve the good of humankind.

Adam Smith's Second Book, *An Inquiry into the Nature and Causes of the Wealth of Nations*

The Wealth of Nations is divided into five parts. Book I (11 chapters in total) describes the causes of improvement in the productive powers of labor, and of the order by which its produce is naturally distributed among the different ranks of the people; Book II (5 chapters in total) examines the nature, accumulation and employment of stock; Book

III (4 chapters in total) distinguishes different progress of opulence in different nations; Book IV (9 chapters in total) elaborates on systems of political economy; Book V (3 chapters in total) discusses the revenue of the sovereign or commonwealth, which is closely related to our subject here. In Book V, Chapter 1 is on the expenses of the sovereign or commonwealth. Specifically, Part 1 is on the expense of defense, Part 2 on the expense of justice, Part 3 on the expenses of public works and

论功劳与过失，即论奖赏与惩罚的对象；第三篇，论我们品评自己情感与行为的基础，并论义务感；第四篇，论效用对赞许感的影响；第五篇，论社会习惯与时尚对道德赞许与谴责等情感的影响；第六篇，论好品格；第七篇，论道德哲学体系。

在书中，亚当·斯密用人类的情感和同情心作为基本原理，来阐释正义、仁慈、克己等一切道德情操产生的根源，说明道德评价的性质、原则以及各种美德的特征，并对各种道德哲学学说进行了介绍和评价，进而揭示出人类社会赖以维系、和谐发展的基础，以及人的行为应遵循的一般道德准则。

这里，人类本性、个人行为、自我保存、利己心、内在自我、公正旁观者、自我管制、同情心、内在冲突、逐利者、看不见的手、同感、社会动物等等，成了《道德情操论》的关键词。人类情感作为一只看不见的手，在调节着个人的社会行为，促成利己心与同情心的有机融合，这构成了亚当·斯密人性论的基本内涵。斯密在此书中，第一次运用了他导师弗朗西斯·哈奇森传授的"人们可以通过发现对人类有益的行为来认识从理论上来说什么是好的"的哲理。

亚当·斯密的第二本书《国富论》

《国富论》共分五部分：第一篇，论劳动生产力进步的原因，兼论劳动产品在不同阶级人们之间自然分配的顺序（共11章）；第二篇，论资本的性质、积累和用途（共5章）；第三篇，论不同国家财富的不同发展（共4章）；第四篇，论政治经济学体系（共9章）；第五篇，论君主或国家的收入（共3章）。其中尤其值得注意的是和本书主题相关性较强的第五篇：第一章论君主或国家的开支——第一节论国防开支；第二节论司法开支；第三节论公共工程和公共机构

public institutions with Article 1 on the expenses of public works and institutions for facilitating the commerce of the society, Article 2 on the expense of the institutions for the education of youth, Article 3 on the expense of the institutions for the instruction of people of all ages, and Part 4 on the expense of supporting the dignity of the sovereign. Chapter 2 then probes into the sources of the general or public revenue of the society; and Chapter 3 examines public debts.

The main economic ideas conveyed in *The Wealth of Nations* are: (1) Division of Labor and Value Theory. It includes Division of Labor Theory, Value Theory (value in use and value in exchange; value of labor and the setting of two types of values), Theory on the Three Sources of Revenue (namely wages, profit and rent), and Market Price and Natural Price. (2) Income and Allocation Theory. This includes Wages Theory, Profit Theory, and Rent Theory. (3) Regeneration of Social Capital Theory. This comprises "What is regeneration of social capital", "Premise on the theory of Regeneration of Social Capital", and "The core problem in the regeneration of social capital is the problem in realizing the aggregate social product", etc.

The main ideas presented in *The Wealth of Nations* are that a seemingly chaotic free market is in fact a self-adjusting mechanism producing types and quantities of products determined by what society needs most urgently, leading everyone through pricing, demand and supply, and competition just like an invisible hand, to follow market rules conscientiously. In Adam Smith's own words, "As every individual, therefore, endeavors as much as he can both to employ his capital in the support of domestic industry, and so to direct that industry that its produce may be of the greatest value; every individual necessarily labours to render the annual revenue of the society as great as he can. …and he is in this, as in many other cases, led by an invisible hand to promote an end which was no part of his intention. … By pursuing his own interest, he frequently promotes that of the society more effectually than when he really intends to promote it."**3** As seen here, the mechanism of price, demand and supply, and competition, being the invisible hand, is governing the behavior of commodity producers/enterprises, leading to an organic integration of egoism and altruism, henceforth, forming the basic connotation of the free economy. Adam Smith has taken the concept of "an invisible hand" from *The Moral Sentiments* and aptly applied to *The Wealth of Nations*, in the self-adjustment and self-regulation of market economy, demonstrating once again his mentor

的开支（第一项是便利社会商业的公共工程和公共机构；第二项是青少年教育机构的开支；第三项是对所有年龄层次的人进行教育的机构的开支）；第四节论维护君主尊严的开支。第二章论一般收入或公共收入的来源。第三章论公债。

《国富论》包括的主要经济思想有：第一，分工和价值理论，包括分工理论、价值理论（使用价值和交换价值、劳动价值及两种价值规定）、三种收入理论（工资、利润、地租）、市场价格与自然价格理论。第二，收入与分配理论，包括工资理论、利润理论、地租理论。第三，社会资本再生产理论，包括什么是社会资本再生产、社会资本再生产理论的前提、社会再生产运动的核心问题是社会总产品的实现问题⋯⋯

《国富论》的中心思想是：看起来似乎杂乱无章的自由市场实际上是一个自行调整的机制，自动倾向于生产社会最迫切需要的商品种类和数量，它通过价格机制、供求机制和竞争机制，就像一只看不见的手，在冥冥之中让每个人自觉地按照市场规则行动。用亚当·斯密的话来说就是："各个人都不断地努力为自己所能支配的资本找到最有利的用途。固然，他所考虑的不是社会的利益而是自身的利益，但他对自身利益的研究自然会或者毋宁说必然会引导他选定最有利于社会的用途。""在这场合，像在其他许多场合一样，他受着一只看不见的手引导，去尽力达到一个并非他本意想要达到的目的。""他们促进社会的利益，其效果往往比他们真正想要实现的还要好。"**3** 在这里，价格、供求、竞争机制，作为一只看不见的手，在调节着商品生产者/企业的社会行为，促成利己性与利他性的有机融合，构成了自由经济的基本内涵。亚当·斯密把《道德情操论》

Francis Hutcheson's philosophy that people themselves could discover what is ethically good by discovering the actions that serve the good of humankind.

Under the premise of economic liberalism mentioned in *The Wealth of Nations*, Adam Smith points out the government functions in a free economy society, covered mainly in Chapter 1 of Book V. This chapter deals with expenses of defense, justice, and public works and public institutions (expenses of education included), etc. It also summarizes the three main functions of the government, that is, ensuring national security, maintaining justice and order, and providing public goods. Amongst these, the profit of erecting and maintaining public works such as roads, bridges, navigable canals, and harbors could never repay the expense to any individual, therefore the duty should be taken by the state.[4] Henceforth, the government plays the role of a night watchman. This particular role of the government is mentioned in Book V of *The Wealth of Nations*, generalized by later generations as "small government".

The book established Adam Smith as the forefather of classical economics, and the founder of classical economics and market value theory. On this basis, later generations have made up for Adam Smith's deficiencies such as the inadequacies of the division of labor theory, the inherent contradictions in the value theory system and the weaknesses in the market economy theory, leading to the mainstream neoclassical economics of today; and his overview of the functions and roles of the government in the market economy still exerts its influence some 240 years later. Traditional economists still adopt "small government", "night watchman state", and "provision of public goods" to keep tabs on the roles of modern countries in the market economy.

Analysis of the Contents of Adam Smith's Third Book

Adam Smith completed his first book, *The Theory of Moral Sentiments* in 1759 and his second book, *The Wealth of Nations* in 1776. Thereafter, he returned from London to Scotland, and worked at the customs where his father had worked previously, a place considered then to be the true source of wealth, and an important import and export trading place where national interests are highly concentrated. There, he observed and contemplated, hoping to write a third book on the subject of "the

中的"看不见的手"的概念，运用到了《国富论》的市场经济自行调节中，提出了"看不见的手"理论，再一次展现了他导师弗朗西斯·哈奇森传授的"人们可以通过发现对人类有益的行为来认识从理论上来说什么是好的"的哲理。

在《国富论》提出的经济自由主义前提下，亚当·斯密指出了经济自由社会里的政府职能——它主要集中在《国富论》的第五篇第一章中，涉及国防开支、司法开支、公共工程和公共机构开支（包括教育开支）等等。这里概括了政府的三种职能，即保护国家、维护公正与秩序、提供公共物品。其中，提供公共物品，比如道路、桥梁、运河和海港，被认为是资本家无利可图的工程，需要由政府去保证。[4] 因此，政府起着一个"守夜人"的作用，这就是亚当·斯密在第五篇涉及并被后来人概括为"小政府"的角色。

《国富论》奠定了亚当·斯密作为古典经济学鼻祖的地位，他被戴上了古典经济学开创者、市场价值理论创立者等桂冠。在这一基础上，后来者弥补了亚当·斯密分工理论存在不足之处、价值理论体系存在内在矛盾、市场经济理论存在弱点等缺陷，才有了今天占据主流的新古典经济学。而亚当·斯密对市场经济中政府的职能和作用的概述，也一直影响着240多年后的今天。传统经济学界的人们仍然在用"小政府""守夜人""提供公共物品"来规约着现代国家在市场经济中的职能。

亚当·斯密的第三本书内容分析

在1759年完成第一本书《道德情操论》、1776年完成第二本书《国富论》之后，亚当·斯密从伦敦回到了苏格兰，效仿他父亲，担任海关官员。在海关这个当时被认为是财富的真正源泉、国与国利益高度集中的进出口贸易要地，他一边观察一边思考，期望能够写

general principles of law and government, and of the different revolutions they have undergone in the different ages and periods of society."[5] Regrettably, he had passed away before his third book was completed, and furthermore, his manuscripts were all destroyed.

What could be the contents of Adam Smith's third book? References need to be made once again to the philosophy instructed by his mentor, Francis Hutcheson, that people themselves could discover what is ethically good by discovering the actions that serve the good of humankind. Henceforth, in *The Moral Sentiments*, through analyzing a person's selfishness and sympathy for others in society, Adam Smith formulated the basic connotation of human nature theory and the characteristics of morality; in *The Wealth of Nations*, through investigating industries' egoism and altruism in the market, Smith formulated the basic connotation of the free economy and the characteristics of industries' commercial behaviors; then, through analyzing national and human interests, would his third book on "government and law" be on the basic national economic functions and the characteristics of management practice of government (law)? At the center of Adam Smith's political economics is the concept of the "invisible hand": as to human's moral behaviors, Adam Smith suggested that the "invisible hand" integrates selfishness and sympathy, which is guiding human moral sentiments; as to industries' commercial behaviors, Adam Smith suggested that the "invisible hand" integrates egoism and altruism, which is the guiding mechanism on pricing, demand and supply, and competition for industries. In that case, as to government management practice, what would the "invisible hand" be? Analyzing Adam Smith's own academic thoughts and the philosophy imparted by his mentor in conjunction, it appears that Adam Smith was investigating "behavioral science"; or was perhaps revealing human nature, industries in the market, and state management by investigating "behavioral science" and "behavioral economics". Regrettably, he only left footprints on two of his three giant steps in his two masterpieces.

We can at least conclude that had Adam Smith completed his third masterpiece, his analysis on government functions and management would not be merely confined to what was described in the first chapter of Book V of *The Wealth of Nations*. Apart from national protection and maintaining justice and order, government's provision of public goods would definitely not be confined to just the four types of infrastructure—roads, bridges, navigable canals and harbors, which yield no profit to

出关于"法律与政府的原则，以及法律与政府在不同历史时期所经历的改革"的第三本书。[5] 但遗憾的是他未及写完便与世长辞，所有手稿资料也被销毁了。

那么亚当·斯密第三本书的内容会是什么呢？这又需要回到他导师弗朗西斯·哈奇森传授的哲理中来——"人们可以通过发现对人类有益的行为来认识从理论上来说什么是好的"。于是，《道德情操论》通过分析社会中个人的利己心与同情心，勾画出人性论的基本内涵和人的道德行为特征；《国富论》通过分析市场中企业的利己性与利他性，构建了自由经济的基本内涵和企业的商业行为特征；那么，他的第三本书聚焦于"政府与法律"，是否也会通过分析国家利益与人类利益，从而得出国家的基本经济职能和政府（法律）的管理行为特征呢？贯穿亚当·斯密政治经济学的核心概念是"看不见的手"：对于个人道德行为，这只"看不见的手"是利己心与同情心的融合，它引导着人们的道德情操；对于企业商业行为，这只"看不见的手"是利己性与利他性的融合，它引导着企业的价格、供求和竞争机制；那么，对于政府的管理行为，亚当·斯密要揭示的这只"看不见的手"又是什么呢？将亚当·斯密的学术思想与他导师传授的哲理结合起来分析，似乎亚当·斯密是在研究"行为科学"，或者是通过研究"行为科学""行为经济学"来揭示个人人性、企业市场和国家管理的。很可惜他的三步棋却只下完两步。

但至少我们可以说，如果亚当·斯密有幸完成了第三本书，他对政府职能和管理行为的分析，绝不会仅仅停留在《国富论》第五篇第一章的几点描述上。除了保护国家、维护公正与秩序之外，政府所提供的公共物品也绝不会局限在道路、桥梁、运河、海港等四

capitalists. What is regrettable is that even today, over 200 years later, various economic thoughts on government functions and management practice have not gone beyond what Adam Smith had described in *The Wealth of Nations.*

The limitations of research on government functions and its characteristics of behaviors when Adam Smith wrote *The Wealth of Nations* was understandable. Firstly, the Industrial Revolution had just started, small handicraft workshops were just shifting to large-scale industries using machineries, urbanization was still in its infancy, and people still focused on industries, industrial resources, and industrial revolution. Just as Adam Smith had criticized mercantilism, which viewed trade as the only source of wealth, and physiocracy, which viewed agriculture as the only wealth-creator by pointing out that all the material production departments create wealth, *The Wealth of Nations* lacked the recognition and application of urban infrastructure and urban resources. Because of limitations of the times, Adam Smith restricted government functions and management practice only to industrial economy. Secondly, faced with industrial economy, namely, industries, commodities, pricing, demand and supply, and competition, governments would naturally restrict their roles as night watchmen in ensuring national security, justice, and order, and in providing a conducive market, and nothing else.

The problem now is precisely that after the completion of *The Wealth of Nations* in 1776, Adam Smith shifted his attention from the study of human behavior to the study of industry behavior, then to the study of government behavior, and began writing on "general principles of government and law" in 1790, more than ten years after the completion of *The Wealth of Nations.* Why did Adam Smith work for the customs after he completed *The Wealth of Nations*? Was it just to take care of his mother? Was it to make more money? From the trajectory of his life, these were obviously not the main reasons. When Adam Smith completed *The Moral Sentiments* at the age of 36, he became a private teacher to the son of the Chancellor of the Exchequer, and gained a salary for life. To research for *The Wealth of Nations*, he socialized with London's business circle, and completed the masterpiece when he was 53. Thereafter, he chose to work for the customs, where a country's import and export could be observed, and presumably began to research on domestic and international economic situations, and the "government behavior" derived from them. This manifested that his life

类基础设施（且它们是资本家无利可图的工程）的范畴内。然而令人遗憾的是，两百多年后的今天，各类经济学理论仍然把政府的职能和管理行为局限在当年亚当·斯密《国富论》的描述上。

我们可以理解亚当·斯密撰写《国富论》时对政府职能及行为特征探研的局限性：一则，他所处的时代才刚刚开始工业革命，才刚刚开始从工场手工业转向机器大工业，城市化进程几乎还没有大的发展，人们的目光主要还是集中在产业、产业资源、产业革命上。正如亚当·斯密的《国富论》批判了重商主义只把对外贸易作为财富源泉的错误观点，批判了重农学派认为只有农业才创造财富的片面观点，指出一切物质生产部门（即产业部门）都创造财富一样，《国富论》对城市基础设施、城市资源的认识和运用几乎微乎其微，时代的局限性使亚当·斯密把政府职能与管理行为圈定在产业经济之中。二则，既然是面对产业经济，即面对企业、商品、价格、供求与竞争，政府理所当然只是保护国家安全、公正、秩序，提供良好市场环境的"守夜人"角色，而不是其他。

现在的问题恰恰在于，在1776年完成了《国富论》之后，亚当·斯密从研究人的行为转到研究企业的行为，又转到研究国家政府的行为，而且在《国富论》完成十多年之后的1790年着手撰写《政府与法律论》。那么，亚当·斯密在完成了《国富论》后，为什么要去海关任职？难道只是为了照顾他母亲？难道是为了多赚钱谋生？从他的人生轨迹来分析，显然这都不是主要原因。亚当·斯密36岁完成了《道德情操论》，后成为英国财政大臣儿子的私人教师，获得终身俸禄。为研撰《国富论》，他出入伦敦商业圈，于53岁完成了此一巨著。之后他选择到反映国家进出口贸易状况的经济重地——海关任职，应该是开始探研国家与国际经济状况，以及由

choices were mainly correlated with his academic interest. Why did it take him 14 years to research for his third book? Of course, during his research, Adam Smith was also responsible for some school matters. More importantly, however, in my opinion, he tried to apply further the philosophy of his mentor, Francis Hutcheson, that people themselves could discover what is ethically good by discovering the actions that serve the good of humankind to the rules of government management and operation.

If the essence of *The Moral Sentiments* was the guidance of "an invisible hand", which is the amalgamation of individuals and society, selfishness and sympathy; and the essence of *The Wealth of Nations* was the promotion of "an invisible hand", which is the amalgamation of industries and market, egoism and altruism; then, what was the driving force behind a government's behavior attributes and nature? What was regulating the internal restraints between countries? For a government, there are national interests as well as international interests; it has national attributes as well as international attributes; it embodies partial (micro) demand while expecting overall (macro) balance. The essence is the contradiction of national interests of one country against another, and even against human interests. Furthermore, when a state pursues and protects its own interests, apart from political and military means, what kind of economic means are there at its disposal? How does a state pursue its own interests? Possible routes include "protection" and "competition". While "protecting" its own interests should be promoted by mutual rules, how should it "compete" for its own interests? In what areas should it compete? I think these were the difficult questions encountered by Adam Smith in his third book, which he endeavored to solve. However, he couldn't or had no time to answer these questions. As a consequence, there exist the fallacy of traditional economics and the shortcomings in Adam Smith's market theory. That is, there is only one subject—"industry" with industry supply and demand, and industry competition in the market. This fallacy in market theory lasts even to this day. Many problems in modern economy are not problems of the market, but fallacies in traditional market theory, problems that the much revered and esteemed Adam Smith left behind.

此产生的"国家政府行为"。这说明他的人生选择主要与学术取向有关。那么为什么第三本书的研究长达 14 年之久？当然，这期间亚当·斯密也肩负其母校的相关事务，但我个人认为更重要的原因是，他长时间在海关工作，是在探寻如何将他导师弗朗西斯·哈奇森的哲理——"人们可以通过发现对人类有益的行为来认识从理论上来说什么是好的"——进一步运用到国家政府的管理及运行规律上来。

如果说《道德情操论》的精髓与内核是个人与社会、利己心和同情心的融合形成的"看不见的手"的引导，《国富论》的精髓与内核是企业与市场、利己性和利他性的融合形成的"看不见的手"的推动，那么，一国政府的行为属性、内在本质靠什么来牵引？国家与国家之间的内在牵制力靠什么来规约？就政府属性而言，一国既有国家利益，又从属于全球利益；既有一国属性，又含国际属性；既体现局部（微观）需求，又期望整体（宏观）平衡：这内在本质、精髓和内核应该就是一国政府的国家利益与他国政府的国家利益乃至人类利益的内在矛盾运动。进一步说，一国政府为了维护或争取国家利益，除了政治、军事的手段之外，经济上还有什么手段？应如何去争取其利益？可能的途径是"维护"与"竞争"："维护"自己的利益要靠共同规则来推动；而靠"竞争"来争取自己的利益又应怎么做？在哪些领域竞争？我想，这就是亚当·斯密的第三本书碰到并试图解决的难题。但最终他还是未能解决或来不及回答这些问题，于是，就有了传统经济学的缺陷和亚当·斯密市场理论的不足，即市场只有一个主体——企业，市场只存在企业供求与企业竞争。这种市场理论的缺陷一直延续至今。现代经济的许多问题，不是市场的问题，而是传统市场理论的问题——人们崇拜亚当·斯密，而亚当·斯密来不及回答、解决的问题也遗留至今。

3. The Deficiencies in Adam Smith's Theories and Emergence of John Maynard Keynes' Theories

Adam Smith is the forefather of classical economics and the founder of market value theory. The core of his theory and even its deficiencies have influenced generations that came and went. Many economists that followed, including the renowned Professor Alfred Marshall who published *Principles of Economics* in 1890, made "Economics" an independent discipline, proposed a series of new categories and concepts, boldly innovated and promoted the study of economics to a new level, and in doing so, formed the school of Neoclassical Economics. However, in my opinion, these were just reforms and innovations, and synthesized theories under the original framework established by Adam Smith. The new school merely studied commodities, pricing, demand and supply, competition in terms of industries, industrial economy and industrial resources; it was restrained to the relationships between the markets (industries) and governments—the "Goldbach's conjecture" in economics, though the discussions were deepened or extended by changing perspectives or innovating categories. Thus the government was limited and only deemed as the "night watchman" or "small government" who provided security, fairness, order and public goods.

The biggest contribution made by Adam Smith's *Wealth of Nations* was its elaborate description of market attributes, industries and their relationships with the government in the industrial economy. Under the guidance of "an invisible hand", the market attributes and government functions in the industrial economy were clearly defined. This is the reason why Adam Smith's economic thoughts are everlasting! However, it could not distinguish other forms of economies from industrial economy or had not done so; it had not detailed the complete connotation of the market system, the boundaries (or scope) of the market, and the effectiveness of the market, nor had it intricately defined the clear relationships between governments and the market, etc. The constraints of the times and the uncompleted third book lay behind the big flaw in Adam Smith's economic theory.

John Maynard Keynes, with his unique experiences in academia and politics, completed *The Economic Consequences of the Peace* in 1919 after World War I; to deal with the world economic crisis of 1929-1933 and promote Roosevelt's "New Deal" in the United States, he completed *The General Theory of Employment, Interest and Money* in 1936. The deficiencies

三、亚当·斯密理论的缺陷与凯恩斯理论的崛起

亚当·斯密不愧为古典经济学的鼻祖和市场价值理论的创立者，其理论内核的合理与不足，都整整影响了几代人。后有众多经济学家，包括著名的阿尔弗雷德·马歇尔教授（1890 年出版《经济学原理》），将经济学作为一门独立的学科，提出了一系列新的范畴和概念，大胆创新，推动经济学研究迈上了一个新的台阶，即形成了新古典经济学派。但依我所见，这仍然是在亚当·斯密原来确立的框架下的一种改革创新、一种集大成论，仍然只囿于产业、产业经济、产业资源来论商品、价格、供求、竞争，只囿于产业经济中的政府与市场（企业）关系，虽然不断深化或改换角度、创新范畴来扩展其论述，但仍然把政府与市场关系这一经济学中的"哥德巴赫猜想"局限一隅，即政府只是提供安全、公平和秩序以及公共物品的"守夜人""小政府"角色。

亚当·斯密《国富论》最大的贡献是详述了产业经济中的市场属性、企业主体及其与政府的关系，在"看不见的手"的牵引下，产业经济中的市场属性与政府职能得以界定，这是亚当·斯密经济学思想长青的原因！但他无法或还没有区分出产业经济之外的其他经济类型，没有细分出市场体系的完整内涵、市场的界限（或范围）以及市场的有效性，没有细致界定出政府与市场的明晰关系，等等。时代的局限性与第三本书研撰的未遂，导致亚当·斯密经济学理论存在重大缺陷。

而凯恩斯以其"亦学亦政"的独有经历，在第一次世界大战后的 1919 年完成了《〈凡尔赛合约〉的经济后果》，为应对 1929—1933 年的世界性经济危机和助推美国罗斯福新政，又于 1936 年完成了《就业、利息和货币通论》，等等。亚当·斯密经济学理论中的

in Adam Smith's economic theory, or what had remained unexplored, led to Keynes' success; whilst Keynes' theory had made breakthroughs in economics, it was also stuck in its deficiencies and contradictions.

缺陷或还未探研之处，成就了凯恩斯的成功；而凯恩斯在经济学上有了新发展之余，也同样陷入了其经济学理论的缺陷和矛盾之中难以自拔。

CHAPTER 2   THE CONTRIBUTIONS AND DEFICIENCIES OF KEYNESIAN ECONOMICS

1. The Main Experiences of Keynes

John Maynard Keynes (1883-1946), born and raised in Cambridge, England, was highly proficient and competent in mathematics and economics. From 1902 to 1906, aged 19 to 23, Keynes studied at Cambridge University; after graduation, from 1906 to 1908, Keynes worked as a clerk in the India Office. Keynes returned to work in Cambridge University in 1908. In 1913, aged 30, Keynes published his first work, *Indian Currency and Finance*. From 1913 to 1914, he worked for the Royal Commission on Indian Currency and Finance.

From 1915 onward, that is, during the First World War, Keynes worked for the Treasury and later took charge of foreign financial relations. In May of 1919, aged 36, as the chief representative of the British Treasury as well as an advisor to Prime Minister David Lloyd George, Keynes attended the Paris Peace Conference, during which he attempted to reduce the huge amount of compensation Entente Powers had demanded from Germany. The claim was refused and Keynes resigned. In 1919, Keynes returned to Cambridge University and published the book, *The Economic Consequences of the Peace*; thereafter, he published a series of articles and works such as *A Treatise on Probability* in 1921, *A Revision of the Treaty* in 1922, *A Tract on Monetary Reform* in 1923, "Does Unemployment Need a Drastic Remedy?" in 1924, and *The End of Laissez-Faire* in 1926, and *A Treatise on Money* in 1930, etc.

In October of 1929, the Wall Street Stock Market crashed, and a world economic depression started. In 1930, Keynes became a member of the Economic Advisory Council. In 1931, at the invitation of the University of Chicago, Keynes travelled to Chicago to discuss crisis-combating measures with American economists. From 1932 to 1933, Keynes advocated continually government's intervention in stimulating economic growth; in 1934, Keynes visited President Roosevelt to promote the New Deal on his second trip to the United States. In February of 1936, *The General Theory of Employment, Interest and Money* was published.

In September of 1939, the Second World War started; in 1940, Keynes was given a position at the Treasury again and became a consultant of the Chancellor. From 1942 to 1944, Keynes actively engaged in building post-

贰 凯恩斯经济学的贡献与缺陷

一、凯恩斯主要经历

生长于英国剑桥的约翰·梅纳德·凯恩斯（1883—1946），擅长数学和经济学。1902—1906 年（19—23 岁），他在剑桥大学学习。毕业后，即 1906—1908 年，他在英国印度事务部任文职官员。1908 年，他回到剑桥大学工作。1913 年（30 岁），凯恩斯发表了他的第一部著作《印度货币与财政》。1913—1914 年，他担任过皇家印度财政和货币委员会成员。

1915 年开始（32 岁），即第一次世界大战期间，凯恩斯加入英国战时财政部，后期主要负责英国对外财政关系。1919 年 5 月（36 岁），凯恩斯以英国财政部的首席代表和首相劳合·乔治的顾问的身份参加了巴黎和会，期间，他试图阻止协约国对德国设置过高的赔款额，遭到失败后辞职。1919 年，凯恩斯回到剑桥大学，后发表《和约的经济后果》一书。此后，凯恩斯发表了系列文章和著作，其中主要的有：《概率论》（1921 年），《和约的修正》（1922 年），《货币改革论》（1923 年），《失业需要大力补救吗？》（1924 年），《自由放任政策的终结》（1926 年），《货币论》（1930 年），等等。

1929 年 10 月，华尔街股市崩盘，世界经济大萧条开始。1930 年，凯恩斯成为政府经济顾问委员会成员。1931 年，凯恩斯受邀去美国芝加哥大学，同美国经济学家讨论应对危机的措施。1932—1933 年，凯恩斯持续倡导通过政府干预刺激经济增长。1934 年，凯恩斯再次去美国，并面见罗斯福总统，促推罗斯福新政。1936 年 2 月，凯恩斯发表《就业、利息和货币通论》。

1939 年 9 月，第二次世界大战爆发。1940 年，凯恩斯再次进入财政部，成为英国政府财政大臣顾问。1942—1944 年，凯恩斯积

war economic order, from which the later International Monetary Fund (IMF), the World Bank and the Bretton Woods system were derived. In February of 1946, Keynes went to the United States to attend the first meeting of the World Bank and International Monetary Fund. In April of 1946, John Maynard Keynes passed away.

2. Characteristics of Keynes' Economic Thoughts

Keynes' strengths in mathematics and economics, coupled with his rich experiences in academia and politics, led him to contemplate and explore economics in a unique way. For example:

(1) Earlier in his book, *The Economic Consequences of the Peace* in 1919, Keynes had already made a detailed analysis of pre-war Europe, the Paris Peace Conference, the items of the Treaty of Versailles, especially those on war reparations, and the prospect of Europe after signing the Treaty and remedies, etc. He believed that the huge claims Entente Powers demanded would destroy Germany's economy, thereby leading to further conflicts in Europe. He proposed to revise relevant items of the Treaty, resolve debts between countries, make international loans available, and improve relations with Russia to remedy hidden troubles brought about by the Treaty.[1] Through *The Economic Consequences of the Peace*, we can see that: (i) Keynes predicted profoundly the serious consequences that might be brought about by government actions that did not conform to economic logic. Hence, he was trying to prevent and remedy such situations. (ii) Keynes analyzed government actions and attempted to change the possible consequences with government's economic policies and measures. In doing so, he raised to a higher level the general public's (especially of that time) awareness and acceptance of economics. (iii) Keynes described the roles and functions of the government from the perspectives of state power and overall economic trends, thereby breaking away from the traditional economic theory and objectively analyzing how government's policies directly affected national economy.

(2) Faced with the situation of a million unemployed Britons in 1924, Keynes, in his article, "Does Unemployment Need a Drastic Remedy?", proposed the government should spend 100 million pounds per year to stimulate economic growth, especially in investing in and building housing, roads, and electric energy facilities, etc. Keynes further suggested that national savings should be spent on domestic infrastructure

极参与建立战后国际经济秩序，后来的国际货币基金组织、世界银行和布雷顿森林体系皆发源于此。1946 年 2 月，凯恩斯到美国参加世界银行和国际货币基金组织的首次会议。1946 年 4 月，凯恩斯与世长辞。

二、凯恩斯特色经济思想

凯恩斯擅长数学和经济学，且在学界、政界均有丰富经历，这使他的经济学思考与研究别具一格。举例来说：

第一，在 1919 年的《和约的经济后果》一书中，凯恩斯详尽分析了战前欧洲状况、巴黎和会谈判、《凡尔赛和约》的条款尤其是赔款事宜，以及《和约》签订后的欧洲前景与补救措施。他认为，协约国对德国的巨额赔款要求将毁灭德国经济，从而导致欧洲进一步的冲突。凯恩斯提出修改《凡尔赛和约》的有关条款，解决各国之间的债务问题，进行国际贷款，改善与俄国的关系，以补救《和约》带来的隐患。[1]从这本书中我们可以看到，首先，凯恩斯深刻地预见了政府行为不符合经济逻辑时可能带来的严重后果，因此力图阻止与修正。其次，凯恩斯分析政府行为，并试图运用政府的经济手段改变可能产生的后果，从而把人们（尤其在当时）对经济学的认知和接受程度提高到了一个更新的阶段、更高的水平。再次，凯恩斯从国家权力和整体经济趋势的角度，阐述了政府在其中扮演的角色、发挥的作用，从而与传统经济理论决裂，开启了政府政策直接影响国家经济的客观分析。

第二，1924 年，面对英国失业人数已达一百万的状况，凯恩斯在《失业需要大力补救吗？》一文中提出，政府每年应支出一亿英镑来促进经济增长，特别是用来投资建设住房、道路、电力能源设施等，国家的储蓄应投资于国内的公共基础设施，而不是国外。政

instead of foreign investment. Governments should do what the private investors could not do or have not done yet, and increasingly raise their effectiveness.[2] Here, (i) Keynes further suggested that government's measures to stimulate economic growth could be to increase domestic investments in constructing infrastructure such as housing, roads, and electric energy facilities. (ii) The operation organizations of public infrastructure are semi-autonomous entities, invested by private funds and administered by the government. The investment and construction of public goods could effectively stimulate economic growth. (iii) Thus, governments should not do things which private investors have already done. It doesn't matter whether they do better or worse than the private investors. But instead, they should do the things that modern society needs to do but has not yet started doing. Henceforth, Keynes has achieved a breakthrough in the field of economics by looking into the effects of government's investment in infrastructure construction on stimulating economic growth, and attempting to explain these under a theoretical framework.

(3) Keynes published *The General Theory of Employment, Interest and Money* in 1936, which is divided into 6 Books made up of 24 chapters. Book I is Introduction, explaining mainly the effective demand principle; Book II is Definitions and Ideas, elaborating mainly on the definitions of income, saving and investment, and the meaning of further investigation; Book III talks about the Propensity to Consume, elaborating mainly on marginal propensity to consume and the multiplier; Book IV investigates the Inducement to Invest, elaborating mainly on marginal efficiency of capital, liquidity preference, etc.; Book V is on Money-wages and Prices, elaborating mainly on money-wages, pricing and the employment function; Book VI is Short Notes Suggested by the General Theory, elaborating mainly on trade cycle, mercantilism, and the social philosophy towards which the general theory might lead. Some key issues worthy of note are: (i) Keynes, being a student of Professor Marshall in

Cambridge, at this point held the view that the classical and neoclassical economic theories represented by Adam Smith and Alfred Marshall respectively, which state that an equilibrium state of full employment can be reached through self-adjustment mechanism of market demand and supply forces, cannot hold true. (ii) The level of employment in a country is determined by effective demand. Effective demand refers to the aggregate demand when aggregate supply price and aggregate demand price are in equilibrium. As aggregate supply will not change

府应该去做私人投资者还没有或还未能去做的事，并不断提高政府效率。[2] 由该文可知，首先，凯恩斯进一步明确提出，政府促进经济增长的措施包括在国内加大住房、道路、电力能源等基础设施投资建设。其次，这些公共基础设施的运营组织应属于私人投资和国家管理之间的半自治实体，而公共物品工程投资建设能有效促进经济增长。再次，对政府而言，重要的不是去做私人投资者已经做过的事，做得比他们好或差都不重要，而是应去做现代社会需要但还没有人去做的事。这一阶段，凯恩斯的经济学研究已经从发挥政府作用进一步引申到政府投资基础设施建设对经济增长的促进作用，并试图在理论上有所解释，有所突破。

第三，1936 年，凯恩斯发表《就业、利息和货币通论》。全书共分六篇二十四章。第一篇，引论，主要阐述有效需求原理。第二篇，定义与观念，主要阐述收入、储蓄、投资的定义和进一步考察的意义。第三篇，消费倾向，主要阐述边际消费倾向和乘数。第四篇，投资诱导，主要阐述资本边际效率、流动性偏好等。第五篇，货币工资与价格，主要阐述货币工资、价格、就业函数等。第六篇，《通论》引起的几点思考，主要略论经济周期、重商主义及《通论》可能导向的社会哲学等。由这部著作可知，第一，作为剑桥大学马歇尔教授的学生的凯恩斯，此时观点鲜明地认为，以亚当·斯密和马歇尔为代表的古典经济学和新古典经济学理论，即借助市场供求力量能够自动调节、实现充分就业的均衡状态，不可能成立。第二，他认为一国的就业水平是由有效需求决定的。有效需求是指商品总供给价格与总需求价格达到均衡时的总需求，而总供给在短期内不会有大的变动，因此，导致就业不足的根源在于有效需求不

significantly in the short run, the root cause of underemployment lies in insufficient effective demand. (iii) Effective demand or aggregate demand is the sum of consumption demand and investment demand. Insufficient effective demand or aggregate demand is thus due to insufficient consumption demand and investment demand. (iv) Hence, Keynes advocated government's intervention in the economy. Through policies, the government can stimulate consumption and increase investment in order to attain full employment. Keynes believed that as consumption tendency is relatively stable in the short run, to attain full employment, the government must focus on increasing investment demand. Changes in investment will produce a multiplier effect on changes in income and output, with national income increasing a few times. (v) Keynes suggested that the government should increase investment with fiscal policies rather than monetary policies. Especially during periods of economic depression, the government should adopt expansionary fiscal policies, that is to increase fiscal expenditure, reduce taxes and issue bonds. Keynes also suggested that investment policies should work in concert with consumption demand. Keynes felt that the government should also control investment, in order to prevent fluctuations of the economy brought about by it. (vi) The government must think of ways to increase effective demand, and increase consumption demand by improving equal income.

As can be seen, (i) in his *General Theory of Employment, Interest and Money*, Keynes found a new field to help promote economic growth for a country—this field is not in foreign trade advocated by mercantilism, nor in agricultural production favored by physiocrats, nor in industrial economy as Adam Smith described, but in public projects and goods that governments provide to the society that bring no profits to private investors, namely, investment in the construction of roads, bridges, navigable canals, habors, housing, power energy and other infrastructure as Adam Smith described in Article 1, Part 3, Chapter 1, Book V of *The Wealth of Nations*. (ii) The government should intervene in the development of the national economy, especially in situations of imbalanced aggregate demand and insufficient effective demand. The government should intervene in investments in infrastructure. (iii) And the government should adopt proactive fiscal policies like increasing fiscal expenditures, reducing taxes and issuing government bonds, to increase fiscal budgets for construction of housing, roads and other public projects. (iv) Keynes' characteristic economic thoughts, being an independent economic theory system, took shape. Keynes'

足。第三，有效需求或总需求是消费需求与投资需求之总和。有效需求不足或总需求不足是消费需求与投资需求不足的结果。第四，为解决需求不足问题，凯恩斯主张政府干预经济，通过政府的政策，来刺激消费和增加投资，以实现充分就业。因为凯恩斯认为，消费倾向在短期内是相对稳定的，要实现充分就业就必须从增加投资需求着手。投资的变动会使收入和产出的变动产生一种乘数效应，从而促进国民收入成倍增长。第五，凯恩斯所主张的政府扩大投资，是以财政政策为主，而不是以货币政策为主。尤其是在经济萧条时期，政府应采取扩张性的财政政策——增加财政开支、减少税收和发行公债。同时凯恩斯又提出，投资政策要结合消费需求来互动，国家也要控制投资，以消除投资对经济造成的波动性影响。第六，凯恩斯提出，政府要想办法促进有效需求，要推进收入均等化以增加消费需求。

综上可知，首先，凯恩斯在《就业、利息和货币通论》中找到了一国促进经济增长的新领域。这领域不是在重商主义所倾向的对外贸易中，不是在重农学派所偏向的农业生产中，也不是在亚当·斯密所描述的产业经济中，而是在亚当·斯密《国富论》第五篇第一章第三节第一项中所描写的那类不能给私人投资者带来利润收益而由政府向社会提供的公共工程、公共物品中——道路、桥梁、运河、海港、房屋建筑、电力能源等基础设施投资。其次，凯恩斯认为，政府要干预国家经济的发展，尤其是在总需求不平衡、有效需求不足的情形下。而政府干预的手段和切入点就在于上述基础设施投资。再次，政府干预的手段是积极的财政政策，即上文所说的增加财政开支、减少税收、发行公债，从而把更多的财政预算用于前

theory, together with classical economics dominated by Adam Smith and neoclassical economics dominated by Alfred Marshall, formed the two sides of the economic system. One side focused on supplying commodities, forming industrial economics with enterprises being the subjects, each abiding by the rules of market economy. The other side focused on supplying public works and public goods, forming infrastructure economics or urban economics. Keynes did not make clear who the subjects were in infrastructure economics or urban economics: it could be the government, private investors or economic associations. Keynes again did not make clear the rules by which they abided, or maybe they also abided by the rules of market economy.

3. Roosevelt's New Deal

As described earlier, Keynes visited the United States on numerous occasions. In 1934, Keynes met President Roosevelt, and discussed and promoted his New Deal. On the one hand, President Roosevelt was very appreciative of Keynes' views; but on the other, Keynes was under hostility from American advocates of laissez-faire economy.

At the heart of Roosevelt's New Deal were the three Rs, a series of economic policies implemented by Franklin Roosevelt after he was elected President in 1933: "Recovery", "Relief", and "Reform", otherwise known as the "Three Rs New Deal". It would be most opportune to mention here that the failure of Hoover's government in combating the economic crisis was due to the government's pursuance of a laissez-faire policy, and its objection to intervening in the national economy, which in turn aggravated the damage done by the economic crisis and plunged the American economy to rock bottom. Increasing public displeasure and dissatisfaction led to public outcries for reform growing louder by the day; with the election slogan of the "New Deal", Roosevelt won widespread support and defeated Herbert C. Hoover to become the 32nd President of the United States.

Apart from revamping the banking and financial industries, revitalizing manufacturing industries and modifying agricultural policies, establishing a social security system and building emergency relief agencies, the most important measure in Roosevelt's New Deal was to promote "Work Relief", that is to put in massive efforts to build public works and increase employment in order to stimulate production and consumption.

述房屋、道路建设等公共工程。最后，作为一个独立的经济学理论体系的凯恩斯特色经济思想已经形成。其理论与以亚当·斯密为主的古典经济学和以马歇尔为主的新古典经济学一道，形成经济学体系的两侧。一侧是：以提供商品为主→形成产业经济→企业是产业经济的主体→企业共同遵循市场经济规则。一侧是：以提供公共工程、公共物品为主→形成基础设施经济或城市经济→对于基础设施经济或城市经济的主体，凯恩斯含糊不清，或是政府，或是私人投资者，或是经济联合体→对主体共同遵循的规则，凯恩斯也含糊不清，或许也是遵循市场经济规则？

三、罗斯福新政

正如前面所述，凯恩斯曾多次前往美国。尤其是 1934 年，凯恩斯在美国面见了罗斯福总统，共同讨论、促推"罗斯福新政"。一方面，罗斯福总统十分欣赏凯恩斯的观点，另一方面，凯恩斯在美国也遭遇了经济自由放任派的敌意。

罗斯福新政即 1933 年富兰克林·罗斯福任美国总统后实行的一系列经济政策，其核心是三 R：复兴、救济和改革——也称三 R 新政。在此我们不得不说的是，当年美国胡佛政府应对危机失败，是由于其采取自由放任政策，反对国家干预经济，从而加剧了经济危机的危害，使美国经济跌入谷底。人民不满情绪日益高涨，全国上下要求改革的呼声越来越强烈，罗斯福以"新政"为竞选口号，赢得了广泛支持，因此击败胡佛，成为美国第 32 任总统。

除了整顿银行和金融业、复兴工业、调整农业政策、建立社会保障体系、建立急救救济署等，罗斯福新政最重要的措施就是推行"以工代赈"，大力兴建公共工程，增加就业，刺激生产和消费。

Work Relief was a measure to revamp the previous federal scheme which merely transferred relief in cash and in kind across all states purely as a relief effort, to one that provided employment in public works construction to the unemployed, especially to fit and healthy young people aged from 18 to 25, with high unemployment rate. Such public works projects included flood control, soil and water conservation, road construction, and various types of work in forestation (tree planting, forest protection, fire break and forest watchtowers setup), as well as various public and civil works. This measure not only revamped the provision of relief across the country and encouraged the unemployed to develop the sense of self-reliance and independence, but also spurred the construction and development of public and civil works in the United States, and stimulated production and consumption, alleviating the economic crisis and social conflicts brought about by the Great Depression.

The first measure of Roosevelt's New Deal was to urge the Congress to pass the plan of "Civilian Conservation Corps". The plan recruited a first batch of 250 thousand people to work in 1500 camps across the various states in the country. Before the United States was involved in the Second World War, more than two million youths had worked in this project, opening up more than 7.4 million acres of state-owned forests and a large number of state-owned parks. Each person worked for an average of 9 months each session; most of their salaries was spent on supporting themselves and their families, thus expanding the scope of relief and correspondingly increasing the purchasing power across the whole society.

During the era of the New Deal, there were various institutions of work relief across the United States, generally divided into two systems: (1) the Public Works Department (with a budget of USD 4 billion allocated by the government), which was responsible for planning long-term objectives for public works, and (2) the Civil Engineering Department (with a budget of USD 1 billion allocated by the government), running 180,000 small-scale projects across the nation, including school buildings, bridges, dikes, sewerage systems, post offices and administration agencies. Employment for 4 million people was provided and a vast number of unemployed unskilled workers went back to work. Several new work relief programs were established subsequently. The most famous were the Works Progress Administration, which received a Congressional grant of USD 5 billion and the National Youth Administration, which targeted the youth of the nation. Both programs collectively employed a

"以工代赈"即联邦把向各州提供救济款物的单纯救济改为给失业者提供建设公共工程工作机会的救济形式,尤其侧重吸纳失业率偏高的、年龄在 18—25 岁、身强体壮的青年人,在全国范围内从事植树护林、防治水患、水土保持、道路建筑、开辟森林防火线和设置森林瞭望塔等大量公共和民用工程建设。这些措施既完善了救济工作,促进失业者自力更生,又推动了全美民用工程和公共工程事业的建设和发展,刺激了生产和消费,缓解了大萧条带来的经济危机与社会矛盾。

罗斯福新政的第一项措施,就是促请国会通过"民间资源保护队计划"。该计划第一批招募了 25 万人,在遍及各州的 1500 个营地劳动。到美国参与第二次世界大战前,先后有 200 多万青年在这个项目中工作过,他们开辟了 740 多万英亩[3]国有林区和大量国有公园。平均每人每期干 9 个月,月工资中拿出绝大部分做赡家费,这在整个社会扩大了救济面和相应的购买力。

新政期间,全美设有名目繁多的工赈机关,综合起来可分成两大系统:一是以着眼长期目标的工程为主的公共工程署(政府先后拨款 40 多亿美元),二是民用工程署(投资近 10 亿美元)。如民用工程方面,全国兴建了 18 万个小型工程项目,包括校舍、桥梁、堤坎、下水道系统、邮局和行政机关等公共建筑,先后吸引了 400万人工作,为广大非熟练失业工人找到了用武之地。后来又继续建立了几个新的工赈系统。其中最著名的是国会拨款 50 亿美元兴办的工程兴办署和专门针对青年人的全国青年总署,二者总计雇佣人

total of 23 million people, providing employment for half of the nation's workforce.

By the onset of World War II, the Federal Government had already provided USD 18 billion for various projects and comparatively inexpensive direct relief efforts. The United States government already built nearly 1,000 airports, more than 12,000 sports fields, and more than 800 school buildings and hospitals, not only creating employment for craftsmen, unskilled laborers and architects, but also providing a variety of jobs for thousands of unemployed artists. That was by far the grandest and most successful relief program the United States government has ever implemented. These funds, through various channels, stimulated private consumption and investment through government's investment.

The measures of Roosevelt's New Deal, especially a large number of public and civilian relief projects, such as the Tennessee Valley Comprehensive Development Project, not only greatly alleviated unemployment and stimulated economic recovery, but more importantly, created a new model for the government to intervene in the economy or stimulate economic growth. The use of active fiscal policies, combined with massive public works construction and provision of public goods, provided the theoretical basis and implementation means for the government's intervention in the economy or exploration for a new model of economic growth. Investments, especially infrastructure investments in public works and public facilities brought great benefits to the American economy, establishing Roosevelt as the most popular American president after Abraham Lincoln.

4. Contributions and Deficiencies of Keynesian Economics

There have been widespread media reports in recent years that Donald Trump's economics resembles Roosevelt's New Deal. According to "The Essence of Trump's Administration is Roosevelt rather than Reagan", an economic review published on March 7, 2017 in *The Weekly-*

Economist of Japan, although Trump's Administration is often considered similar to Reagan's, Trump's policies are in fact more akin to Roosevelt's New Deal. "During the election campaign, both Reagan and Trump used the slogan, 'Make America Great Again' and ultimately achieved overwhelming victories. Furthermore, Reagan also talked about tax reductions and deregulations. In terms of patriotic slogans and some economic policies, Trump's Administration and that of Reagan do have

员达 2300 万，占全国劳动力的一半以上。

到第二次世界大战前夕，联邦政府支出的种种工程费用及数目较小的直接救济费用达 180 亿美元，美国政府借此修筑了近 1000 座飞机场、12,000 多个运动场、800 多座校舍与医院，不仅为工匠、非熟练工人和建筑师创造了就业机会，还给成千上万的失业艺术家提供了形形色色的工作，是迄今为止美国政府最宏大、最成功的救济行动。这些钱通过不同渠道，成为以政府投资刺激私人消费和个人投资的"引动水"。

罗斯福新政的措施，尤其是"以工代赈"修建的一大批公共工程和民用工程项目，比如田纳西河流域工程，不仅大大缓解了失业问题，刺激了经济复苏，更重要的是开创了国家干预经济或国家促进经济增长的新模式。积极财政政策与大力兴建公共工程设施、提供公共物品相结合，为国家干预经济或探寻经济增长新模式提供了理论依据和实施手段。投资——主要是以基础设施投资为主的公共工程、公共物品投资建设，使美国经济受益极大，罗斯福也因此成为自亚伯拉罕·林肯以来最受欢迎的总统，载入美国史册。

四、凯恩斯经济学的贡献与缺陷

近年不断有媒体报道："特朗普经济学"更像"罗斯福新政"。其中，日本《经济学人》周刊 2017 年 3 月 7 日刊登经济评论文章《特朗普政府的本质是罗斯福而非里根》称："虽然有人认为特朗普政府与里根时代类似，但实际上其政策与罗斯福的'新政政策'更为相似。……里根在选战中，与特朗普一样提出'恢复强大的美国'口号，最终实现了压倒性的胜利。另外，里根也提出减税和放松管制。从爱国性的口号和部分经济政策上来看，特朗普政府与里

their similarities. However, ...the economic policies implemented by the Reagan's Administration, apart from tax reductions and deregulations, also included interest rates hikes, revaluation of the Dollar and fiscal tightening. ... Reagan's economic policies focused on supply side rather than demand side, allowed industries to participate fully in market competition through thorough deregulation. ... If compared to the past, Trump's polices are similar to Democrat Roosevelt's New Deal following the 1929 global panic. The objective of the New Deal was to eliminate the extreme shortage in demand and unemployment, it was an economic policy centered on huge public expenditures and based on Keynesian demand side ideas. ... During the election campaign, Trump publicly committed USD 1 trillion to infrastructure investment, with the aim of strongly stimulating demand side. Although the United States has now recovered from the Lehman crisis, and almost approached full employment, nevertheless, there are still problems of mismatches in employment. Trump's policies can be said to be a 'New Deal', judging from the emphasis on demand side and deliberate attempts to employ workers. ... As to the movement of US interest rates, there could be a similar trend to the era of Roosevelt. ... Hence, in order to maximize the effectiveness of the policies, Trump is attempting to intervene in exchange rate movements (at least verbally), correcting excessive appreciation in the US dollar and high interest rates."[4]

Indeed, from the Roosevelt Administration to the Trump Administration, the economic rationale behind those measures to stimulate economic growth with massive amounts of infrastructure investments originated from the series of Keynesian theories, especially "Does Unemployment Need a Drastic Remedy?" of 1924 and *The General Theory of Employment, Interest and Money* published in 1936. Keynes' unique life experiences in academia and politics, and his pioneering "government intervention" economic thoughts, have made a great contribution to world economic theory and economic system.

Take *The General Theory of Employment, Interest and Money* as an example. It is generally believed that if Adam Smith's *Wealth of Nations* is the Bible of economic liberalism, then Keynes' *General Theory of Employment, Interest and Money* is the treasure of state interventionism. (1) Keynes reinterpreted the concept of full employment, and pointed out the three types of unemployment that existed in reality, namely,

根政府有一定的相似性。然而，……里根政府实施的经济政策除了减税和放松管制外，还包括上调利率、美元升值和紧缩财政。……里根政府的经济政策重视的不是需求，而是供给侧。通过彻底地放松管制，让企业彻底参与市场竞争。……如果与过去比较，特朗普的政策反而酷似1929年世界大恐慌后就任的民主党总统罗斯福的'新政政策'。新政政策目的是消除大恐慌后需求极度不足和工人失业问题，所实施的以巨额公共事业支出为中心的经济政策，正是立足于凯恩斯型需求侧的想法。……特朗普在选举期间就公开承诺进行总额1万亿美元规模的基础设施投资，试图强烈刺激需求侧。现在，美国虽然已经从雷曼危机中复苏，接近完全就业水平，但雇佣上仍然存在错配问题，从重视需求侧、有意向劳动者分配工作的角度看，特朗普的政策可以说恰恰是新政。……关于左右今后美国经济的利率动向，很可能会出现与罗斯福时代相似的走势。……因此，特朗普试着对汇率进行口头介入，通过纠正美元过度升值和利率过高情况，最大限度地发挥政策的效果。"[4]

的确，从罗斯福政府到特朗普政府，均采取大量投资基础设施建设以刺激经济增长的措施，其经济理论均源于凯恩斯的系列论述，尤其是1924年的《失业需要大力补救吗？》和1936年的《就业、利息和货币通论》等。凯恩斯"亦学亦政"的特殊人生经历和开创性的"政府干预"经济思想，对世界经济学理论的发展、体系的完善作出了重大贡献。

仍以《就业、利息和货币通论》为例，普遍的看法是，如果说亚当·斯密的《国富论》是经济自由主义的圣经的话，那么，凯恩斯的《就业、利息和货币通论》便是国家干预主义的宝典。该书主要论述了如下要点：第一，凯恩斯重新解释了充分就业概念，指出现实中存在自愿失业、摩擦失业和非自愿失业三类，非自愿失业的

voluntary unemployment, frictional unemployment, and involuntary unemployment. The existence of involuntary unemployment meant that the traditional employment theory is invalid. (2) Keynes brought up the principle of effective demand, and pointed out that the level of employment depends on the effective demand of society, which is in equilibrium with aggregate supply. (3) Keynes suggested a simple national income determination theory, and stated that the main factors deciding national income and employment rate are three psychological laws (marginal propensity to consume, marginal efficiency of capital and liquidity preference) and money supply. (4) Keynes suggested the law of diminishing marginal propensity to consume, the law of diminishing marginal efficiency of capital, and the liquidity preference theory. (5) Keynes put forward the multiplier theory, and stated that initial increases in investments can lead to increased induced investments, and through the chain effect, ultimately to effective demand increases in society many times over the initial investments, and vice versa. (6) Keynes put forward a theory of economic cycles, suggesting that an economic cycle mainly consists of four stages: prosperity, depression, recession and recovery, caused by the fluctuations in the investment rate, whilst the fluctuations in the investment rate are due to changes in the capital marginal efficiency. In addition, Keynes studied the price theory, the wage theory, and international trade theory, etc. Thus, Keynes' contribution to the revolution of economic theory, known as the "Keynesian Revolution", is publicly acclaimed as the equivalent of Copernicus' contribution to astronomy, Darwin's to biology, and Einstein's to physics.

Keynes' *General Theory of Employment, Interest and Money* summed up and integrated a large number of economic concepts from a macro perspective, opening a new chapter in the development of economics in the 20th century. The above analyses have shown that: (1) Keynes' unique experiences in academia and politics allowed him to discover a new field in the promotion of national economic growth in the field of public works and public goods investment centered on infrastructure, instead of "foreign trade" advocated by mercantilism, or "agriculture and animal husbandry" advocated by the physiocracy, or the "commodity production sectors" and "industrial economy" of Adam Smith. (2) The government is the primary body in the field of infrastructure investment. To put it another way, the government is the primary body to intervene in the economy and promote economic growth in this field. (3) The main measures of the government in infrastructure investment are

存在意味着传统就业理论的失效。第二，凯恩斯提出了有效需求原理，指出就业量实际上取决于与总供给相均衡的社会有效需求的大小。第三，凯恩斯提出了简单的国民收入决定理论，认为决定国民收入和就业水平的因素主要是三大心理变量（边际消费倾向、资本边际效率和流动性偏好）和货币供应量。第四，凯恩斯提出了上述三大心理变量的运行规律，即边际消费倾向递减、资本边际效率递减和流动性偏好规律。第五，凯恩斯提出了乘数理论，认为初始的投资增加可以引发诱致性投资增加，通过连锁式效应，最终可以带来数倍于初始投资的社会有效需求扩张，反之亦然。第六，凯恩斯提出了经济周期理论，认为经济周期主要包括繁荣、萧条、衰退和复苏四个阶段，这是由于投资率波动引起的，而投资率的波动又主要在于资本边际效率的变动。此外，凯恩斯还研究了物价理论、工资理论、国际贸易理论等等。因此，凯恩斯经济学理论的创见被誉为"凯恩斯革命"——一场像哥白尼在天文学上、达尔文在生物学上、爱因斯坦在物理学上一样的革命。

凯恩斯《就业、利息和货币通论》的出现，从宏观的视角对大量经济概念进行了归纳和整合，使经济学的发展在 20 世纪翻开了崭新的一页。如上所说，第一，凯恩斯在"亦学亦政"的特殊经历中找到了一国促进经济增长的新领域——不是重商主义的"对外贸易"，不是重农学派的"农业和畜牧业"，不是亚当·斯密的"商品物质生产部门"和"产业经济"，而是以基础设施投资为主的公共工程、公共物品投资领域。第二，基础设施投资领域的第一主体，或者说国家在此领域干预经济/促进经济增长的第一主体，是政府。第三，政府在基础设施投资领域运用的主要政策手段是财政政策而

fiscal policies rather than monetary policies. Hence, Keynes' economics extended beyond the limits of classical economics and neoclassical economics: On the one hand, classical and neoclassical economics followed the logic of "formation of the commodity price—formation of the industrial economy which centers on the commodity production sectors—persistence of the enterprises as the main body of the free economy—all the main bodies abiding by the market rules" to boost economy. On the other hand, Keynes and the Keynesian school followed the path of "government investment in public projects and public goods—government investment mainly in infrastructure or the development of urban economy—government as the main body of infrastructure investment—government adoption of active fiscal policies" to effectively promote economic growth. From the trajectory of economic growth, it was clear that Keynes and later Keynesians did push the development of economics beyond the limits of product-price analyses, which is the extremely successful and unique contribution of Keynes and Keynesian economics.

However, with the development of Keynesian theories and related government policies, we find some problems. (1) Keynes did not, in basic economics theory, strictly distinguish the public works, public goods and material goods in essence. Instead, he consciously or subconsciously placed public works and public goods into the framework of commodity-price analysis. (2) There were no strict definitions and distinctions between infrastructure and urban economy with material production and industrial economy. In fact, the motives for Keynes to put forward government intervention was to solve the problems of unemployment and economic growth; the government intervened with active fiscal policies and investing large sums of money in public works and public goods centered on infrastructure investment, which belonged to urban economy. Urban economy, as it turned out, had not fully developed during Adam Smith's era. Limitations of the times led to Adam Smith's definition of infrastructure and urban economic development only as public goods, which private investors were unable to get profits from, but could only be provided by the government. In Keynes' times 160 years later (from *The Wealth of Nations* of 1776 to *The General Theory of Employment, Interest and Money* of 1936), although he defined such public works and public goods as a semi-autonomous area between private investors and the state, he did not specifically suggest that these

非货币政策。于是，凯恩斯经济学的发展就突破了古典经济学和新古典经济学的边界：古典经济学和新古典经济学遵循"商品价格形成→形成围绕物质生产部门的产业经济→始终坚持企业为自由经济的主体→主体共同遵循市场规律"的思路来推动经济增长；凯恩斯及凯恩斯主义则借助"国家投资公共工程和公共物品→以基础设施投入或城市经济拓展为主→基础设施投资领域的第一主体是政府→政府运用积极财政政策"的路径，有效推动经济增长。由此，从经济增长的运行轨迹上来说，凯恩斯及后来的凯恩斯主义确实使经济学的发展跳出了商品—价格分析的限制，这是凯恩斯及凯恩斯主义极为成功且独树一帜的贡献。

但随着凯恩斯理论及相关政策的深化与推动，我们发现凯恩斯理论存在一些问题：第一，在基础的经济学理论当中，凯恩斯并没有在本质上严格区分公共工程、公共物品与物质商品，而是有意无意又自然而然地把公共工程、公共物品装进了商品—价格分析的框架之中。第二，没有严格区分和界定基础设施、城市经济与物质生产、产业经济的不同点。其实，凯恩斯最早提出政府干预的动因是解决失业问题，促进增长，而政府干预是通过积极的财政政策，在以基础设施投资为主的公共工程、公共物品领域大量投资，这主要属于城市经济范畴，而这又恰恰是亚当·斯密时代还没有重大发展、没有深入涉及的范畴。时代的局限性使亚当·斯密把基础设施、城市经济拓展只定义为公共物品，且是私人投资者不能赚取利润、需要靠政府提供的公共物品。160年后的凯恩斯时代（从1776年的《国富论》到1936年的《就业、利息和货币通论》），虽然他把此类公共工程、公共物品定义在私人投资者和国家之间的半自治领域，

did not belong to industrial economy, but rather, urban economy. Urban economy can be seen in both a broad sense and a narrow sense. In a broad sense, urban economy included not only industrial economy (operational), livelihood economy (non-operational), but also public works and public goods economy which centered on infrastructure investment and development (quasi-operational). In a narrow sense, urban economy referred specifically to public works and public goods economy which centered on infrastructure investment and development. Different from industrial economy, it was but a new economic field, a new resource generation field. Mixing urban economy and industrial economy into one would cause a series of contradictions in economics, especially market economic theories. (3) Keynes did not strictly distinguish between the main participants in urban economy (infrastructure investment) and those in industrial economy. The main participants of commodity production in industrial economy were the industries; whilst the main participants in urban economy (the field of infrastructure investment) would firstly be the government, but at the same time, private investors and alliance investors. Keynes' analysis of effective demand included investment demand and consumption demand, insufficient investment demand resulting from decline in capital marginal efficiency and liquidity preference. The former referred to a decline in return on investment and the latter to preference of people to retain cash. From Keynes' analysis of the decline in investment profit margins, infrastructure investors not only included the government, but also private and alliance investors, as they jointly participated in investment, following the rules and operating mechanism of the market. Derived from this was the concept of "return on investment (ROI)" in urban economy (infrastructure investment), whose participants included the government, private investors and investor union, its operation under market rules in the fields of public works and public goods. However, as Keynes and Keynesian economics did not distinguish between government's participation/intervention in urban economy and enterprises' participation in industrial economy, therefore arose the problem in its economics of the vague roles of the government and industries in industrial economy or market economy. Consequently, there arose a series of theoretical and practical disputes against the so-called "government intervention" by the defenders of classical and neoclassical economics, or the so-called defenders of market economy. (4) To elaborate, Keynes and Keynesian economics did not

但并没有旗帜鲜明地提出这不属于产业经济而属城市经济范畴。城市经济有广义与狭义之分——广义城市经济既包括产业经济（经营性），又包括民生经济（非经营性），还包括以基础设施投资和拓展为主体的公共工程、公共物品经济（准经营性）；狭义城市经济专指以基础设施投资拓展为主体的公共工程、公共物品经济，它不同于产业经济，而属于一个新的经济领域，一种新的资源生成领域。把城市经济与产业经济混为一谈，会带来经济学，尤其是市场经济理论的一系列矛盾，难以自圆其说。第三，凯恩斯没有严格区分基础设施投资领域／城市经济的参与主体与产业经济的参与主体。产业经济中商品生产的主体就是企业；而城市经济／基础设施领域的投资主体首先是政府，但同时又包含私人投资者和投资者联盟。凯恩斯认为，有效需求包括投资需求和消费需求，其中投资需求不足是因为资本边际效率递减和流动性偏好，前者是指投资利润率下降，后者是指人们保留现金的偏好。这里凯恩斯对投资利润率下降的原因分析中，基础设施建设的投资主体显然既包含了政府，又包含了私人和联盟投资者，他们共同参与投资、共同遵循市场运作机制。因此才会有"投资利润率"的概念，即在城市经济／基础设施投资领域，参与主体包括政府、个人、联盟三类投资者，经济运行依靠市场规则，范围主要包括公共工程和公共物品。但由于凯恩斯及凯恩斯主义没有区分城市经济中的政府参与／政府干预与产业经济中的企业参与，而把它们混为一谈，于是就出现了在其经济学说中政府与企业在产业经济或市场经济中同分一杯羹的问题，这使得亚当·斯密古典经济学与马歇尔新古典经济学的维护者，或者说所谓市场经济的捍卫者，站出来拼命反对所谓的"政府干预"，从而产生了一系列理论和实际问题的争论。第四，进一步说，凯恩斯及

further clarify whether market rules were limited to the production of commodities in industrial economy, or also included infrastructure investment-centered public works and public goods in urban economy. Thereby, whether governments, as one of the investors, should also follow market rules in the investment of public works and public goods was not clarified. (5) To analyze further, as governments had participated in urban economy—the investment of public works and public goods, were they in competitive relationships with other regional governments, private investors, and alliance investors? How should governments' roles be defined and differentiated in the development of industrial economy and urban economy? Before these questions were effectively solved, having found a new field that can promote national economic growth, Keynes and Keynesian economics then rushed to adopt related policies and measures and study the practical results to help solve problems in this field. They did not address some fundamental economic issues, thereby, resulting in ambiguity and confusion in assumptions and later analyses, and creating an "ambiguous area" which led to endless controversies and contradictions in later generations.

To sum up, (1) Keynes' theory abandoned the support provided by Adam Smith's theories, established its own system with a unique style, but yet consciously or subconsciously relied on the support of Adam Smith's market theory of industrial economy. The key points of Adam Smith's theories included: "selfishness" and "sympathy" integrating to form "an invisible hand" in *The Moral Sentiments,* and "egoism" and "altruism" integrating to form "an invisible hand" in *The Wealth of Nations.* Keynes found a new field that can promote national economic growth—the development and utilization of infrastructure resources and urban resources. However, there was a lack of rational support as far as government functions and roles of a nation were concerned; or perhaps, he had no chance to do the research yet. (2) The regulatory methods of Keynes and the Keynesian school to promote economic growth embodied the principles of balanced supply, effective demand, optimal allocation of resources, and benign economic development, etc. However, the theory did not point out that with the prosperity of the nation and progress of its science and technology, there arose the problem of the development of urban resources and international resources like space resources, deep sea resources and polar resources. In national economic growth, the new

凯恩斯主义也没有明确市场规则是否只局限在产业经济/商品生产中，还是也包括在城市经济/作为基础设施投资的公共工程和公共物品中，因而也没有明确作为参与主体之一的政府在公共工程、公共物品的投资中是否也应遵循市场规则。第五，更深入分析的话，政府参与城市经济/以基础设施投资为主的公共工程、公共物品投资，那么它与区域内其他政府、私人投资者、投资者联盟是否也是竞争关系？政府在产业经济发展中的角色与在城市经济开拓中的角色到底如何区分、如何界定？这类问题都没有得到有效的解决，凯恩斯及凯恩斯主义在找到了一国促进经济增长的新领域之后，就急急忙忙着手于研究此领域相关的政策措施与实效问题，推动解决当时的实际问题，而把该理论中需要首先澄清的基础问题搁置一旁。这就导致其理论在前提假设乃至后面的分析上有含混的问题，产生了"模糊区域"，因此后人争论不休，以其矛攻其盾，矛盾百出。

综上可知，第一，凯恩斯理论抛弃了亚当·斯密的理论支撑，自成系统，独树一帜，但又有意无意地依赖亚当·斯密的产业经济市场理论作为支撑。亚当·斯密理论支撑的要点，在《道德情操论》中是"利己心"与"同情心"有机融合的"一只看不见的手"，在《国富论》中是"利己性"与"利他性"有机融合的"一只看不见的手"，而凯恩斯找到了一国促进经济增长的新领域——基础设施资源、城市资源的开发和利用，但在论述政府职能和国家角色时，其理论却又缺乏合理内核的支撑，或尚未来得及研究。第二，凯恩斯或凯恩斯学派促进经济增长的调控方式无不体现着供给均衡、有效需求、优化资源配置、经济良性发展等原则，但在理论上却忽略了，随着一国的繁荣、科技的进步，出现了城市资源甚至是国际资源如太空资源、深海资源、极地资源等的发掘问题，国家经济增长的课题中新增了"新生资源"或"资源生成"的问题，需要进一步

subject of new resources and resource generation needed to be further studied. Scarcity and generation of resources are twins in the allocation of resources in economics. (3) The development of economic theories lags behind the changes in economic reality. Keynes adopted Adam Smith's theory on the allocation of industrial resources, but yet did not explore problems on the generation of urban resources/infrastructure resources, thereby considering problems in isolation. Keynesian economics at this time, being practical, prescribed a cure only on the symptoms instead of on the root cause of the problems. In my opinion, this is where the real problem of Keynes' theories lies. (4) The generation and effective allocation of new resources need a system of rules and regulations for support and guarantee. The regulations would help the government, as one of the main subjects in the development and utilization of new resources, determine what to do with the development and utilization of current resources—industrial resources, as well as how to regulate the development and utilization of new resources—urban resources. It was precisely such lack of rules and regulations that had become another weakness in Keynes' theories. (5) The foundation of economic theories is subject to "evolution paradigms". Hence, we should draw lessons and experiences from successful cases of economic practices, learn from the dynamic deductive process history has taught, and use "resource scarcity" and "resource generation" from the core principles of "resource allocation" in economics as a starting point to further analyze and develop modern market theory and modern economics system.

研究。这里，资源稀缺与资源生成，是经济学中资源配置的一对孪生儿。第三，经济理论的发展滞后于经济现实的变化。凯恩斯借用了亚当·斯密产业资源配置的理论，却又不去讨论城市资源／基础设施资源的生成问题，这样就产生了"就问题论问题""就政策论政策"的情况，此时的凯恩斯经济学作为致用之学，就出现那种"头疼医头，脚疼医脚"的药方了。我想，这应该是凯恩斯理论真正的问题所在。第四，新的资源生成、资源的有效配置，需要制度建设的配套与保障。有了制度建设才能确定，作为新生资源开发和利用主体之一的政府，应该如何面对原有资源（产业资源）的开发和利用，应该如何调控新生资源（城市资源）的开发和利用。而配套的"制度建设"的欠缺，又成为凯恩斯理论的另一缺陷。第五，经济学理论基础受"演化范式"的规范。因此，我们应借鉴经济实践中的成功案例，借鉴历史的动态演绎过程，以经济学核心原则"资源配置"中的"资源稀缺"和"资源生成"为切入点，分析、演化出现代市场理论乃至现代经济学体系。

CHAPTER 3   SCARCITY AND GENERATION OF RESOURCES

1. Scarcity and Generation of Resources are a Pair of Twins in Resource Allocation.

Faced with massive unemployment in Britain in the 1920s and the Great Depression in the United States and even the whole world in the 1930s, the master economist Keynes, with his unique experiences in academia and politics, found an effective solution and discovered a new path and a new field for a country's economic growth, namely, apart from stimulating industrial economy, enhancing effective demand by investing in infrastructure to effectively solve the problem of unemployment and promote a country's economic recovery and growth. However, to implement these measures required the government to be the main body in initiating investment, therefore contradicting Adam Smith's definition of "night watchman state".

Why couldn't Keynes and the subsequent Keynesian school explain and solve this problem under the principles and framework of economics? This required one to start with Adam Smith's *Wealth of Nations*.

In *The Wealth of Nations*, Adam Smith first put forward two assumptions when discussing economic activities of human society, namely, the egoism of economic activities and resource scarcity. Commodity economy integrates egoism and altruism to form the "invisible hand", forming the system of commodities, prices, demand and supply, and competition, and eventually forming the market rules; resource scarcity leads to a universal rule in the selection of the control target in economy: the optimized allocation of resources and the healthy development of economy. With regard to the two assumptions, the "invisible hand" and the market rules have long become the Bible of classical and neoclassical economics; and "resource allocation" and "resource scarcity" have been taken as the starting point for economic research by both liberal economics and Keynesian economics. Just as P. A. Samuelson said, "Economics is the study of how societies use scarce resources to produce valuable goods and services and distribute them among different individuals."[1]

Hence, when traditional economics discusses resource allocation, it cannot escape the association with resource scarcity. Resource allocation

叁 资源稀缺与资源生成

一、资源稀缺与资源生成是资源配置中的一对孪生儿

亦学亦政的经济学大师凯恩斯，面对上个世纪 20 年代英国的大量工人失业和 30 年代美国乃至世界的经济大萧条，找到了解决此类问题的有效方法，发现了一国促进经济增长的新路径、新领域，即除了刺激产业经济发展外，利用基础设施投资，扩大有效需求，能有效解决失业问题，促进一国经济复苏和经济增长。然而，由于推行此措施的投资主体首先来自政府，于是就有了与亚当·斯密定义的政府只是"守夜人"的观点相矛盾的争议。

为什么凯恩斯及之后的凯恩斯主义未能在经济学原理或者说经济学范畴内去解释、解决这一问题？这还要从其鼻祖亚当·斯密的《国富论》说起。

亚当·斯密的《国富论》在论述人类社会的经济活动时，首先提出了两个假设——经济活动的利己性和资源稀缺。商品经济的"主观为己、客观为他人"的利己性与利他性有机融合，成为一只"看不见的手"，形成商品、价格、供求、竞争体系，并最终形成市场规则；资源稀缺使经济领域的调控目标无不服从一个原则——资源的优化配置与经济的良性发展。这两个假设中，"看不见的手"及市场法则早已成为古典经济学、新古典经济学的圣经，而"资源配置及稀缺法则"，无论是自由主义经济学派，还是凯恩斯主义经济学派，都将其作为经济学研究的出发点。于是就有了萨缪尔森所说的："经济学研究的是一个社会如何利用稀缺的资源生产有价值的商品，并将它们在不同的个体之间进行分配。"[1]

因此，传统经济学一论及资源配置，就必然与资源稀缺联系起来。资源配置本身的定义就是：对相对稀缺的资源在各种不同用途

is itself defined as the choice made after comparing the various purposes that relatively scarce resources can be used for. According to traditional economics, at a certain stage of social economic development, compared to people's needs, resources tend to be relatively scarce, thereby requiring society to rationally allocate these limited and relatively scarce resources, so as to utilize the least amount of resources to produce the most suitable and useful goods and services, and maximize the benefits. Taking a step further, whether or not resources can be allocated rationally has become an extremely critical factor in determining the success or failure of a country's economic development.

Here, we are neither denying the importance of resource allocation, nor the necessary connection between resource allocation and resource scarcity, nor that the law of resource scarcity has become the starting point for economic research. However, we cannot study resource allocation without discussing, contemplating and exploring the problem of "resource generation". The current situation is quite different from that of Adam Smith's time: (1) When Adam Smith published *The Wealth of Nations* in 1776, the Industrial Revolution just started in Britain. At that time, what Adam Smith referred to as resource allocation was merely the allocation of industrial resources such as people, money and material associated with the production, exchange, and consumption of goods, and not others. (2) The urban infrastructure in Britain around 1776 was still rather backward, consisting of nothing more than roads, bridges, canals and ports. It was inadequate to be used to solve massive unemployment and economic crisis as in Keynes' era more than a hundred years later. (3) The construction of modernized infrastructure we have in modern society involves not only a series of investment projects in hardware and software, but also a series of projects in the development and construction process of intelligent cities. These have become the new field and new resources to promote a country's economic growth, thereby giving rise to the issue of resource generation. This new field of resource generation could be referred to as "urban resources"; different from traditional industrial resources in nature and allocation, they promote economic growth from a different route.

The introduction of urban resources and resource generation is crucial for economics for it can untangle a contradiction in Keynesian theories: finding a new field to promote a country's economic growth on the one hand, and being restricted to using industrial economic

上加以比较作出的选择。传统经济学认为，在社会经济发展的一定阶段内，相对于人们的需求而言，资源总是表现出稀缺性，这要求人们对有限的、相对稀缺的资源进行合理配置，以便用最少的资源耗费，生产出最适用的商品和劳务，获取最佳的效益。进一步说，资源配置合理与否，已经成为决定一个国家经济发展成败的极其重要的影响因素。

在这里，我们不否认资源配置的重要性，不否认资源配置与资源稀缺的必然联系，也不否认资源稀缺法则已经成为经济学研究的出发点。但问题在于，我们研究资源配置，就不能不去讨论、思考、发掘"资源生成"的问题。因为当前的情况和亚当·斯密时代已大不一样：首先，亚当·斯密1776年发表《国富论》时，英国工业革命才刚刚开始。此时亚当·斯密所说的资源配置，只是指与商品生产、交换、消费相联系的产业资源中人、财、物的配置，而非其他。其次，1776年前后，英国的城市基础设施还相当落后，仅仅局限于简单的道路、桥梁、运河和港口等，根本无法像一百多年后的凯恩斯时代那样，承担起缓解国家大量失业和经济萧条的重要作用。最后，现代社会的现代化基础设施建设，不仅包括系列硬件投资项目，还有系列软件投资项目，乃至更进一步的智能城市开发与建设过程中的系列工程。这些现代化基础设施建设构成了促进一国经济增长的新的领域、新的资源，由此产生了"资源生成"问题，而这个新的资源生成领域可以被称为"城市资源"，它有别于传统产业资源的性质和配置方式，从另一路径发挥着促进经济增长的积极作用。

城市资源与资源生成概念的提出对经济学的关键性在于，它能够解决凯恩斯理论遗留的矛盾，即凯恩斯一方面找到了一国促进经

ideology to analyze and solve problems on the other. Being a pair of twins in resource allocation theories in economics, resource generation and resource scarcity are two inseparable aspects that are closely related to economic development and progress of the times. Urban resources (needless to say, there will be international resources such as space resources, deep sea resources, polar resources, etc. subsequently) differ from industrial resources that Adam Smith studied during his time, in their nature, contents and functions. Each of them exerts different effects on the economic practice and the theories of economics. We should rectify the situation in traditional economics where there was no research, discussion nor analysis on resource generation, or its effects on economic development and theories of economics. We should abandon traditional economics' habit of merely using the theories and methods of industrial resources allocation to understand, contemplate, and explain the effects of the new-born resource generation, which emphasized efficient allocation of resources based only on resource scarcity and discussed merely equilibrium and disequilibrium in distributions. These resulted in the economic theories' development deviating from reality or lagging behind changes in economic reality, leaving resource generation and its corresponding institutional construction and regulation setting void. These are the problems we should solve at the moment.

2. From Resource Generation to Generative Resources

Generative resources, generated from "resource generation", featured as dynamic, economic and productive, are economic resources like industrial resources.

Resource generation is not arising out of plan, but rather pre-exists or arises from the objective needs of the times. It becomes dynamic when it can be produced to generate revenue. A mountain which sits idle, as an example, is a static natural resource, but once developed into a dynamic production factor, it becomes an important economic resource.

Land, mines, water, forests, grasslands, and other static landscapes are natural resources; once developed, they become economic resources; this is a fact long known to all. Urban infrastructure – hardware, software, and development and construction of intelligent cities – is to cater for the objective needs of the times, and possesses the characteristics of resource generation. It is another generative resource following industrial

济增长的新领域，另一方面又囿于产业经济的思维方法去分析解决问题。资源生成与资源稀缺，应该是经济学资源配置理论中的一对孪生儿，是该理论紧密结合经济发展和时代进步的不可分割的两个方面。城市资源（当然以后还有太空资源、深海资源、极地资源等国际资源）在性质、主体、作用上均不同于亚当·斯密当年研究的产业资源，二者在经济实践和经济学理论中均发挥着不同的作用。传统经济学中没有人去研究、讨论、分析的资源生成问题及其对经济发展、对经济学理论的影响，应该引起我们的重视。传统经济学习惯性地用产业资源配置的原理、方法去了解、思考、解释资源生成这个新生事物的作用，只从资源稀缺法则出发强调资源的有效配置，围绕着均衡与非均衡做文章，使经济学理论的发展脱离现实，或远远滞后于经济现实的变化，从而使资源生成和与之相匹配的制度建设、规则制定一直成为空白，这都是我们目前应该着力解决的问题。

二、从资源生成到生成性资源

资源生成派生的生成性资源与产业资源一样同属经济资源，它具备三大特性：动态性、经济性、生产性。

资源生成不是计划设定的产物，而是原已存在或随着时代进程的客观需要而出现的事物，它由静态进入动态，直至具备经济性和生产性。比如，一座山体，矗立在那里，是静态的自然资源，开发起来，进入动态，即生成生产要素，就是重要的经济资源。土地、矿产、水、森林、草原等静态景观是自然资源，动态开发则成为经济资源，这点大家早已知晓。随着时代进程的客观需要而存在和发展的城市基础设施——包括硬件、软件乃至更进一步的智能城市开发建设，也符合资源生成的范畴特性，它是继产业资源之后的又一

resources—urban resources. Of course, there are space resources which are similar (there are actually many more usable resources in outer space than on earth). Just within the solar system, there are vast deposits of mineral resources on celestial bodies such as the Moon, Mars and other asteroids; on Jovian planets and the comet, there is an abundance of hydrogen energy; in planetary and interplanetary spaces, there exist vacuum resources, radioactive resources and vast temperature difference resources; furthermore, through flights of spacecraft, orbital resources, micro-gravity resources and others can be generated. In their static states, these are natural resources, but once developed and utilized, they become productive factors, and are important and treasured economic resources. With regard to the generation, development and utilization of such resources, can national governments not play a role as one of the subjects? Can we still explain and promote it only using traditional theories of industrial economy? Obviously not. In reality, the government plays a different role in the generation, development and utilization of urban resources from what it plays in the development of industrial economy.

Urban resources can be defined in a broad and a narrow sense.

Firstly, cities are not randomly built, most of which are gradually formed in the process of historical development. Secondly, cities are neither static nor fixed; most of them gradually expand through dynamic interactions. Furthermore, cities are not single-functional. Most of them include the functions of hardware and software infrastructure, and even modernized intelligent cities in a three-dimensional development pattern. All the conditions on which the building, existence and development of cities depend are deemed as urban resources.

Hence, from an economic perspective, urban resources in a broad sense contain industrial resources, livelihood resources, and infrastructure resources or public works resources. Urban resources in a narrow sense are what we will discuss at length: Why did Keynes find a new field to boost the economic growth of a nation, but couldn't explain it by price theory and industrial economic theory? Why did the previous Roosevelt Administration or the incumbent Trump Administration invest in infrastructure construction in their attempt to solve economic depression and promote economic growth? (Infrastructure construction has become a measure pursued globally to promote economic growth; for instance, China has invested in infrastructure construction of "Belt

生成性资源——城市资源。当然之后还有与此类似的太空资源（太空中可利用的资源比地球上可利用的资源要多得多）：仅从太阳系范围来说，在月球、火星和小行星等天体上，有丰富的矿产资源；在类木行星和彗星上，有丰富的氢能资源；在行星空间和行星际空间有真空资源、辐射资源、大温差资源；利用航天器飞行，还可派生出轨道资源和微重力资源等。这些太空资源如保持静止状态，则属自然资源，若得以开发利用，则生成生产要素，成为重要、宝贵的经济资源。对这类资源的生成、开发和利用，国家政府能不作为主体之一发挥作用吗？我们还能囿于传统的产业经济原理来解释与推动吗？显然不能。值得注意的是，城市资源的生成、开发与利用，政府在其中扮演着不同于在产业经济发展中的角色。

城市资源有广义与狭义之分。

首先，城市不是随意设立的，大多数城市是随着时代进程，在客观的历史发展中逐渐形成的。其次，城市不是静态固定的，大多数城市是随着时代进程，在动态的聚合交往中逐步扩大的。再次，城市不是单一功能的，大多数城市是随着时代进程，在立体发展格局中囊括了基础设施硬件、软件乃至现代化智能城市功能的。城市设立、存在和发展的一切条件，堪称"城市资源"。

因此，从经济学角度定义，广义的城市资源包括了产业资源、民生资源和基础设施／公共工程资源，而狭义的城市资源则是我们要重点分析的。为什么凯恩斯找到了一国经济增长的新领域，但又很难用商品价格理论、产业经济理论去解释它？为什么罗斯福政府或现在的特朗普政府解决经济萧条、促进经济增长的首要措施是投资基础设施建设（基础设施建设已成为当今世界各国努力推动的促进经济增长手段，比如中国对"一带一路"沿线国家的基础设施建

and Road" nations.) These questions could be answered by the research into urban resources in their narrow sense. As important generative resources, urban resources in their narrow sense include investment and construction of hardware and software infrastructure, as well as the development and operation of intelligent cities in the process of further modernization. It is a new economic field whose theories are worth developing, whose market rules are worth exploring, whose government-market relationship is worth studying to discover a new engine for national and even global economy. It is related to and different from theories of industrial economics. Modern economists really should not just rely on theories of industrial economics to explain or promote the development of urban economy and urban resources.

Urban infrastructure, as generative resources, refers to public work facilities that provide public services for social production and residents' living, and is a public goods system to ensure smooth running of national and regional social economic activities and residents' daily lives. It includes not only hardware public facilities such as roads, railways, airports, communications, water, electricity, gas and others, but also software public services such as education, science and technology, health care, sports, culture and others. With the progress of urban modernization, it also includes the series of development and construction of intelligent cities. To put it in detail, hardware mainly refers to the six major systematic engineering infrastructure: (1) energy supply system, such as electricity, gas, natural gas, liquefied petroleum gas, heating, etc; (2) water supply and drainage system, such as water resource protection, water plants, water distribution system, drainage and sewerage; (3) transportation system, divided into external transport facilities (e.g., aviation, railways, shipping, coaches and highways) and internal ones (e.g., roads, bridges, tunnels, subways, light rails, public transportation, taxis, parking facilities, and ferries); (4) posts and telecommunications system, such as postal service, telegraphs, landline phones, mobile phones, internet, radio and television, etc; (5) environmental protection and sanitation system, such as landscaping, garbage collection and disposal, pollution control, etc; (6) defense and disaster prevention safety system, for disasters such as fire, flood, earthquake, typhoon, sand storm, ground subsidence, air defense, etc. Software mainly refers to administrative management, culture and education, health care, commercial services, financial insurance, social welfare, and other infrastructure for social services. With the progress of urban-rural integration, software also

设的投资）？这些都能在对狭义的城市资源的研究中得到解答。作为重要的生成性资源，狭义的城市资源包括基础设施硬件、软件的投资建设，以及更进一步的现代化进程中智能城市的开发和运作，这是真正值得我们开发其理论、探索其市场规则、研究其中的政府与市场关系从而挖掘出国家乃至世界经济发展新引擎的经济学新领域。它与产业经济理论有联系，但更有区别，现代经济学家不应该再囿于产业经济理论来解释或推动城市经济、城市资源的开发建设。

作为生成性资源的城市基础设施指的是为社会生产和居民生活提供公共服务的公共工程设施，是用于保证国家和地区社会经济活动和人们日常生活正常进行的公共物品系统。其范围不仅包括公路、铁路、机场、通信、水电煤气等硬件公共设施，而且包括教育、科技、医疗卫生、体育、文化等软件公共设施，并且伴随着城市现代化的进程，还包括更进一步的智能城市的系列开发和建设等。具体来说，硬件公共设施多指六大系统工程性基础设施：第一，能源供应系统，包括电力、煤气、天然气、液化石油气和暖气等。第二，供水排水系统，包括水资源保护、自来水厂、供水网管、排水和污水处理。第三，交通运输系统，分为对外交通设施和对内交通设施。前者包括航空、铁路、航运、长途汽车和高速公路；后者包括道路、桥梁、隧道、地铁、轻轨高架、公共交通、出租汽车、停车场、轮渡等。第四，邮电通信系统，如邮政、电报、固定电话、移动电话、互联网、广播电视等。第五，环保环卫系统，如园林绿化、垃圾收集与处理、污染治理等。第六，防卫防灾安全系统，如消防、防汛、防震、防台风、防风沙、防地面沉降、防空等。软件公共设施主要是指行政管理、文化教育、医疗卫生、商业服务、金融保险、社会福利等社会性基础设施。同时，随着城乡一

includes four main types, namely infrastructure for rural production, rural daily living, construction of ecological environment, and rural social development. With the progress of urban modernization, the development and construction of intelligent cities has become a new part of urban infrastructure. The urban infrastructure, as new generative resources, are fundamental, non-trading and quasi-public goods in economics, become a new field that could promote national economic development and open a new path to reforming economics theories.

3. Three Types of Resources in Cities

Back to reality, the 21st century is a century marked by the co-existence and co-prosperity of economic development, urban construction, and social livelihood. In practice, governments manifest their economic functions through the allocation and management of various resources. In other words, governments would classify from an economic perspective natural resources, human resources, capital resources, industrial resources, urban resources, and public goods resources that exist in reality within their territories, optimize their allocation, and make parallel policies. There are three major resources in cities:

(1) Resources that relate to economic development, otherwise known as "operational resources" in market economy, are mainly industrial resources in regional economy in various countries. As the economic geographical and natural conditions differ, regions would choose one from the primary industry, secondary industry, and tertiary industry as the lead in their economic development. In reality, needless to say, in the process of the development of the primary and secondary sectors, there have been numerous cases of successful development of the tertiary sector, such as logistics, exhibition, finance, tourism, intermediary service, and retail trade. In traditional economics, companies and enterprises are related to these resources, or in other words, are the main

bodies in the development of industrial economy. There are three types of governmental institutions in China that coordinate, monitor, and manage such resources: (i) development and reform, statistics and prices; (ii) (a) treasury, finance, taxation, industry and commerce; (b) industry, transport, security, energy and tobacco; (c) science and technology, information, private communications, intellectual property rights; (d) commerce, customs, maritime affairs, ports, postal service, quality

体化的进程，这类基础设施还包括了乡村生产、生活、生态环境建设和社会发展等四大类基础设施。伴随着城市现代化的进程，开发和建设智能城市系列工程成为了城市基础设施建设的新内容。这些城市基础设施作为新的生成性资源，在经济学上具有基础性、非贸易性和准公共物品性，成为促进一国经济增长的新领域和创新经济学理论的新路径。

三、城市的三类资源

回到现实，21 世纪是经济发展、城市建设、社会民生同生同长、协同繁荣的世纪。各国政府经济职能的发挥，在实践中表现为对国家各类资源的一种调配、管理，即各国政府对国家现实存在的自然资源、人力资源、资本资源、产业资源、城市资源和公共物品资源等进行经济学分类并优化配置、配套政策。其中，城市主要存在三类资源：

第一类是与经济发展相对应的资源，在市场经济中被称为"可经营性资源"。它以各国区域经济中的产业资源为主。因为经济地理和自然条件不同，所以各区域一般会选择三大产业中的某一产业作为主导方向。当然在各国区域经济的现实发展进程中，也不乏在发展第一产业或第二产业的过程中产生强盛的物流业、会展业、金融业、旅游业、中介服务业和商贸零售业等第三产业的成功案例。传统经济学中对应此类资源的机构，或者说在产业经济发展中发挥主体作用的机构，主要是公司企业。在中国，政府协调、监督、管理此类资源的机构主要有三种。第一种是发展改革、统计、物价部门。第二种又细分为四类：其一，财政、金融、税务、工商部门；其二，工业、交通、安全、能源、烟草部门；其三，科技、信息、专用通信、知识产权部门；其四，商务、海关、海事、口岸、邮政、

inspection, foreign affairs, tourism; (iii) audit, territorial supervision, food and pharmaceutical supervision and management, etc. The governmental institutions of coordinating, supervising and managing may be similar or different across different nations, but they share the main principles of "invigoration" in resource allocation; that is, to plan and guide, to support and coordinate, to supervise and manage. This is already commonly agreed upon in theory.

(2) Resources that relate to social livelihood, otherwise known as "non-operational resources" in market economy, are mainly the social welfare and public goods in various regions, including economy (guarantee), history, geography, image, spirit, idea, emergency, security, relief and other social needs in regions. In traditional economics, the government and social enterprises are related to these resources, to put it another way, are the main organizations in the provision of social welfare and public goods. The governmental institutions in China that coordinate, monitor, and manage such resources are: (i) (a) finance, audit, public sectors; (b) literature and history, counseling, archives; (c) civil affairs, social security, poverty alleviation; (d) women and children, Federation of Disabled Persons, the Red Cross, etc.; (e) ethnic groups, religions, overseas Chinese affairs; (ii) geology, earthquake, meteorology; (iii) (a) emergency, safety and security, air defense; (b) people's armed forces, public security, judiciary, supervision organs; (c) fire brigade, armed police, border defense, coast guards and anti-smuggling, etc. Similar governmental institutions may have different names in different nations, but they share the main principles of resource allocation, namely, "social guarantee, general underpinning; fairness and justice, effective promotion". This is also consistent in practice and cognition.

(3) Resources that relate to urban construction, otherwise known as "quasi-operational resources" in market economy, are mainly the urban resources across various regions. These are mainly public service systems to ensure the smooth running of national or regional social

economic activities, the software and hardware infrastructure to provide public service for social production and residents' daily living, namely the urban infrastructure described above in "resource generation", including transportation, posts and telecommunications, power and water supply, landscaping, environmental protection, education, science and technology, culture, health, sports and other urban public works and

质检、外事、旅游部门。第三种是审计、国土监察、食品药品监督管理部门。世界各国政府的协调、监督、管理机构各有异同，但调配此类资源的政策原则主要是"搞活"，即：规划、引导；扶持、调节；监督、管理。这点在理论认识上已经是共识。

第二类是与社会民生相对应的资源，在市场经济中被称为"非经营性资源"。它以各区域的社会公益产品、公共物品为主，包括：经济（保障）、历史、地理、形象、精神、理念、应急、安全、救助，以及区域的其他社会需求。传统经济学中对应此类资源的机构，或者说在提供社会公益产品、公共物品的过程中发挥主体作用的机构，主要是政府和社会企业。在中国，政府协调、监督、管理此类资源的机构主要有三种。第一种细分为五类：其一，财政、审计、编制相关机构；其二，文史、参事、档案相关机构；其三，民政、社保、扶贫相关机构；其四，妇女、儿童、残联、红十字会等相关机构；其五，民族、宗教、侨务相关机构。第二种是地质、地震、气象相关机构。第三种细分为三类：其一，应急、安全、人防相关机构；其二，人民武装、公安、司法、监察相关机构；其三，消防、武警、边防、海防与打私相关机构。世界各国的此类协调、监督、管理机构形同名异，且调配此类资源的政策原则主要都是"社会保障、基本托底；公正公平，有效提升"。这点在实践和认识上也很一致。

第三类是与城市建设相对应的资源，在市场经济中被称为"准经营性资源"。它以各区域的城市资源为主，主要包括保证国家或区域的社会经济活动正常进行的公共服务系统和为社会生产、居民生活提供公共服务的软硬件基础设施，即上文谈到"资源生成"时所提及的城市基础设施，如交通、邮电、供电供水、园林绿化、环境保护、教育、科技、文化、卫生、体育事业等城市公共工程设施

public life service facilities. The quality of the software and hardware infrastructure directly affects the appearance, characteristics, taste, functions and effects of a nation or region. The completeness of the software and hardware infrastructure shall promote the development of social, economic and other undertakings across nations and regions, and push the optimization of urban spatial distribution and structure. The reason why I classify these resources as quasi-operational resources is that they don't have clear definitions in traditional economics. They belong to the "cross-over region" between the government and enterprises, that is, the investment and development of urban infrastructure, as an undertaking to promote economic development and social livelihood, can be undertaken by either enterprises or the government. The governmental institutions in China that coordinate, monitor, and manage such resources are: (i) state-owned assets, major projects; (ii) land resources, environmental protection, urban and rural construction; (iii) human resources, public resource transactions; (iv) education, science and technology, culture, health, sports, press and publication, radio, film and television, research institutions, etc.; (v) agriculture, forestry, water conservation, marine fisheries, etc. The urban quasi-operational resources are the basis for investigating resource generation and investment in infrastructure, and deepening the economic theory analysis.

Theories and practices have taught us: (1) Pertaining to operational resources—industrial resources and industrial economy, resources should be allocated by the market to enterprises, society and various domestic and foreign investors by taking capitalization measures as much as possible. Governments should then design their policies in accordance with the principles of "planning and guidance, support and coordination, supervision and management". (2) Pertaining to non-operational resources—public goods and livelihood economy, in other words, in areas out of reach of enterprises, governments should be responsible for the supply, allocation, management and development of such resources in all facets, and design governmental policies following the principles of "fairness and justice, general underpinning, effective promotion". This is the reason why the national treasury, which is derived from and to be used by the public, should weaken its constructive treasury functions and instead, strengthen its public (public benefits) treasury functions. (3) Pertaining to quasi-operational resources—(narrowly defined as) urban resources and urban economy, governments should determine whether

和公共生活服务设施等。这类基础设施的软硬件水平，直接影响着一个国家或区域的外形、特征、品位、功能和作用。完善的软硬件基础设施将促进各国、各区域的社会、经济等各项事业发展，推动城市空间分布形态和结构的优化。我之所以称这类资源为准经营性资源，是因为这一部分在传统经济学中还属于"模糊板块"，可被归类为政府与企业的"交叉领域"，也就是说，城市基础设施的投资建设是可由企业来承担，也可由政府来完成的促进经济发展和社会民生的事业。在中国，政府协调、监督、管理此类资源的机构主要有五种：第一种是国有资产、重大项目相关机构。第二种是国土资源、环境保护、城乡建设相关机构。第三种是人力资源、公共资源交易相关机构。第四种是教育、科技、文化、卫生、体育、新闻出版、广播影视、研究院所等相关机构。第五种是农业、林业、水利、海洋渔业等相关机构。我们要研究的"资源生成""基础设施投资"、我们要深化的经济学理论分析，就植根于这一城市准经营性资源。

综上，理论与实践告诉我们：首先，对于可经营性资源，即产业资源、产业经济，各国应遵循市场配置资源的原则，发挥其作用，尽可能地通过资本化的手段，把它交给企业、社会和各类国内外投资者，各国政府应按照"规划、引导；扶持、调节；监督、管理"的原则去配套政策。其次，对于非经营性资源，即公共物品、民生经济等企业达不到的领域，各国政府应责无旁贷地、全面地承担起责任，提供、调配、管理和发展此类资源，按照"公平公正、基本托底、有效提升"的原则去配套政策，确保其基本保障。这也就是为什么取之于民、用之于民的国家财政要弱化其建设性财政职能、强化其公共（公益）性财政作用的缘故。最后，对于准经营性资源，即（狭义的）城市资源、城市经济，各国则应根据区域发展

these are to be developed and allocated as operational resources or to be operated and managed as public welfare undertakings, depending upon the direction of regional development, treasury status, capital flows, demand of enterprises and the acceptability and affordability of the public amongst other reasons.

4. The Investment Entities of Urban Infrastructure

The investment, development, and management of urban infrastructure, i.e. quasi-operational resources, present problems in its implementation across various nations: that of determining the investment carrier and of operating the investment fund.

(1) Pertaining to the problem of determining the investment carrier – if we put the urban infrastructure, i.e. quasi-operational resources, into the market system for its investment, development, operation and management, then, governments can set up the carrier of urban infrastructure construction projects through sole proprietorships, joint ventures, cooperation, shareholding systems and even state-owned but privately-operated enterprises. Such equity structures, in accordance with market demand, social supply and objective trends of domestic and international economic development, can not only finance effectively, optimize structure, stabilize economic and social development, but also effectively regulate and control the market according to forecast, and avoid massive losses by preventing certain regional governments from problems in the construction and development of urban infrastructure. The problems include huge wastes of urban resources, wasteful repeated construction of urban infrastructure, low-level, low-standard and disorderly operation of urban economic management. These problems arise from certain regional governments providing for society public goods for free service and sharing; investing without profiting; constructing without managing and operating; focusing on social benefits only but ignoring economic benefits. Hence, during the

selection of the investment, development, operation and management methods of urban infrastructure (quasi-operational resources), regional governments across the world should, with regard to existing urban infrastructure resources, reform the ownership structure of "stock assets" carriers, and build up and operate carriers adaptable to capital market financing means according to market rules and objective demands of economic development; in other words, they could transform the "stock assets" carriers into state-owned but privately-run, shareholding, joint venture, cooperation forms, or auction off to investors home and abroad

方向、财政状况、资金流量、企业需求和社会民众的接受程度与承受力等因素，来确定其是按可经营性资源来开发调配，还是按公益性事业来运行管理。

四、城市基础设施的投资主体

在各国的实践中，城市基础设施即准经营性资源的投资、开发、管理，存在着确定投资载体、运营投资资金的问题。

首先，关于确定载体问题，如果我们把城市基础设施即准经营性资源放入市场体系中去投资、开发、运营和管理，那么，各国政府可以以独资、合资、合作、股份制甚至国有民营等方式组建城市基础设施建设项目的载体。此种股权组建方式不仅能根据市场需求、社会供给和国内外经济发展的客观趋势有效融资，优化结构，促进经济和社会稳步发展，而且能根据对市场的预测进行有效调控，防范某些区域政府在城市基础设施建设和发展中"只为社会提供无偿服务型、共享型的公共物品；只投入、不收益；只建设、不经营；只注重社会性，而忽视经济性；只注重公益性，而忽视效益性：从而造成城市资源的大量损耗，城市基础设施建设的重复浪费，城市经济管理的低层次、低水平和无序性运转"的问题，以避免重大损失。因此，在城市基础设施即准经营性资源的投资、开发、运营、管理方式的选择过程中，各国的区域政府应对原已存在的城市基础设施资源——"存量资产"的平台载体进行产权改造，按照市场规则和经济发展的客观要求，建立并运行与资本市场融资手段相适应的载体。也就是说，将存量资产的平台载体改制为国有民营、股份制、合资、合作形式，或拍卖给国内外投资者去经营、管

to operate and manage, making them equity carriers which conform to market economy rules and participate in market competition. With regard to newly added urban infrastructure projects, or "incremental assets", governments should organize the platform carriers in sole proprietorship, joint venture, cooperation or share-holding forms right from the beginning, and lay the foundation for equity carriers and their development conditions according to market rules, thus turning them into participants in the competition for resource investment, urban development and operation. Steps need to be taken to avoid returning to the old path where government is the sole equity investor in the investment, development, and operation of incremental assets.

(2) Pertaining to the problem of the operation of investment funds— if we invest, develop, operate and manage the urban infrastructure (quasi-operational resources) in the market system, regional governments across the world can solve the problem by capital market financing, for example, issuing bonds or convertible bonds, issuing stocks, setting up project funds or utilizing investment projects by local and foreign funds, back-door listing projects as entities, securitization of project assets, project merger and acquisition, leasing, mortgage, swaps, auction, etc. Governments can also make use of charging and pricing power and use DBO (design-build-operate), BOT (build-operate-transfer), BOO (build-operate-own), BOOT (build-operate-own-transfer), BLT (build-lease-transfer), BTO (build-transfer-operate), TOT (transfer-operate-transfer), amongst others, to implement the capital operation of franchise rights. Governments can also implement or alternately implement different capital operations, according to the different characteristics and conditions of quasi-operational resources, i.e., infrastructure projects— such as using the "PPP" (public-private partnership) model to build equity carriers, or using "PPC" (port-park-city) as a development model to create a rather perfect infrastructure investment and construction economic circle integrating infrastructure, logistics, finance and industrial

park facilities. Utilizing BOT, TOT, or other ways to exercise franchising rights, and as conditions mature, the project company can be transformed into a publicly listed company. Through the issuance of stocks or bonds, urban infrastructure projects can be further strengthened and expanded, thereby helping regional governments to overcome their capital bottleneck, enhancing the investment, development, operation, and management of urban infrastructure, and achieving scientific and

理，使其成为符合市场经济规则的股权载体，参与市场竞争。对于新增城市基础设施项目——"增量资产"的平台载体，各国则应从一开始就以独资、合资、合作或股份制等形式组建，使其能够按照市场规则奠定好股权载体基础和发展条件，成为资源投资、城市开发运营的竞争参与者，要防止增量资产的投资、开发、运营重回政府作为唯一股权投资主体的老路。

其次，对于资金运营问题，如果我们把城市基础设施即准经营性资源放入市场体系中去投资、开发、运营和管理，各国的区域政府则可以主要通过资本市场融资的方式去解决。比如发行债券或可转换债券，发行股票，设立项目基金或借力于海内外基金投资项目，以项目为实体买壳上市，项目资产证券化，项目并购组合、捆绑经营，租赁，抵押，置换，拍卖，等等。政府也可以通过收费权、定价权等手段，运用 DBO（设计—建设—经营）、BOT（建设—经营—移交）、BOO（建设—经营—拥有）、BOOT（建设—经营—拥有—转让）、BLT（建设—租赁—转让）、BTO（建设—转让—经营）、TOT（转让—经营—移交）等方式实施特许经营权的资本运营。政府还可以根据各准经营性资源即基础设施项目的不同特点和条件，采取不同的资本运营方式，或交叉运用不同的资本运营方式。如采用 PPP（政府和社会资本合作）方式建构股权载体，或以 PPC（港口公园式城市）形式作为开发模式，打造出一个较为完美的基础设施、物流、金融和园区相融合的基础设施投资建设经济圈，并结合 BOT 或 TOT 等特许经营权运营方式，在条件成熟时改组项目公司为上市公司，通过发行股票或债券，进一步把城市基础设施项目做强做大。这类措施的目的均是使政府克服资金瓶颈的制约，提升城市基础设施的投资、开发、运营、管理水平，使其科学

sustainable development. The effects of the limited public finances would be multiplied, more effectively satisfying the ever increasing demand of the public on public goods and public welfare undertakings.

To sum up, in the process of the investment, development, operation and management of quasi-operational resources, namely, urban infrastructure, the mode of "government promotion, enterprise participation and market-based operation" implies the following three principles from the beginning—(1) regional governments are one of the main competition subjects in urban economy; (2) regional governments should and must rely on market rules and act according to market regulations in the investment, development, operation and management in this field; (3) at the same time, regional governments are also the national representatives in the investment, development, operation and management thereof, taking on the functions of guiding, coordinating and supervising. Hence, for the investment, development, operation and management of quasi-operational resources or urban infrastructure, governments should follow the above-mentioned principles to design their policies.

地、可持续地发展，使国家有限的公共财政起到"四两拨千斤"的作用，更有效地满足社会民众日益增长的对公共物品、公益事业的需求。

综上所述，在准经营性资源即城市基础设施的投资、开发、运营和管理过程中，"政府推动、社会参与、市场运作"的方式，从一开始就奠定了以下三个原则：第一，各国的区域政府是城市经济的竞争主体之一。第二，在这一领域的投资、开发、运营、管理中，政府应该或者说必须依靠市场规则，按市场规律办事。第三，在上述过程中，各国的区域政府同时又是国家的代表，起着引导、调节、监督者的作用。因此，对准经营性资源即城市基础设施的投资、开发、运营和管理，各国政府应按以上原则来配套政策。

CHAPTER 4   THE DUAL ATTRIBUTES OF GOVERNMENT

1. The Three Functions of Regional Governments

There are two fatal deficiencies in traditional economic market theory, namely, that government, market and society are independent bodies, and government has always been placed out of the market ever since the era of Adam Smith; and that the functions of government are single and restricted to those of public affairs and the provision of public goods and services to society and the public, and do not involve promoting economic development or competing in urban infrastructure construction. These theories have seriously restricted the performance of regional governments' functions across the world.

Maintaining stability, promoting development and handling emergencies are the three basic duties of governments throughout the world.

Through surveying regional governments across the world, economic development, urban construction and social livelihood are deemed as the three main economic functions. Regional governments at all levels making diligent efforts to explore and playing positive roles during the process of China's reform and opening up is such an example.

Firstly, regarding economic development, many regional governments have made fruitful exploration. In as early as 2005, Shunde District in Foshan City, Guangdong Province, China, achieved a regional GDP of 60.1 billion RMB, the secondary industry accounting for 61%, amongst which household appliances and household electronics accounted for 70% of total industrial output, with the household electrical appliance industry mainly dominated by the three giants Midea, Kelon and Galanz. Faced with this situation, to prevent the risk of regional economic crisis brought about by mismanagement in certain enterprises in a single industry, the Shunde government, based on practice, scientifically put forward and implemented a "Triple-Three Strategy" for its industrial development, that is, to guide and support the coordinated development of the primary, secondary and tertiary industries; within each industry, to guide and support more than three pillar industries; within each pillar industry, to guide and support more than three leading enterprises; to perfect the industrial chain, form industrial clusters, and promote sustainable development.[1] Faced with problems of weak foundation and

肆 政府双重属性

一、区域政府的三大职能

传统经济学的市场理论有两个致命的缺陷：一是认为政府、市场、社会三者是各自独立的，从亚当·斯密开始至今，都把政府置于市场之外。二是认为政府的职能是单一的，只涉及公共事务职能，只为社会和民众提供公共物品，而不存在促进经济发展、参与城市基础设施建设竞争的职能。这些理论，严重影响了世界各国区域政府职能作用的发挥。

纵观世界各国，稳定、发展、对突发事件的处置，是其三大根本任务。

纵览各国区域政府，经济发展、城市建设、社会民生，是其三大经济职能。在中国改革开放的过程中，各级区域政府作出了努力探索、发挥出积极作用就是例证。

首先，关于经济发展，很多区域政府作出了卓有成效的探索。早在 2005 年，中国广东省佛山市顺德区的区域生产总值就达到 601 亿元人民币，第二产业占比为 61%，而其中家用电器和家用电子产品又占其工业总产值的 70%，并且家电行业主要由美的、科龙、格兰仕三家巨头垄断。面对这一状况，为避免因单一产业、个别企业经营不善而引发区域性经济危机的风险，顺德政府结合实际，科学地提出并实施了"三三三"产业发展战略：引导和扶持第一、第二、第三产业协调发展；在每一个产业中，引导和扶持三个以上的支柱行业；在每一个行业中，引导和扶持三个以上的龙头企业；完善产业链，形成产业集群，促进可持续发展。[1]

shortage of funds during the growing of a large number of medium-sized, small and micro enterprises, the Shunde government innovated and set up a credit guarantee fund for medium-sized, small and micro enterprises. The regional government arranged special quota funds, and cooperated with professional guarantee agencies and commercial banks to provide guarantee and loans to growing medium-sized, small and micro enterprises which would otherwise have problems securing loans from banks due to a lack of collateral.[2] It has been proved that the Shunde government's guidance, regulation and fore warning in the economic field have promoted the fine development of the primary industry, optimum development of the secondary industry, and accelerated development of the tertiary industry; promoted the transformation and upgrading of traditional industries, the growth of emerging industries, and the rapid growth of high-tech industries; and formed a situation where big, medium-sized and small industries developed in gradient, and industrial clusters complemented one another. Shunde has managed to maintain its leading position till this day amongst over 2,800 counties in China.

Western developed nations are also stepping up their efforts to guide, promote and regulate the development of industrial economy. The NNMI (National Network for Manufacturing Innovation), is one of the US government's most important measures to re-industrialize the country. Following the international financial crisis, the United States announced "A Framework for Revitalizing American Manufacturing", passed the United States Manufacturing Enhancement Act of 2010, and launched the Advanced Manufacturing Partnership (AMP) in June 2011. And in March 2012, the National Network for Manufacturing Innovation was launched, with responsibilities held by various mutually related Institutes for Manufacturing Innovation (IMIs)[3], which have common goals with respective focuses. The United States invested a total of 1 billion US dollars to establish 15 IMIs across the nation, and further in July 2013, proposed that within 10 years, the target was to establish

45 IMIs, and included and implemented the proposal in the budget for the fiscal year 2015. The NNMI has the following main characteristics. Firstly, guided by national strategic objectives and in accordance with regional and industrial needs, it organized research and development projects relatively independently. Secondly, with resource optimization and redistribution as its core, it combined "top-down" and "bottom-up" measures to carry out the integration of existing innovative resources. Thirdly, it was guaranteed by public and private cooperation. The federal government shall provide relatively stable support during the

面对大量中小微企业成长过程中基础不强、资金短缺等问题，顺德政府创新思维，设立中小微企业信用担保基金，即区域政府安排定额财政专项资金，与专业担保机构和商业银行联手合作，为那些因缺乏足够抵押物而难以从银行获取贷款的成长型中小微企业提供担保和贷款。[2] 实践证明，顺德政府在经济领域的引导、调节和预警，促进了区域第一产业精细发展、第二产业优化发展、第三产业加快发展，促进了传统产业的改造提升、新兴产业的培植壮大和高新技术产业的迅猛成长，形成大中小企业梯度发展、产业集群优势互补的态势。至今顺德仍然在中国 2800 多个县域经济体中保持着领头羊的地位。

西方发达国家也在加大力度引导、促进和调节产业经济发展。"美国制造业创新网络计划"（NNMI）就是美国实施其"再工业化"战略的重要举措之一。在国际金融危机后，美国发布了《重振美国制造业框架》，通过了《美国制造业促进法案（2010）》；2011 年 6 月启动了"先进制造业伙伴计划"（AMP）；2012 年 3 月启动了 NNMI，由多个具有共同目标、相互关联但又各有侧重的制造业创新研究院（IMI）[3] 负责——美国投入了 10 亿美元在全国各地率先建立 15 个 IMI，2013 年 7 月又进一步提出十年内使 IMI 达到 45 个，并在 2015 年财年预算案中推进实施。NNMI 主要有以下特点：一是以国家战略目标为导向进行建设，根据区域和产业需求，相对独立地组织研发项目；二是以资源优化和再布局为核心，通过"自上而下"和"自下而上"的结合实现已有创新资源的整合；三是以公私

early stages, followed up by supporting funds and other packages from universities, private organizations and others. Fourthly, supported by network governance, each IMI linked regional, federal and international innovative resources, and through the establishment of a leadership council, NNMI promoted coordination and cooperation between IMIs. Henceforth, in the connection of the government with the market, in the process to optimize government investment and coordinate multi-stakeholder relationships, the government demonstrated its investment guidance functions, realized the leverage effects, led the direction for research and development in industries, promoted the layout for high-end manufacturing, and accelerated innovation and commercialization.

Apart from the US, the United Kingdom's Knowledge Transfer Partnership (KTP) scheme is also noteworthy. The plan was launched in 2003. By supporting the partnership between businesses and academic organizations, with talents with certain knowledge and technological skills as the media, the transfer of knowledge, technology and skills from research organizations to businesses was realized, thereby helping businesses elevate their innovation capabilities. KTP's funds not only came from the public funds of government and public organizations, but also from supporting funds of businesses. KTP established the application criteria and approval protocol for funds and an implementation and acceptance evaluation system. KTP expanded the services provided to businesses, prompted businesses' innovative investments, integrated innovative resources from talents, businesses and organizations, and promoted the upgrading and development of the industrial structure.

Secondly, regarding urban construction, regional governments have a lot to do. By 2006, Foshan City, Guangdong Province of China, riding on the strength of the reform and opening up policy, used a three-fold increase in land use for construction to achieve a thirty-fold increase in economic growth. However, at the same time, Foshan also faced the grim reality of an obvious disequilibrium between land supply and demand, which had become the main bottleneck stifling the future development of the city. With the unrelenting efforts in practice by the Foshan government, in 2007, the "Provisions Regarding the Acceleration of Transformation of Outmoded Towns, Outmoded Factory Buildings and Outmoded Villages" was promulgated (abbreviated as "The Three-Outmoded Transformation"). In 2009, the "Foshan Special Plan for the Three-Outmoded Transformation (2009-2020)" was promulgated, and the city's "Three-Outmoded Transformation" land, covering an area of 253,000 *mu* (168.67 million square meters), was formally released to be

合作为保障，联邦政府提供相对稳定的前期支持，大学、私营机构等跟进，配套资金；四是以网络化治理为支撑，每个 IMI 链接区域、联邦和国际创新资源，NNMI 通过建立领导理事会总体推动 IMI 之间的协调合作。由此，在政府与市场的接续中，在优化政府投资与协调多方利益关系的过程中，政府发挥了投资引导作用，实现了杠杆效应，引领了产业研发方向，促进了高端制造业布局，加速了创新和商业化进程。

除了美国，英国的"知识转移伙伴计划"（KTP）也值得关注。该计划 2003 年出台，通过支持企业和学术机构之间的伙伴关系，以掌握一定知识和技术的人才为媒介，实现知识、技术、技能从研究机构向企业转移，从而帮助企业提升创新能力。KTP 的资金既来源于政府和公共机构的公共资金，又来自于企业的配套资金，KTP 设立资金申请标准和审批程序，确立实施和验收评价体系。KTP 拓展了对企业提供的服务，带动了企业的创新投入，整合了来自人才、企业、机构等的创新资源，促进了产业结构的提升与发展。

其次，关于城市建设，区域政府也大有可为。截至 2006 年，中国广东省佛山市借助改革开放之势，用 3 倍的建设用地增加率换取了 30 倍的经济增长，同时也直面严峻现实——土地供需矛盾凸显已成为未来城市发展的主要瓶颈。佛山政府在实践中不断摸索，于 2007 年出台《关于加快推进旧城镇旧厂房旧村居改造的决定》（简称《三旧改造》），2009 年出台《佛山市"三旧"改造专项规划（2009—2020）》，正式推出全市"三旧"用地 25.3 万亩 [4]，按照"政府出政策，所有者（使用者）出土地，开发商出资金"的市场化改

utilized in adherence to the market reform model of "the government setting policies, owners (users) contributing land, and developers contributing capital". Within the first three years, 35.7 billion RMB was successfully introduced, 730 "Three-Outmoded Transformation" projects were launched, covering an area of approximately 30,000 *mu* (20 million square meters), and added a total area of 23.99 million square meters of new buildings. The "Three-Outmoded Transformation" characterized by "government facilitation, market operation and enterprise participation" rapidly improved the regional construction, greatly enhanced the efficiency of land use, and at the same time promoted the adjustment and improvement in the structures of land use and industries. This was acclaimed and popularized by Guangdong and the rest of the nation as the "Foshan Experience"[5]. Following closely behind in 2010, the Foshan government put forward a development plan of "Integration of Informatization, Industrialization, Urbanization and Internationalization for an Intelligent Foshan". This involved the use of information technology to promote industrialization, urbanization and internationalization, to enhance the overall competitiveness of Foshan. Through vigorous development of intelligent transportation, intelligent environmental protection, intelligent land monitoring, intelligent public security, intelligent urban management, intelligent education, intelligent medical treatment, intelligent culture, intelligent commerce, intelligent government affairs, etc., the goal of urban security, efficiency, convenience, green and harmony was fully attained by the Foshan government, thereby promoting the transition of regional industrialization, accelerating the process of urbanization and furthering its internationalization.[6]

During the process of modernization of urban governance, the government plays an important role. This is also an unavoidable topic in Western developed nations. The nirvana of Germany's "Industrial Toxic Capital", the Ruhr Industrial Zone, is an example. Whilst bringing

Germany massive economic contributions, it has at the same time, created massive pollution. To combat pollution, the Nordrhein-Westfalen and German government formulated an outline. From 1968 to 1979, and then to 1989, came a long "trilogy": the adjustment of industrial structure, the development of new industries, and ecological revamp, repair and environmental improvement of the industrial heritage. The Ruhr Industrial Zone finally attained jointly the inheritance of regional culture, industrial transformation and upgrading, infrastructure transformation, and urban development. The old industrial zone has become a modern-styled urban industrial zone suitable again for living, commerce and development.

造模式，头三年就成功引入社会资金 357 亿元人民币，启动"三旧"改造项目 730 个，项目占地约 3 万亩，新增建筑面积达 2399 万平方米。"政府推动、市场运作、企业参与"的城乡"三旧"改造，迅速改善了区域建设面貌，大大提升了土地使用效率，同时促进了土地利用结构和产业结构的调整与完善，被广东省和国家推广为"佛山经验"[5]。紧接着，2010 年，佛山政府提出"四化融合，智慧佛山"发展规划，以信息化带动工业化，以信息化提升城镇化，以信息化加快国际化，全面提升佛山的城市综合竞争力。通过大力发展智能交通、智能环保、智能土地监控、智能治安、智能城管、智能教育、智能医疗、智能文化、智能商务、智能政务等，佛山政府全面实现了城市安全、高效、便捷、绿色、和谐的目标，推动了区域的工业化转轨，加速了城市化进程，提升了国际化程度。[6]

在城市治理的现代化的过程中，政府扮演着重要角色，这也是西方发达国家绕不开的话题。如德国"工业毒都"鲁尔区的涅槃即是一例。鲁尔工业区在为德国经济作出巨大贡献的同时也带来了严重污染，就如何治理污染问题，北威州和德国政府制定纲要，从 1968 年到 1979 年，再到 1989 年，漫长的"三部曲"——产业结构调整，发展新兴产业，工业遗产的生态改造、生态修复、环境改善之后，鲁尔区最终实现了区域文化传承、产业转型升级、基础设施改造、城市提升发展的统一，这个老工业区成为宜居、宜商、宜发展的新型城市工业区。

Finally, regarding social livelihood, the government is duty-bound. In 2016, for example, the Guangdong Provincial Government of China put forward ten things to do that can bring real benefits to people: (1) to strengthen the capability to meet basic needs; (2) to enhance the level of support for disadvantaged groups; (3) to strengthen housing security for the low-income groups who have housing difficulties; (4) to improve the living and production conditions in rural areas; (5) to improve basic medical and health services; (6) to promote fair and equitable distribution of educational resources; (7) to promote entrepreneurship and employment; (8) to strengthen pollution control and management, and ecological construction; (9) to strengthen public security; (10) to prevent and mitigate disasters.[7] Each item was concrete and down-to-earth.

Beginning in the 1970s, the "New Village Movement" in the ROK is another classic example. Faced with the situation that farmers accounted for 70% of the population and that agriculture was on the verge of collapse, the ROK government proposed to launch the New Village Movement to revitalize agriculture. The government made policies and provided goods and materials to facilitate rural construction projects, support the National Agriculture Cooperative Federation (NACF) to establish and run their own cooperative finance, spared no effort to push forward the movement, created the renowned "Han River Miracle", and realized enormous growth in the economy. The ROK's experience has set an example for solving the problems of livelihood in a country, especially where there are serious urban and rural imbalances.

2. The Dual Roles of Regional Governments

The three major economic functions of regional governments as described above are essentially the three major missions of governments in governing their regional economies; or from an economics viewpoint, a management or policy arrangement by which governments manage the three types of economic matters in their respective regions; or as it can be said, an allocation or optimization of the three types of economic resources in their respective regions. In any case, to realize these three economic functions, the government needs to make relevant policies, in order to achieve the best economic development and social stability at the least cost, help the nation achieve prosperity and strength, and the public live and work in peace and contentment.

As has been analyzed earlier, with regard to the operational resources, which is industrial economy, or traditional market-operated field, regional governments should follow the principles of "guidance, coordination

最后，关于社会民生，政府更责无旁贷。比如 2016 年，中国广东省政府提出的十件民生实事是：第一，巩固提升底线民生保障水平；第二，加大对困难弱势群体帮扶力度；第三，强化低收入住房困难群体住房保障；第四，改善农村生产生活条件；第五，改善基层医疗卫生服务；第六，促进教育资源公平均衡配置；第七，促进创业就业；第八，加强污染治理和生态建设；第九，强化公共安全保障；第十，抓好防灾减灾。[7] 可谓件件具体，事事落实。

而始于上世纪 70 年代的韩国 "新村运动" 是另一经典案例。面对当时农民比例约占 70%、农业一度处于崩溃边缘的现状，韩国政府提出开展复兴农业的新村运动，通过政策引导和物资支援，扶持农村建设项目上马，支持农协自办合作金融，全力推进新村建设，创造出闻名遐迩的 "汉江奇迹"，实现了经济腾飞。韩国的经验对一国解决民生问题，尤其是城乡严重失衡问题具有典型意义。

二、区域政府的双重角色

上述区域政府的三大经济职能，实质上就是政府管辖本区域经济的三大使命，或者从经济学的角度来看，就是政府对本区域三类经济事务的一种管理，或称制度安排，也可以说对本区域三类经济资源的一种调配，或称优化。总之，政府为实现这三大经济职能，需要配套相关政策，以求用最小的成本换取最佳的经济发展和社会稳定效果，使国家繁荣富强、广大民众安居乐业。

前面已经分析过，对第一类可经营性资源，即产业经济，或者说传统意义上的市场营商领域，区域政府应按照 "引导、调节、监

and supervision" to make policies. With regard to the non-operational resources, which are public goods, or social public welfare undertakings, regional governments should follow the principles of "general underpinning, fairness and justice, and effective promotion" to make policies. With regard to the quasi-operational resources, namely urban infrastructure, which belong to "ambiguous areas", or "overlapping areas" in the traditional market theory system, this is precisely the point where we might achieve breakthroughs in traditional economics system or traditional governmental governance. The economies in various nations have proceeded from the "factor-driven" to the "investment-driven" stages, and are currently progressing towards the new "innovation-driven" stage. The various problems that have arisen in the current economic operation are not fully manifested as "market failure" or "government failure", but are demonstrated more as deficiencies in traditional economics system or traditional market theory, and the void in modern economics system or modern market theory.

To realize the three main economic functions as described above, regional governments ought to excel in dual functions.

Firstly, regional governments play the "quasi-enterprise" or "quasi-micro" roles. The planning, guidance and support of operational resources, that is, industrial economy, by regional governments, and their participation and competition in quasi-operational resources, that is, urban infrastructure investment and operation, have led them to become the centralized agency of non-governmental bodies within the region. Through the innovation of values, institutions, organizations, technologies and other methods, a region competes with other regions to realize maximum regional economic benefits. As such, regional governments are playing the "quasi-enterprise" and "quasi-micro" role. On the one hand, regional governments and enterprises manifest differences in behavioral purposes, development modes, regulatory factors, and assessment criteria. But on the other hand, both regional governments and enterprises are resource allocators in certain categories, within which they exercise internal management. Competitive mechanism between different regional governments and between enterprises persists, and becomes the driving force for the development of both the nation and enterprises; their actions in industrial economy must adhere to the rules of market economy—at this point, the regional governments' regional jurisdictions shift towards regional management rights. They allocate resources to maximize regional benefits, with a focus on the solicitation

督"的原则去配套政策；对第二类非经营性资源，即公共物品，或者说社会公益事业，区域政府应按照"基本托底、公平公正、有效提升"的原则去配套政策；而第三类准经营性资源，即城市基础设施，在传统市场理论体系中，属于一个"模糊板块"或"交叉领域"——这正是我们突破传统经济学体系或传统政府治理方式的关键点。世界各国的经济发展从"要素驱动"走到"投资驱动"，目前正处于走向"创新驱动"的新阶段，当前现实经济运行中反馈出来的多种问题，并不全表现为"市场失灵"或"政府失灵"，而更多地体现出了传统经济学体系或传统市场理论的缺陷，以及现代经济学体系或现代市场理论的空白。

为实现上述三大经济职能，区域政府需扮演好双重角色：

首先是区域政府的"准企业"或"准微观"角色。区域政府对可经营性资源即产业经济的规划、引导和扶持，以及对准经营性资源即城市基础设施投资运营的参与和竞争，使其成为本区域内非政府主体的集中代理，其通过理念创新、制度创新、组织创新和技术创新等方式，与其他区域展开竞争，以实现本区域经济利益最大化。此时，区域政府扮演着"准企业""准微观"的角色。一方面，区域政府与企业表现出了行为目的、发展方式、管制因素和评价标准上的不同。但在另一方面，区域政府与企业又都是一定范畴内的资源调配者，它们都在一定范畴内实施内部管理，竞争机制在各区域政府之间和在各企业之间始终存在，并成为国家和企业二者发展的原动力，它们在产业经济领域都必须遵循市场经济规则——此时区域政府的区域管辖权转为了区域经营权，区域政府以区域利益最大化为中心进行资源调配，重点主要集中在城市基础设施项目的招

of investment, development, investment, operation and management of urban infrastructure projects. Regional governments' actions are subject to both political and economic constraints; regional governments' effectiveness can elevate the region's competitive advantage and complete the region's economic transition and social transformation in advance. To sum up, "quasi" means "not belonging to a certain category, but to a certain extent, possessing certain attributes or functions of this category". Regional governments are not enterprises, but to a certain extent, possess characteristics of enterprises. Consequently, regional governments simultaneously take on certain "quasi-enterprise" and "quasi-micro" roles.

Secondly, regional governments play the "quasi-national" or "quasi-macro" roles. The regulation, supervision and management of operational resources, that is, industrial economy, by regional governments, and their allocation of non-operational resources, that is, public goods or public welfare undertakings under the principles of "general underpinning, fairness and justice, and effective promotion", qualify them to be centralized agencies of national government in their local regions. Regional governments regulate economy through the means of planning, investment, and consumption, and the systems of price, taxation, interest rate, exchange rate, and law, while maintaining social stability through the provision of basic social guarantee, public service, etc. As such, regional governments are playing the "quasi-national" or "quasi-macro" roles. As agents of the national government, regional governments, with the publicness and force bestowed on them, perform the political, economic, urban, social, and other functions of their regions. On economic development and urban construction, regional governments are charged with the responsibilities of studying and formulating the medium- and long-term plans for regional economic and social development; promoting the dynamic balance between aggregate supply and aggregate demand in the region; implementing national economic policies, formulating regional industrial and technical policies; investing vigorously in infrastructure construction; providing public goods and services; effectively adjusting income distribution and redistribution; whilst maintaining regional aggregate economic growth, structural dynamic equilibrium, and effective urban upgrading, upholding at the same time regional market rules and order, regulating prices, controlling unemployment rates, and promoting harmonious and sustainable development of society. In practice, regional governments' "quasi-national" or "quasi-macro" roles manifest mainly in the fiscal revenue and expenditure activities. On the revenue side, regional governments

商、开发、投资、运营和管理上。区域政府的行为除了受到政治约束外也受到经济约束，区域政府的有效作为能提升本区域的竞争优势，并率先实现本区域的经济转轨和社会转型。综上所述，"准"意味着不属于某个范畴，但却在一定程度上承担或具备了这个范畴的某些属性或职能。区域政府不是企业，但又在一定程度上具有企业的行为特征。因此区域政府兼具一定的"准企业""准微观"角色。

其次是区域政府的"准国家"或"准宏观"角色。区域政府对可经营性资源即产业经济的调节、监督和管理，以及对非经营性资源即公共物品或公益事业的调配——"基本托底、公平公正、有效提升"，使其成为本区域国家政府的集中代理，其通过规划、投资、消费等手段，价格、税收、利率、汇率、法律等体系调控经济，通过提供社会基本保障、公共服务等方式维护社会稳定。此时，区域政府扮演着"准国家"或"准宏观"的角色，即区域政府代理国家政府，以其被授予的公共性和强制力，履行本区域的政治职能、经济职能、城市职能和社会职能等。就经济发展、城市建设而言，区域政府的职责有：研究和制订本区域经济社会发展的中长期规划；促进本区域总供给与总需求的动态平衡；执行国家经济政策、制定区域产业政策和技术政策；大力投资基础设施建设；提供公共物品和服务；有效调节收入分配与再分配；既保持本区域经济总量增长、结构动态平衡、城市有效提升，又维护本区域市场规则、秩序，调控物价，控制失业率，促进社会和谐、可持续发展。在实际运行中，区域政府的"准国家"或"准宏观"角色又重点体现在财政收支活动上。收入方面，区域政府利用财政税收收入、转移支付

use treasury revenue from tax collection, transfer payments, equity and others to maintain their own operation and perform various functions. On the expenditure side, it mainly includes the following: social consumption expenditures by fiscal purchases, including administration management expenses, national defense security expenses, science, education, culture and health service expenses, as well as industry, transportation, commerce, agriculture and other departmental expenses; fiscal investment expenditures by governmental investment, including infrastructure investment, scientific and technological research development investment, and policy-based financial investment (to support industries in urgent need of development) and others; and transfer expenditures mainly on the provision of social security, treasury subsidy and others. Social consumption and treasury investment expenditures, being purchase expenditures, directly affect the allocation of social resources and various factors; their scale and structure roughly demonstrate the strength and scope of regional governments' direct involvement in resource allocation, and reflect regional governments' ability to directly regulate social resources within a period of time and the degree of their influence on social economy and others. Transfer expenditures on the other hand, indirectly affect the allocation of social resources and various factors, and assist the implementation of social equity policies.[8]

Finally, the dual roles of regional governments are dialectically unified. The concept of "region" is a relative one. As far as the world is concerned, every nation is a "region". As far as a nation is concerned, every city is a "region". The dual roles of regional governments in each nation have their own inherent attributes: Firstly, governments' institutional supply, which includes the provision of governmental policies, laws and others, aims at ensuring various public goods and social benefits services are fairly, justly and effectively put into place. Secondly, governments' economic regulation, which includes governments' support for industrial development, investment in urban infrastructure construction and others, aims to effectively guide the transformation and upgrading of industries and the urban modernization, to promote scientific, coordinated and sustainable economic and social progress in the region. So to speak, the dual roles of regional governments are dialectically unified. It is precisely the dual roles that amend the deficiencies of traditional economics system or traditional market theory, and open a new chapter on modern economics system and modern market theory. Modern market theory tells us that enterprises are the main market

收入、股权收入和其他收入，维持自身运转和履行各项职能。支出方面则主要包括以下几类：以财政购买形式安排的社会消费性支出，包括行政管理费、国防安全费、科教文卫事业费以及工交商农部门事业费等；以政府投资方式安排的财政投资性支出，包括基础设施投资、科技研究发展投资、政策性金融投资（支持急需发展的产业）等；主要由社会保障支出和财政补贴支出等组成的转移性支出。社会消费性支出和财政投资性支出作为购买性支出，直接影响社会资源和各类要素的调配，其规模和结构大致体现出区域政府直接介入资源调配的力度和范围，反映出区域政府在一定时期直接调节社会资源的能力以及对社会经济等的影响程度；转移性支出则间接影响着社会资源和各类要素的调配，并辅助社会公平政策的实施。[8]

　　最后，区域政府的双重角色是辩证统一的。区域是个相对概念：对于全球而言，每个国家就是一个区域；对于国家而言，每个城市就是一个区域。各国区域政府的双重角色有其自身的内在属性：一是政府的制度供给。它包括政府的政策供给和法规供给等，目标是保障各类公共物品和公益服务得以公平、公正、有效地实施。二是政府的经济调节。它包括政府对产业发展的扶助和对城市基础设施建设的投入等，目标是有效引导产业转型升级和城市现代化发展，促进该区域经济社会的科学、协调、可持续进步。可以说，区域政府的双重角色是辩证统一的。正是这种双重角色，修正了传统经济学体系或传统市场理论的缺陷，书写了现代经济学体系和现代市场理论的新篇章。现代市场理论告诉我们：企业是产业经

competitors in the industrial economy, whereas regional governments are the main market competitors in the urban economy. The development of modern economics system has revealed that apart from microeconomics, which has enterprises as object of study, and macroeconomics, which has the nation or the world as object of study, there should also be mezzoeconomics, which has regional governments as object of study.

3. The Dual Competitors in Market Competition

From the above analysis, we can see that:

Firstly, there are external possibilities for regional governments to participate in competition. As already known, the publicness of regional governments' management functions is mainly manifested through taxation, industry and commerce, public security and other supervision measures, which are necessary for guaranteeing regional public expenditure and maintaining regional market and social stability; and their openness, fairness and justice are ensured by legislation, judiciary, administration, and other means. The regional governments' mandatory management functions are mainly manifested through the three super-economic mandatory powers of legislation, judiciary and administration, as well as the economic mandatory power to control over money and affairs. From the outside, it appears that regional governments' management functions are manifested through the three main economic areas of economic development, urban construction and social livelihood; however, in essence, these management functions are the effectiveness of regional governments' allocation of the various tangible and intangible resources the regions already or may potentially possess. The management practice across the world and the success of China's reform and opening up have already told us that, regional governments should first ensure that the provision of regional social benefits services and public goods meets the standards of "general underpinning, fairness and justice, and effective promotion". On this basis, in order to prevent urban resources, especially urban infrastructure from laying idle and wasted, or large-scale damage of infrastructure, poor quality of urban construction, and disorderly urban management due to investing without profiting, constructing without managing and operating, and focusing only on public benefits and neglecting economic returns, regional governments, through market mechanism, would in part or a majority of areas, invest, develop, and manage urban infrastructure—known as quasi-operational resources. In the process of transforming quasi-operational resources into

济中的主要市场竞争主体，区域政府是城市经济中的主要市场竞争主体。现代经济学体系的发展也已揭示，除了以企业为研究对象的微观经济学和以国家（或全球）为研究对象的宏观经济学，还应该有以区域政府为研究对象的中观经济学。

三、市场竞争的双重主体

综合上述分析，我们可知：

首先，区域政府参与竞争具有外在可能性。我们知道，区域政府管理职能的公共性主要体现在税务、工商、公安等监管措施上，这是保证区域公共开支、维护区域市场与社会稳定所必需的，其公开、公平、公正性是由立法、司法、行政等手段保障的；区域政府管理职能的强制性则主要表现为立法、司法、行政三项超经济性强制权，以及财权、事权等经济性强制权。从外在看，区域政府的管理职能体现在经济发展、城市建设、社会民生三大经济领域；而实质上，此管理职能是区域政府对其区域内已经和可能拥有的各类有形资源与无形资源的有效调配。世界各国的管理实践和中国改革开放的成功经验都告诉我们，各区域政府在确保本区域社会公益服务和公共物品供给"基本托底、公平公正、有效提升"的基础上，为防范城市资源尤其是城市基础设施闲置浪费，或"只投入、不收益；只建设、不经营；只注重公益性、忽视效益性"而造成基础设施大量耗损或城市建设低质运作、城市管理无序进行的问题，都会在局部或大部分领域，通过市场机制投资、开发、管理城市基础设施这一准经营性资源。在这"准经营性"向"可经营性"转变的过

operational resources, the carrier of urban infrastructure investment—the equity nature and structure of infrastructure project companies (for example, sole proprietorships, joint ventures, partnerships, jointstock companies, even state-owned privately-run enterprises and others) must be set to comply with market rules and regulations; the financial management of urban infrastructure investment, whether through BOT, PPP or other franchised means, or through public listing and issuance of bonds or stocks to expand and consolidate the infrastructure construction projects, must go through market competition. From the very beginning, the method of "government promotion, enterprise participation, and market operation" has bestowed regional governments with external possibilities to participate in urban economic construction and development competition.

Secondly, regional governments' participation in competition is inherently inevitable. On one hand, regional governments' implementation of "general underpinning, fairness and justice, and effective promotion" policies on non-operational resources, that is, public goods or social benefits undertakings; and "coordination, supervision, and management" policies on operational resources, that is, industrial economy, lead regional governments to become centralized agents for national government in their respective regions. Regional governments maintain stability through basic social guarantee, public services and other measures, and coordinate the economy through planning, investment, consumption, price, taxation, interest rate, exchange rate, law and other means. In practice, regional governments mainly utilize treasury revenues and expenditures to realize its publicness and mandatory power. At this point, regional governments play the "quasi-national" and "quasi-macro" roles. On the other hand, regional governments' participation and competition in the investment and operation of quasi-operational resources, that is, urban infrastructure, and planning, guidance and support of operational resources, that is, industrial economy, lead regional governments to become centralized agents for non-governmental bodies in their regions. Regional governments compete with each other through various innovative measures, carry out resource allocation for the maximization of regional benefits, with emphasis on attracting investment, developing, investing, operating and managing urban infrastructure construction projects. Regional governments, like enterprises, are the resource allocators and participants within a certain category (urban economy or industrial economy), market competition mechanism being the driving force for

程中，城市基础设施投资的载体，即基础设施项目公司的股权结构及其性质（如独资、合资、合作、股份制甚至国有民营等）的确立就必须符合市场规则；城市基础设施投资的资本运营——不管是通过 BOT、PPP 之类特许经营的方式，还是通过上市并发行债券、股票的方式以促进基础设施建设项目做强做大，都必须通过市场竞争。"政府推动、社会参与、市场运作"的方式，从一开始就使得各区域政府参与城市经济建设与发展的竞争具有了外在可能性。

其次，区域政府参与竞争具有内在必然性。一方面，区域政府对非经营性资源即公共物品或公益事业实施的"基本托底、公平公正、有效提升"政策和对可经营性资源即产业经济实施的"调节、监督、管理"政策，使其成为本区域内国家政府的集中代理。区域政府通过社会基本保障、公共服务等方式维护稳定，通过规划、投资、消费、价格、税收、利率、汇率、法律等手段调控经济。在实际运行中，区域政府主要利用财政收支活动来实现其公共性和强制力。此时，区域政府扮演着"准国家""准宏观"的角色。另一方面，区域政府对准经营性资源即城市基础设施投资运营的参与和竞争，以及对可经营性资源即产业经济的"规划、引导、扶持"，使其成为本区域内非政府主体的集中代理。区域政府通过各种创新方式与其他区域展开竞争，并以区域利益最大化为中心进行资源调配，重点集中在城市基础设施建设项目的招商、开发、投资、运营和管理上。它与企业一样都是一定范畴（城市经济或产业经济）内的资源调配者和参与主体，市场竞争机制成为其发展的原动力，市

development, market rules being the code of conduct they must adhere to. Consequently, at this point, regional governments are playing the "quasi-enterprise" and "quasi-micro" roles. Regional governments' dual roles and the competitive forces arising as a result, profoundly indicate that regional governments' participation in competition is inherently inevitable.

Finally, there exist dual competitors in market competition. Through the analysis of the economic activities of the regional governments, we can reposition the three types of economic functions of the regional governments, distinguish the allocation means of the three regional resources in economics, effectively affirm the different positions of governments and enterprises in urban or industrial economy, and explore and study the dual roles and special effects of regional governments at the microeconomic and macroeconomic levels, which will compose a new chapter in the development of modern market economy theory: Firstly, there is the aforementioned theory on the dual roles of regional governments. Secondly, note the theory on the dual competitors in market competition. On the one hand, the dual-competitor theory clarifies the existence in modern market system of two competitors, namely, enterprises and regional governments. On the other hand, it also tells us that regional governments' competition is mainly concentrated in the investment, development, operation and management of urban infrastructure, that is, in the competition for various tangible and intangible resources in urban economic development. Its objective is mainly to optimize the allocation of urban resources of the regions and enhance urban economic efficiency and rates of return, and the policies and measures revolve mainly around the leading edges and sustainable development of regional urban economy. There is basically no competition between enterprises and regional governments in industrial economy as enterprises compete mainly in industrial economy whilst regional governments compete mainly in urban economy. Enterprise competition and government competition each occurs in different fields, and together they constitute the dual competitors in modern market economic system, co-existing and complementing each other. Thirdly, note the theory of "strong-strong mechanism" in a mature market economy, which comprises a strong effective government and a strong efficient market. In modern market economy theory, we need not only a "strong market", where the market determines the allocation of resources in industrial economy and urban economy, and the market rules and regulations have fundamental effects on competition therein; but also a "strong government", that is, the regional government is one of the main

场规则成为其必须遵循的行为准则。因此，此时的区域政府扮演着"准企业""准微观"的角色。区域政府的双重角色以及由此生发的各区域竞争力，深深地表明区域政府参与竞争具有内在的必然性。

最后，市场竞争存在双重主体。通过对区域政府经济活动的分析，我们能够重新定位区域政府的三类经济职能，在经济学上区分三类区域资源配置的方式，有效确立政府与企业在城市经济或产业经济中的不同主体地位，探索、研究区域政府在微观和宏观层面的双重角色与特殊作用，这将书写出现代市场经济理论发展的新的一页：第一是上文论述过的区域政府双重角色理论。第二是市场竞争双重主体理论。一方面，双重主体理论直接阐明了在现代市场体系中存在两个竞争主体——企业和区域政府；另一方面，它又告诉人们，区域政府的竞争主要集中在城市基础设施投资、开发、运营和管理领域，即对城市经济发展中各种有形资源或无形资源的竞争，其目的主要在于优化本区域城市资源配置，提高城市经济效率和回报率，其政策措施主要围绕着区域城市经济的领先优势和可持续发展来配套。企业的竞争主要发生在产业经济中，区域政府的竞争主要发生在城市经济中，企业与政府在产业经济中基本不存在竞争关系。企业竞争和政府竞争各自发生在不同领域，共同构成现代市场经济体系中的双重竞争主体，相辅相成。第三是成熟市场经济"双强机制"理论，即"强式有为政府＋强式有效市场＝成熟市场经济"。现代市场经济理论不仅需要书写"强市场"，即市场决定产业经济、城市经济中资源配置的方式，市场规律与法则对产业经济、城市经济中的竞争起根本性作用；而且需要书写"强政府"，即区

competitors in urban economy, who relies on and acts in accordance with market rules and regulations, and at the same time, needs to plan, guide, support, regulate, supervise and manage industrial economy because of its dual roles. A strong-strong mechanism integrating strong effective government and strong efficient market is the real mature mechanism that develops in practice. A modern market mechanism should not just focus on the promotion and development of industrial economy, but also on the allocation of resources, regional competitive forces, and regional sustainable development in urban economy. Together they construct a complete system of modern market economy, and guide the development of economic practices and the progress of economic theories across the world.

4. Thoughts from Three Case Studies

The following are three cases cited in my research on whether various nations across the world need to explore or implement top-level arrangement of national finance, which are not necessarily related to the content of this chapter on "dual attributes of government". Nevertheless, from another perspective, that of monetary and financial competition amongst nations in the global economy, it incites thoughts on why the United States government, whilst advocating liberal economy in theory, interferes frequently and proactively takes the lead in global economic system competition, resulting in their current status in the world economy. What does this imply?

The first case is the US monetary and financial system established by Alexander Hamilton. Hamilton was the first US Treasury Secretary from 1789 to 1795. During his tenure, Hamilton advocated rebuilding the national credit destroyed in the war, improving the financial system, establishing a complete financial management system, and creating favorable conditions for the development of industry and commerce, hence building the five pillars of the US monetary and financial system:

a unified government bond market, a central bank-led banking system, a unified mintage system (gold and silver bimetallism), a tax collection system based mainly on tariff and consumption tax, and financial and trade policies to encourage the development of the manufacturing industry. They have become the solid foundation upon which the modern monetary and financial system of the United States is built, which in turn ultimately leads the global economy.[9] On this matter, we need to consider:

> 域政府是城市经济的竞争主体之一，它依靠市场规则，按市场规律办事，同时政府双重属性的本质又需要它对产业经济实施规划、引导、扶持、调节、监督和管理。强式有为政府与强式有效市场相结合的双强运行机制，才是真正在实践中发展成熟的现代市场机制。现代市场机制的着眼点不仅仅在产业经济的提升发展上，而且在城市经济的资源配置、区域竞争力和区域可持续发展上。它们共同构筑起现代市场经济的完整体系，引领着世界各国经济实践的发展和经济学理论的进步。

四、三个案例阅思

下述三个案例，是我在研究世界各国是否需要探讨或进行国家金融顶层布局时引用的案例，与此章内容"政府双重属性"没有必然联系。但它们却从另一个角度——国家在全球经济中进行货币金融竞争的角度，引发人们去思考：为什么在经济学理论上力主自由主义经济的美国政府，却又在全球经济体系竞争中频频干预，主动引领，从而有了当今美国在世界经济中的地位？它说明了什么？

第一个案例是亚历山大·汉密尔顿对美国货币金融体系的构建。汉密尔顿于 1789—1795 年任美国第一任财政部长，任职期间力主重建战争中被破坏的国家信用，健全金融体系，建立完备的财政管理制度，创造有利条件促进工商业发展，从而构建了美国货币金融体系的五大支柱——统一的国债市场、中央银行主导的银行体系、统一的铸币体系（金银复本位制）、以关税和消费税为主体的税收体系，以及鼓励制造业发展的金融贸易政策，这些成为美国现代货币金融体系的扎实基础，使其最终成长为主导全球经济的美国金融系统。[9]对此，我们需要思考的是：为什么两百多年前的汉密尔顿的

Why did Hamilton's "financial thinking" over 200 years ago already emphasize so heavily on "national credit"? Why did he think that for the United States to become a prosperous and powerful country, it must have a solid confederation of states and a strong central government? Why do contemporaries regard Hamilton as the greatest Treasury Secretary in American history?

The second case is the international financial system established on the Bretton Woods Conference. In July 1944, the Bretton Woods Conference was convened in New Hampshire, US. John Maynard Keynes, the then head of the British delegation, put forward a plan for the world financial system before the meeting, that is, a world unit of currency (the bancor), a world central bank and the International Clearing Union. Harry Dexter White, chief economist of the US Treasury and chairman of the conference representing the United States, on the other hand, in light of the logic that political power takes precedence over economy, adopted political and diplomatic measures at crucial stages of the conference, which eventually led to the establishment of three working committees revolving around their political objectives, discussing respectively the International Stability Fund, the International Bank for Reconstruction and Development and other issues on international financial cooperation. Subsequently, the International Monetary Fund (IMF), the World Bank (IBRD), and the Bank for International Settlements (BIS) were formally established; these organizations established the post-war international financial order.[10] What is worth considering is: Why has the result of the 44-nation wrestling in the Bretton Woods Conference dominated the international financial system for more than 70 years, with its impact still felt today?

The third case is the US dollar internationalization system established by the Marshall Plan. This program, led by the United States, was launched in April 1948 and terminated in 1951. During this period, European countries established the Organization for Economic

Cooperation and Development to match the Marshall Plan, and created a counterpart fund to solve the problem of currency conversion. US aid to Europe included funds, technology, personnel and other aspects. Amongst them, financial aid flowed like this: the US provided US dollars to European countries, while European countries used US dollars as foreign exchange to purchase US goods; apart from Germany, European countries basically did not repay the aid funds; apart from Germany, who used the aid funds for private enterprises reinvestment, most European

"金融思维"就已如此高度强调"整体国家信用"？为什么他认为美国要成为一个繁荣富强的国家，"必须建立一个坚固的诸州联盟和一个强有力的中央政府"？为什么当代人把汉密尔顿视为美国历史上最伟大的财政部长？

第二个案例是布雷顿森林会议构建的国际金融体系。1944 年 7 月，布雷顿森林会议在美国新罕布什尔州召开。时任英国代表团团长的凯恩斯在会前提出了世界金融体系的"三个一"方案，即一个"世界货币"，一个"世界央行"，一个"世界清算体系"联盟。而以美国财政部首席经济学家怀特为会议主席的美国方面，则按照政治力量优先于经济的逻辑，在会议的关键时刻采取政治与外交手段，最终促成了围绕其政治目标而设立的三个工作委员会，分别讨论国际稳定基金、国际复兴开发银行和其他国际金融合作事宜。日后正式成立的"国际货币基金组织"、"世界银行"（国际复兴银行）和"国际清算银行"等奠定战后国际金融秩序的组织均发端于此。[10] 这里值得我们思考的是：为什么布雷顿森林会议中 44 国角力的结果左右了国际金融体系七十余年，至今影响犹在？

第三个案例是马歇尔计划构建的美元国际化体系。该计划由美国主导，1948 年 4 月启动，1951 年终止。此间，欧洲国家成立了"经济合作与发展组织"与马歇尔计划对接，并创立了"对应基金"解决货币转换问题。美国对欧洲的援助包括资金、技术、人员等方面，其中资金援助的流向是：美国援助美元给欧洲国家，欧洲各国将美元作为外汇，购买美国的物资；除德国外，欧洲国家基本上不偿还援助资金；除了德国将援助资金用于私有企业再投资，欧洲各

countries used the funds to fill their fiscal deficit. In this system, the US dollars stagnated in Europe and formed the "Eurodollar". Thus, the global currency system gradually developed from the "gold and silver bimetallism" to the "gold standard", then to the "gold to US dollar and US dollar to other currencies" (fixed exchange rate: 35 US dollars to 1 ounce of gold), and then to the "fixed exchange rate system of US dollar to other currencies" (gold and US dollar decoupled on August 15, 1971), and finally to the "floating exchange rate system of US dollar to other currencies" (established in 1976 by the Jamaica Agreement), and eventually, formed a strong US dollar internationalization system.[11]

All the above case studies illustrate financial thoughts, financial strategies, financial policies, financial systems and financial behavior promoted by the liberal economy-pursuing US government on a national level. During the competition and development of contemporary world economies, the most effective measure taken by the US government against other countries is "financial sanctions". As can be seen, the top-level financial arrangement of developed nations has already commenced. As far as developing countries are concerned, economic exchanges often develop from merchandise trade to general service trade, and then to high-end service trade; economic openness is often promoted from current account to capital account; even the economic free trade zones that many nations have tried to establish develop from trade facilitation to investment and financing facilitation, and then to capital account convertibility. This gap reminds us that it is imperative for regional governments to participate in economic competition and for the nation to participate in financial arrangement and carry out top-level financial design.

国多数将其用于填补财政亏空。在这个体系中，美元滞留欧洲，形成"欧洲美元"。于是世界货币体系逐渐由"金银复本位制"发展到"金本位制"，再到"黄金·美元·他国货币"双挂钩（实施固定汇率：35 美元 =1 盎司黄金），再到"美元与他国货币固定汇率制"（1971 年 8 月 15 日黄金与美元脱钩），最后到"美元与他国货币浮动汇率制"（由 1976 年的《牙买加协定》所确立），最终形成了强势的美元国际化体系。[11]

上述案例均为奉行自由主义经济的美国政府在国家层面推行的"金融思想""金融战略""金融政策""金融体系""金融行为"。在当代世界各经济体的竞争发展中，美国政府对他国最拿手的举措，也是"金融制裁"。可见，发达国家的金融顶层布局早已开始。而对发展中国家来说，经济往来常由商品贸易发展到一般服务贸易，再到高端服务贸易；经济开放则常由经常项目向资本项目推进；就连许多国家尝试设立的经济自由贸易区，也是由贸易便利化发展到投融资便利化，再到资本项目可兑换。这种差距提醒我们：政府参与经济竞争，国家参与金融布局，进行金融顶层设计，已经势在必行！

CHAPTER 5   REGIONAL GOVERNMENT COMPETITION

1. The Broad and Narrow Senses of Government Competition

The concept of "region" is a relative one. Globally, a country is a region. Nationally, a city is a region. Not only do similarities exist between regions, so do differences. Regional government usually refers to the governmental organization that manages the administrative affairs of the region, which has a relatively stable region under jurisdiction, relatively concentrated population and regional governance institutions. Regional government is public and mandatory.

Regional competitiveness refers to the force that can support the sustainable survival and development of a region, i.e., during the process of competition and development of a region, compared with other regions, the ability to attract, compete for, possess, regulate and transform resources, as well as the ability to compete for, possess and regulate the market, namely, the ability to optimize the allocation of resources required for its own development. Put simply, it is the ability to attract resources and compete for market that a region needs for its own development. With the methodology of comparative economics, an index system can be established to analyze and evaluate regional competitiveness, so as to find problems during regional development and factors to enhance competition. Therein lies the positive significance that through studying the ways to enhance regional competitiveness, we would create competitive advantages and optimize the allocation of resources to promote the scientific and sustainable development of the regional economy.

Regional resources or urban resources, defined from the perspective of economics, and as discussed in Chapter 3 "Scarcity and Generation of Resources", have broad and narrow definitions. Broadly speaking, urban resources include industrial resources, livelihood resources and infrastructure resources; narrowly speaking, urban resources refer to urban infrastructure resources, including the investment and construction of hardware and software infrastructure, as well as the investment, development and operation of modern intelligent cities. Henceforth, the regional economy or urban economy in its broad sense includes industrial economy, livelihood economy and the economy based mainly on infrastructure construction; whereas the regional

⑥ 区域政府竞争

一、政府竞争的广义与狭义范畴

区域，是个相对概念。对于全球而言，一个国家就是一个区域；对于国家而言，一个城市就是一个区域。区域之间既有共性、相似性，又有个性、差异性。区域政府，通常指管理此一区域行政事务等的政府组织，拥有相对稳定的地域、相对集中的人口和区域治理机构。区域政府具有公共性和强制性特征。

区域竞争力，是指能支撑一个区域持久生存和发展的力量，即一个区域在竞争和发展的过程中，与其他区域相比较，所具有的吸引、争夺、占有、调控和转化资源的能力，以及争夺、占有和调控市场的能力，也就是其自身发展所需的优化资源配置的能力。简言之，它是一个区域发展所需的对资源的吸引力和对市场的争夺力。我们可以基于比较经济学的方法论，建立指标体系，来分析与评价区域竞争力，由此发现区域发展中的问题，找到提升竞争力的因素。其积极意义在于：通过研究如何提升区域竞争力，我们将创造竞争优势，为本区域经济发展优化资源配置，促进其科学、可持续发展。

区域资源或城市资源，从经济学的角度上去定义，正如我们在第三章《资源稀缺与资源生成》中论述的那样，有广义与狭义之分。广义的城市资源包括产业资源、民生资源和基础设施资源；狭义的城市资源就是指城市基础设施资源，包括基础设施硬件、软件的投资建设，以及更进一步的现代化智能城市的投资、开发及运作等。因此，广义的区域经济或城市经济包括产业经济、民生经济和

economy or urban economy in its narrow sense specifically refers to the investment and development of infrastructure. Consequently, it follows that regional government competition differs in its broad sense and its narrow sense.

Broadly speaking, regional government competition includes the competitions in operational resources (industrial economy), non-operational resources (livelihood economy) and quasi-operational resources (urban economy). Narrowly speaking, regional government competition refers to competition for the investment and construction of quasi-operational resources (infrastructure resources). As far as nations are concerned, their three major tasks are maintaining stability, promoting development and handling emergencies. As far as regional governments are concerned, promoting economic growth, implementing urban construction and protecting social livelihood are their three major economic functions. Regional governments perform these three functions, classify various types of tangible and intangible resources that the regions already have or would potentially have based on economics, allocate resources, make policy measures, and analyze and compare the competition amongst regional governments. In essence, these measures are to discover, create and raise the competitiveness of the regions.

Regional government competition can mainly be divided into three categories:

The first category, competition in livelihood economy, mainly relates to the resources that are associated with the people's livelihood, known in market economy as non-operational resources. These are mainly social public goods resources, including economy (guarantee), history, geography, image, spirit, value, emergency, security, relief, and other social needs of the region. The principles of governments' policies accordingly should be "social guarantee, general underpinning; fairness and justice, effective promotion". The perfection of such policies and measures serves to maintain social coordination and stability, enhance and optimize the environment for the investment and development of the regional economy.

The second category, competition in industrial economy, mainly relates to the resources that are associated with economic growth, known in market economy as operational resources. These are mainly industrial resources, including the primary, secondary and tertiary industries. Due to differences in economic geographical and natural conditions, the pace of development of the primary, secondary and tertiary industries, as well as their focuses, varies in different nations. Nevertheless, many nations have meticulously developed their primary industries, optimized

以基础设施建设为主体的经济；狭义的区域经济或城市经济则专指基础设施投资建设。于是，区域政府竞争也就有了广义、狭义之别。

区域政府竞争，广义上包括对可经营性资源（产业经济）、非经营性资源（民生经济）和准经营性资源（城市经济）的竞争，狭义上则指对准经营性资源即基础设施投资建设等的竞争。对国家而言，稳定、发展和对突发事件的处置，是其三大任务。对各国区域政府而言，经济增长、城市建设、社会民生是其三大经济职能。区域政府履行其三大职能，对该区域已经和可能拥有的各类有形和无形资源进行经济学分类、配置资源、匹配政策措施，以及分析、比较区域政府竞争状况，这些举措的实质都是发现、创造、提升该区域的竞争力。

区域政府竞争主要分以下三大类：

第一类，民生经济竞争，主要涉及与社会民生相对应的资源——在市场经济中被称为非经营性资源，它以社会公共物品资源为主。包括经济（保障）、历史、地理、形象、精神、理念、应急、安全、救助，以及区域的其他社会需求。政府与之相匹配的政策原则应该是"社会保障，基本托底；公平公正，有效提升"。此类政策措施的完善，能维护社会协调稳定，提升和优化区域经济的投资、发展环境。

第二类，产业经济竞争，主要涉及与经济增长相对应的资源——在市场经济中被称为可经营性资源。它以产业资源为主，包括三大产业。由于经济地理和自然条件不同，各国三大产业的发展速率不一，各有侧重。但许多国家都精细发展第一产业，优化发展第二产

the development of their secondary industries, and accelerated the development of their tertiary industries, and continually succeeded. The principles of governments' policies accordingly should be "planning, guidance; support, coordination; supervision, management". The perfection of such policies and measures serves to promote market openness, fairness and justice, to effectively promote the coordinated development of industrial economy, and to increase the overall productivity of the society.

The third category, competition in urban economy, mainly relates to the resources that are associated with urban construction, known in market economy as quasi-operational resources. These are mainly urban resources, including the public service system, which is used to ensure that normal social and economic activities of the nation or region can be carried out; and the software and hardware infrastructure, which is used to provide public services for production and life, such as services in transportation, post and telecommunications, power and water supply, landscaping, environmental protection, education, science and technology, culture, health, sports, press and publication, radio, film, television, and even services for the development and construction of modern intelligent cities. The reasons why they are quasi-operational resources are that their development and management can be carried out by the government in the form of providing public goods—in this regard, they are non-operational resources, being public welfare and livelihood economy in nature, or can also be promoted by the government and enterprises with the assistance of the market—in this regard, they are operational resources, being commodities and industrial economy in nature. In the latter case, urban resources are developed, operated and managed by the government or enterprises in the market environment. The operation depends not only on the financial status of the government, but also on the market demand and the public acceptability. Government practice across the world, including the successful experience of China's reform and opening up, has told us that in order to prevent the urban resources from lying idle and being wasted, or the low-quality and disorderly management of urban construction, regional governments across the world will develop, operate and manage part or even most of the quasi-operational resources, that is, the investment and development projects of infrastructure under the context of market. At this point, its carrier, that is, the equity nature and structure of infrastructure construction projects, must conform to market competition rules; its operation, that is, the investment, operation and management of infrastructure construction projects must be realized through

业，加快发展第三产业，并不断产生成功案例。对此，政府与之相匹配的政策原则应该是"规划、引导；扶持、调节；监督、管理"。此类政策措施的完善，能促进市场公开、公平、公正，有效促进产业经济协调发展，提高社会的整体生产效率。

第三类，城市经济竞争，主要涉及与城市建设相对应的资源——在市场经济中被称为准经营性资源。它以城市资源为主，包括用于保证国家或区域的社会经济活动正常进行的公共服务系统和为生产、生活提供公共服务的软硬件基础设施，比如交通、邮电、供电供水、园林绿化、环境保护、教育、科技、文化、卫生、体育、新闻出版、广播影视乃至更进一步的现代化智能城市的开发建设等。之所以称其为准经营性资源，是因为它们的开发和管理，既可由政府以提供公共物品的方式来实施——此时它是公益性的，是非经营性资源，属民生经济性质；也可由政府和企业借助市场来推动——此时它是商品性的，是可经营性资源，属产业经济性质。后一种情况下，城市资源的经营是由政府或企业在市场环境中开发、运营、管理，其经营情况既取决于政府的财政状况，又取决于市场的需求和民众的可接受程度。世界各国政府的实践，包括中国改革开放的成功经验告诉我们：为防范城市资源闲置浪费或城市建设管理低质无序的问题，各国区域政府都会把部分甚至大部分准经营性资源即基础设施投资建设项目放到市场环境下开发、经营和管理。此时，其载体，即基础设施建设项目的股权性质与结构，必须符合市场竞争规则；其运营，即基础设施建设项目的投资、经营、管理，必须

market competition. Henceforth, by participating in the allocation and competition of quasi-operational resources, that is, the urban economy, the government promotes the comprehensive and sustainable development of urban construction and social economy.

The three types of competition above, that is, the optimal allocation of resources and supporting policies, constitute a big system, and governments compete substantially with one another in a big market system. Consequently, regional governments across the world compete with one another on the effectiveness of their allocation of the three types of resources above and the completeness of their supporting policies and measures, thereby promoting economic growth and development. Competition between regional governments across the world is manifested not only broadly in the three types of economy mentioned above and their supporting policies and measures; but also narrowly in the third type, that is, the investment and construction of the software and hardware urban infrastructure, and even in the development and construction projects of modern intelligent cities, and their supporting policies and measures. This book discusses regional government competition in various chapters, which generally refers to competition in the broad sense, but focuses more on competition in the narrow sense.

2. The Connections and Differences Between Government Competition and Enterprise Competition

The competition between enterprises is reflected predominantly in the competition for industrial resource allocation in industrial economy. The competition between regional governments is reflected predominantly in the competition for urban resource allocation in urban economy. The two systems are relatively independent, complementing each other. Their connections and differences are as follows:

(1) On areas of competition: Enterprises are subjects in microeconomics. Enterprise competition occurs mainly in the commodity market, mainly

in the allocation of industrial resources in the industrial economy. With manufacturers as the subjects, market equilibrium theory is the dominant theory in traditional classical economics. On the premise of maximizing profits, supply, demand, market equilibrium price, perfect competitive market, monopolistic competitive market, oligopolistic market and the different competitive strategies in different market structures are the main factors affecting competition amongst enterprises. Enterprise competition sets the premise and foundation for regional government competition. On the other hand, regional government is the research

通过市场竞争手段实现。由此，政府通过参与准经营性资源即城市经济的调配和竞争，推动城市建设和社会经济全面、可持续发展。

以上三类竞争，即对资源的优化配置和政策配套，是一个大系统，是政府与政府之间在一个大市场体系内的大竞争。因此，各国区域政府在对以上三类资源的调配是否有效、配套的政策措施是否完善上相互竞争，以此推动经济增长与发展。各国区域政府的竞争，既表现为在以上三类经济及其配套政策措施上的广义竞争，又表现为在第三类即城市基础设施软硬件投资建设乃至现代化智能城市开发建设项目及其政策配套措施上的狭义竞争。本书在不同章节阐述区域政府竞争，通常泛指广义竞争，但更集中论述的是狭义竞争。

二、政府竞争与企业竞争的联系和区别

企业之间的竞争主要表现为在产业经济中对产业资源配置的争夺；区域政府之间的竞争主要表现为在城市经济中对城市资源配置的争夺；二者相对独立，两个体系相辅相成。其联系与区别在于：

第一，竞争领域。企业是微观经济学的主体，企业竞争主要是在商品市场的竞争，以产业经济中的产业资源配置为主。以厂商为主体的市场均衡理论是传统古典经济学的主导理论。企业以追求利润最大化为前提，供给、需求、市场均衡价格、完全竞争市场、垄断竞争市场、寡头垄断市场、不同市场结构不同竞争策略等，是企业之间竞争的主要影响因素。企业竞争是区域政府竞争的前提和基础。

subject in mezzoeconomics. Competition between regional governments occurs mainly in the factor market, mainly in the allocation of urban resources in the urban economy. Factor markets include land, capital, talents, property rights, technology and information, and other hardware and software markets. Regional governments need not only to grasp the quantity, quality, structure and distribution of the urban resource factors, but also to formulate policies and systems to coordinate the allocation of urban resource factors in the region, and attract foreign resource factors, thereby optimizing the allocation of resources and increasing regional competitiveness. The competition in the factor market affects the competition of enterprises in the commodity market.

(2) On means of competition: The main means by which enterprises maximize profits are improving labor productivity to effectively influence costs, prices, supply and demand, scale, and optimizing the allocation of industrial resources to minimize costs. On the other hand, regional governments attempt to improve total factor productivity to promote sustainable economic growth for the region. For the regional government, after the simple expansion of tangible factors such as land, projects and capital, the bottleneck of diminishing marginal return on capital makes the "extensive" economic growth unsustainable. When the input of all the tangible factors in the region remains unchanged, regional governments can still inject new driving energy into regional economic development and urban construction by promoting technological innovation, optimizing resource allocation, restructuring and improving intangible factors such as institution, organization, law and the environment.

(3) On path of competition: Enterprise performance is mainly led by input-oriented growth, whose continuous improvement results from the continuous input of production factors by enterprises, such as capital, labor, land, technology, entrepreneurship and others. The strategy of input is initially quantitative expansion, gradually developing to the

stage of quality improvement, and then to the stage of expansionary management, where sustainable and effective input become the key. Regional government performance is mainly led by efficiency-oriented growth. As seen from the development practice of regional governments across the globe, their regional economic growth paths evolve from a "factor-driven stage" (also known as "resource allocation stage"), to an "investment-driven stage" (also known as "efficiency enhancement stage"), to an "innovation-driven stage" (also known as "sustainable growth

区域政府则是中观经济学的研究主体，其相互竞争主要是在要素市场的竞争，以城市经济中的城市资源配置为主。要素市场包括土地、资本、人才、产权、技术和信息等软硬件市场。区域政府一是要掌握城市资源要素的数量、质量、结构、布局，二是要通过制定政策和制度来调控区域内城市资源要素的配置，吸引区域外资源要素，从而优化资源配置，提高区域竞争力。要素市场竞争影响着企业在商品市场的竞争。

第二，竞争手段。企业追求利润最大化，其主要手段是通过提高劳动生产率来有效影响成本、价格、供求、规模，以及通过优化企业资源配置促进成本最小化。区域政府则努力提高全要素生产率，以此促进区域经济可持续增长。对于区域政府而言，经过拼土地、拼项目、拼资本等有形要素的简单扩张后，资本边际报酬递减这一瓶颈使得粗放式经济增长难以为继。在区域内所有有形要素的投入量保持不变时，区域政府还可以通过推动技术创新、优化资源配置、调整结构以及改善制度、组织、法律、环境等无形要素，为区域经济发展、城市建设注入新的驱动力。

第三，竞争路径。企业绩效以投入型增长为主导，其持续提高来自于企业生产要素的不断投入，包括资本、劳动、土地、技术、企业家才能等。企业投入的策略是，初期以数量型外延扩张为主，逐渐发展到质量型提升阶段，再到拓展型管理阶段，持续和有效的投入成为关键。区域政府绩效则以效率型增长为主导。从世界各国区域政府的发展实践来看，其区域经济增长路径经历过"要素驱动阶段"（也称"配置资源阶段"）、"投资驱动阶段"（也称"提高效率阶段"）和"创新驱动阶段"（也称"可持续增长阶段"）。区域政

stage"). Regional governments promote efficiency-oriented economic growth by optimizing the combination of resource factors.

(4) On competition orientation: Enterprises are guided by expanding demand. Enterprise competition needs to be based on market demand; from quantity and structure of demand to enterprise strategies, whether they can meet market demand or not becomes the key to determine the success or failure of enterprises. Regional governments are guided by optimizing supply. Effective allocation of the supply of tangible resource factors such as land, capital, projects, technology and talents, effective coordination of the supply of intangible resource factors such as planning, investment, consumption, price, taxation, interest rate, exchange rate and law, and the promotion of supply-side structural reform through innovation in values, institutions, organizations and technology are the definitive direction for regional governments to develop economy, construct cities and improve livelihood.

(5) On competition mode: Enterprises use the Enterprise Resource Planning (ERP) system to effectively integrate the management of their resources of materials, capital, information and customers, to assist enterprises to achieve effective cross-regional, cross-sectoral and cross-industrial coordination and allocation in the flow of materials, people, money, and information, so as to integrate resources effectively, adjust functions expeditiously and improve productivity, with market as its orientation, and ultimately effectively improve the competitiveness of enterprises. On the other hand, through the District Resource Planning (DRP) system, regional governments can effectively allocate various resource factors within their regions, such as land, population, finance, environment, technology and policies, to assist regional governments' layout around regional planning and development strategies using systematic management ideas and means. They can allocate regional resources and enhance regional competitiveness based on judgment of market changes, thereby fulfilling the optimization of regional total

factor productivity, and even the sustainable regional socio-economic development.

3. The Forms of Regional Government Competition

As can be seen from above, enterprise competition is the competition in industrial resource allocation in the industrial economy, that is, competition in the commodity market, whereas regional government competition is the competition in urban resource allocation in the urban economy, that is, competition in the factor market, dominated

府通过优化组合资源要素，促进区域经济实现效率型增长。

第四，竞争导向。企业以扩大需求为导向。企业竞争需从市场需求出发，从需求量、需求结构到企业战略策略，能否适应市场需求是决定企业成败的关键。区域政府则以优化供给为导向。有效配置土地、资本、项目、技术、人才等有形资源要素的供给，有效调节规划、投资、消费、价格、税收、利率、汇率、法律等无形资源要素的供给，并通过理念、制度、组织、技术创新等手段促进供给侧结构性改革是区域政府发展经济、建设城市、改善民生的确定方向。

第五，竞争模式。企业采用 ERP（企业资源规划）系统，对企业的物质、资金、信息、客户等资源进行有效的一体化管理，以帮助企业在物流、人流、财流和信息流等方面实现跨地区、跨部门、跨行业的有效协调与配置，从而以市场为导向，有效集成资源，快速调剂功能，提高生产效率，最终有效提高企业竞争力。区域政府则可通过 DRP（区域资源规划）系统，有效调配区域内包括土地、人口、财政、环境、技术、政策等在内的各种资源要素，帮助区域政府以系统化的管理思想和手段，围绕区域规划和发展战略来布局，并根据对市场变化的判断，调配区域资源，提高区域竞争力，从而实现区域全要素生产率的最优化，乃至区域社会经济的可持续发展。

三、区域政府竞争的形式

由上可知，企业竞争是在产业经济中对产业资源配置的竞争，即商品市场中的竞争，区域政府竞争则是在城市经济中对城市资源配置的竞争，即以基础设施软硬件为主的要素市场中的竞争。企业

mainly by the software and hardware infrastructure. Competitions between enterprises and between regional governments are the two levels of competition systems in modern market economy; they are mutually independent and interrelated, and together constitute the dual competitors in modern market economy. Firstly, competition at the enterprise level is the basis of all competition in the market economy. Enterprise competition motivates competition among regional governments. Regional government competition is mainly in optimizing resource allocation of institutions, policies, projects and the environment, etc. It is another kind of competition on top of enterprise competition, which in turn influences, supports and promotes enterprise competition. Secondly, enterprise competition system exists only among enterprises. Governments at any level can only play the roles of planner and guide in industrial economy/industrial resource allocation, supporter and coordinator in commodity production, and supervisor and manager of market order, and have no rights to directly intervene in the micro-affairs of enterprises. The competition system of regional government exists only among regional governments, which should adhere to the laws of market economy, and compete in projects, policies and specific affairs in the allocation of urban resources, economic development, urban construction and social livelihood. Regional government competition in the narrow sense is the main driving and leading force behind regional government competition in the broad sense.

The specific forms of regional government competition are as follows:

(1) Competition in projects, of which there are three main types: firstly, major national projects, including key national projects, national science and technology support programs, key national technology infrastructure construction plans, major engineering projects and industrialization projects financed by the state; secondly, social investment projects, such as high-tech industries, emerging industries, equipment manufacturing industries, raw materials industries, and financial, logistics and other

services; thirdly, projects with the introduction of foreign capital, such as intelligent manufacturing, cloud computing and big data, the Internet of Things, construction of intelligent cities and others. During the process of implementing various projects, regional governments can firstly, directly introduce funds, talents and industries; secondly, effectively solve the problems of financing and land expropriation in the region by virtue of the legitimacy of project policies and the rationality of public services; and thirdly, through practical implementation of

之间的竞争和区域政府之间的竞争是现代市场经济中分属两个层面的竞争体系，二者相互独立又相互联系，共同构成现代市场经济中的双重竞争主体：首先，企业层面的竞争是市场经济中一切竞争的基础。企业竞争带动了区域政府间的竞争。区域政府竞争主要是在制度、政策、项目、环境等方面优化资源配置，属于企业竞争层面之上的另一种竞争，它反过来又影响、支撑和促进了企业的竞争。其次，企业竞争体系只存在于企业之间，任何政府都只能是产业经济/产业资源配置的规划、引导者，商品生产的扶持、调节者和市场秩序的监督、管理者，没有权力对企业微观事务进行直接干预。区域政府竞争体系只存在于区域政府间，区域政府需遵循市场经济规律，在城市资源配置、经济发展、城市建设、社会民生等方面展开项目、政策和具体事务的竞争，主要是以狭义的区域政府竞争牵引、带动广义的区域政府竞争。

区域政府竞争的具体形式如下：

第一，项目竞争，主要有三类：一是国家重大项目，包括国家重大专项、国家科技支撑计划重大项目、国家重大科技基础设施建设项目、国家财政资助的重大工程项目和产业化项目。二是社会投资项目，比如高技术产业、新兴产业、装备制造业、原材料产业以及金融、物流等服务业。三是外资引进项目，比如智能制造、云计算与大数据、物联网、智能城市建设等。在实施各类项目的过程中，区域政府一则可以直接引进资金、人才和产业；二则可以凭借项目政策的合法性、公共服务的合理性来有效解决区域内筹资、征地等问题；三则可通过项目落地，引导开发区域土地、建设城市设

projects, guide the development of regional land, construct urban facilities, attract more investment, promote industrial development, optimize resource allocation and enhance policy capacity, and ultimately, promote sustainable regional socio-economic development. Hence, project competition has become the focus of competition and direction of development for regional governments across the world. Project awareness, development awareness, efficiency awareness, advantage awareness, condition awareness, policy awareness and risk awareness have become the necessary requirements for regional governments across the world to participate in competition in market economy.

(2) Competition in the supporting industrial chain: In general, each region has its own industrial base and characteristics, depending mostly on the natural resource endowments of the region. How to maintain and optimize the resource endowments of the region, and how to gather high-end resources from outside the region? The key is the optimization of the industrial structure and effective allocation of the industrial chain; and the breakthrough lies in high-end development of the industries, formation of industrial agglomeration, and leading industrial clusters. The competition of regional government's supporting industrial chain lies mainly in two aspects: first, the factors of production. Low-end or primary factors of production cannot form stable and sustainable competitiveness; only by introducing and investing in high-end factors of production, such as industrial technology, modern information technology, network resources, transportation facilities, professionals, research and development think tanks, etc., can strong industries with competitive advantages be established. Second, the industrial clusters and supporting industries. The theory on regional competitiveness suggests that the effective establishment of supporting industries led by existing industrial base within the region can reduce the transaction costs of enterprises and increase their profitability. The industrial smile curve suggests that most values are concentrated at the two ends of

the industrial value chain, namely, research and development, and the market. An important path to sustainable regional development is to cultivate superior industries, complete the industrial chain, and attract investment in accordance with the industrial structure.

(3) Competition in talents, science and technology: In this field of competition, the most fundamental is to establish the notion that talent resources are the primary resources, and science and technology are the primary productive forces; the most basic is to improve the local talent training system, and increase the investment in local talent training and in science and technology innovation; the most critical is to create

施、扩大招商引资、带动产业发展、优化资源配置、提升政策能力，最终促进区域社会经济的可持续发展。因此，项目竞争成为各国区域政府的竞争重点、发展导向。项目意识、发展意识、效率意识、优势意识、条件意识、政策意识和风险意识，成为各国区域政府在市场经济中参与竞争的必然要求。

第二，产业链配套竞争。一般来说，每个区域都有自己的产业基础和特色——多数取决于本区域内的自然资源禀赋。如何保持和优化区域内的禀赋资源并汇聚区域外的高端资源？产业结构优化、产业链有效配置是其关键；向产业高端发展、形成产业集聚、引领产业集群是其突破点。区域政府的产业链配套竞争主要从两个方面展开：一是生产要素方面。低端或初级生产要素无法形成稳定持久的竞争力，只有引进并投资于高端生产要素，比如工业技术、现代信息技术、网络资源、交通设施、专业人才、研发智库等，才能建立起强大且具有竞争优势的产业。二是在产业集群、产业配套方面。区域竞争力理论告诉我们，以辖区内现有产业基础为主导的产业有效配套，能减少企业交易成本，提高企业盈利水平。产业微笑曲线告诉我们，价值最丰厚的地方集中在产业价值链的两端——研发和市场。培植优势产业，配套完整产业链条，按照产业结构有的放矢地招商引资，是区域可持续发展的重要路径。

第三，人才、科技竞争。这一领域的竞争最根本的是确立人才资源是第一资源、科学技术是第一生产力的理念；最基础的是完善本土人才培养体系，加大本土人才培养投入和科技创新投入；最关键的是创造条件吸引人才，引进人才，培养人才，应用人才。衡量

conditions to attract, bring in, cultivate and utilize talents. The main indicators to measure the competitiveness of scientific and technological talents include regional scientific and technological talent resource index, the number of people engaged in scientific and technological activities per 10,000 people, the number of scientists and engineers per 10,000 people, the number of students enrolled in higher education per 10,000 people, the index of annual input of scientific and technological talents per 10,000 people, the total operating expenditure on scientific and technological activities, the proportion of expenditure on science and technology in GDP, per capita scientific research funds, the percentage of scientific and technological appropriations in local financial expenditure, per capita financial expenditure on education, the total amount of local financial expenditure on education, and the number of full-time teachers employed in higher education, amongst others. Through diligently improving the relevant indicators, regional governments elevate the competitiveness of local talents and science and technology.

(4) Competition in treasury and finance: Regional fiscal competition includes competition in fiscal revenue and fiscal expenditure. The main route of fiscal revenue increase is to promote economic growth and raise tax revenue. Fiscal expenditure includes social consumption expenditure, transfer expenditure and investment expenditure, with its main competition occurring in the area of investment expenditure, including government's investment in infrastructure, research and development of science and technology, policy-based financing (supporting industries in urgent need of development), and others. Fiscal investment expenditure is an important driving force of economic growth. Under the circumstances of limited financial revenue and expenditure, regional governments across the world actively build various platforms for investment and financing, mobilize and attract financial resources such as capital, talents and information from regional, domestic and international financial institutions, to serve regional economic development, urban

construction, and social livelihood. Regional governments also compete with one another for various preferential policies, such as the emphasis of fiscal expenditure, financial measures to absorb capital, etc.

(5) Competition in infrastructure: As mentioned above, the competition in this field includes the construction of the software and hardware urban infrastructure, as well as the development and operation of modern intelligent cities. Infrastructure hardware includes expressways, railways, ports, aviation, and other transport facilities; electricity, natural gas, and other energy facilities; optical cable, network,

科技人才竞争力的主要指标包括区域科技人才资源指数、每万人中从事科技活动的人数、每万人中科学家和工程师人数、每万人中普通高校在校学生数、科技活动经营支出总额、科技经费支出占国内生产总值比重、人均科研经费、科技拨款占地方财政支出百分比、人均财政性教育经费支出、地方财政教育支出总额、高校专任教师数等。各国区域政府通过努力改善、提高相关指标来提高本土的人才和科技竞争力。

第四，财政、金融竞争。区域财政竞争包括财政收入竞争和财政支出竞争。财政收入增长的主要途径是促进经济增长、提高税收；财政支出包括社会消费性支出、转移性支出和投资性支出，其中最主要的财政支出竞争发生在投资性支出领域，包括政府的基础设施投资、科技研发投资、政策性金融投资（支持急需发展的产业）等。财政投资性支出是经济增长的重要驱动力。在财政收支总体规模有限的情况下，各国区域政府积极搭建各类投融资平台，最大限度地动员和吸引区域、国内乃至国际各类金融机构的资金、人才、信息等金融资源，为本区域经济发展、城市建设、社会民生服务。区域政府在各种优惠政策上也展开相互竞争，如财政支出的侧重、吸纳资金的金融手段等。

第五，基础设施竞争。如前所述，这一领域的竞争包括城市基础设施的软硬件建设乃至现代化智能城市的开发运用等。基础设施硬件包括高速公路、铁路、港口、航空等交通设施，电力、天然气

and other information platform facilities; and science and technology parks, industrial parks, business incubation parks, creative industry parks, and other engineering infrastructure. Infrastructure software includes education, science and technology, health care, sports, culture, social welfare and other public infrastructure. Intelligent city development includes big data, cloud computing, the Internet of Things and other intelligent technology platforms. The infrastructure system of a region supports its socio-economic development, and predominantly includes three types, namely, advanced, adaptive and lagging. If the supply of regional infrastructure is moderately advanced, not only will it directly strengthen regional competitiveness, but also create high-quality urban structure, size of facilities, and spatial layout, prompt enterprises in market competition to reduce costs and improve productivity, thereby promoting industrial development. The degree of completeness of regional infrastructure will directly affect the current and future state of regional economic development.

(6) Competition in the environment system: Environment here mainly refers to the ecological environment, humanistic environment, policy environment and social credit system. Developing investment should be in harmony with protecting the eco-system; attracting investment should be coupled with policy services; pursuing wealth should be balanced with repaying the society; legal supervision and social credit should support each other. These are the indispensable development environments for regional government competition. The building of a good environmental system has become the secret of success for regional governments to attract investment, develop projects and promote continuous economic development, as proven by the experience of successful regions both at home and abroad.

(7) Competition in import and export: In an open international economic system, regional import and export competition across the world has become an important link influencing regional

competitiveness. It is mainly manifested in four aspects. Firstly, in the development of processing trade and general trade, regional governments across the world endeavor to reduce the proportion of processing trade and increase that of general trade, in order to enhance the motivation for regional trade in goods and services. Secondly, in foreign investment, regional governments across the world attempt to push for the overseas distribution of enterprises and compete for overseas projects in order to promote the distribution of their regional interests and extend their market chains overseas. Thirdly, in terms of capital export,

等能源设施，光缆、网络等信息化平台设施，以及科技园区、工业园区、创业孵化园区、创意产业园区等工程性基础设施；基础设施软件包括教育、科技、医疗卫生、体育、文化、社会福利等社会性基础设施；智能城市开发包括大数据、云计算、物联网等智能科技平台。一个区域的基础设施体系支撑着该区域社会经济的发展，其主要包括三种类型：超前型、适应型和滞后型。区域基础设施的供给如能适度超前，不仅将直接增强区域竞争力，而且能创造优质的城市结构、设施规模、空间布局，使市场竞争中的企业减少成本，提高生产效益，从而促进产业发展。区域基础设施的完善程度将直接影响区域经济发展的现状和未来。

第六，环境体系竞争。这里的环境主要指生态环境、人文环境、政策环境和社会信用体系等。发展投资与保护生态相和谐，吸引投资与政策服务相配套，追逐财富与回报社会相契合，法制监督与社会信用相支撑，等等，均是区域政府竞争必需、必备的发展环境。良好的环境体系建设成为区域政府招商引资、开发项目、促进经济持续发展的成功秘诀，这已被海内外成功区域的经验所证明。

第七，进出口竞争。在开放型的国际经济体系中，世界各国的区域进出口竞争成为影响区域竞争力的一个重要环节。它主要体现在四个层面：一是在加工贸易与一般贸易的发展中，各国区域政府力图减少加工贸易占比，提高一般贸易比重，以增强区域商品和服务贸易的原动力；二是在对外投资上，各国区域政府力图推动企业在海外布局，竞争海外项目，以促使本区域的利益布局和市场链条

regional governments across the world try to promote capital account convertibility, in other words, under the circumstances of facilitating international current account investment, take various measures to promote the circulation of money capital and facilitate free currency exchange. Fourthly, in terms of import, especially the introduction of high-tech products, industries and projects, regional governments across the world shall fully take preferential policy measures to attract, support and even spare no expense to assist their investment, distribution and production. The result of import and export competition is one of the important factors affecting regional economic growth across the world.

(8) Competition in policy systems: This can be divided into two levels: Firstly, regional governments' foreign policy system, and secondly, the series of regional governments' domestic policies. It also holds true between nations. As policies themselves are public goods, characterized by non-exclusiveness and can be easily imitated, thus, a good competitive policy system must contain the following characteristics. Firstly, it is practical, that is, it is realistic and satisfies the requirements of economic and social development. Secondly, it is advanced, that is, it has predictability, and is leading and innovative. Thirdly, it is operational, that is, policies are clear, pertinent, and implementable. Fourthly, it is organizational, that is, there are specialized agencies and personnel responsible for its implementation. Finally, it is result-oriented, that is, it has mechanisms for its inspection, supervision, assessment and evaluation, including exerting a third-party influence to effectively realize policy objectives. The level of completeness of regional policy systems across the world has a great impact on regional competitiveness.

(9) Competition in management efficiency: The management efficiency of regional government is the overall reflection of its administrative management activities, pace, quality and efficiency. It includes four categories, namely, macro-efficiency, micro-efficiency, organizational efficiency and personal efficiency. As far as administrative

compliance is concerned, regional governments should meet the standards of legitimacy, interests and quality in the competition of management efficiency; as far as administrative efficiency is concerned, regional governments should meet the standards of quantity, time, pace and budget. The competition in management efficiency of regional governments is essentially the competition in their organizational system, principal responsibilities, service consciousness, work skills and technology platforms. Developed regional governments have already in practice pioneered the competition of management efficiency by

延伸至海外；三是在资本输出上，各国区域政府力图推进资本项目可兑换，即在国际经常项目投资便利化的情况下，采取各项措施促进货币资本流通、货币自由兑换便利化等；四是在进口方面，尤其是对高科技产品、产业、项目的引进，各国区域政府全面采取优惠政策措施，予以吸引、扶持甚至不惜重金辅助其投入、布点和生产。进出口竞争的成效是影响世界各国区域经济增长的重要因素之一。

第八，政策体系竞争。它分为两个层次：一是区域政府对外的政策体系；二是区域政府对内出台的系列政策。国家与国家之间也是一样。由于政策本身是公共物品，具有非排他性和易效仿性的特点，因此，有竞争性的好的政策体系一定包含以下特征：一是求实性，即符合实际的，符合经济、社会发展要求的；二是先进性，即有预见性的、超前的、有创新性的；三是操作性，即政策是清晰的、有针对性和可实施的；四是组织性，即有专门机构和人员负责和执行的；五是效果导向性，即有检查、监督、考核、评价机制，包括发挥第三方作用，有效实现政策目标。世界各国区域政策体系的完善程度对区域竞争力的影响也极大。

第九，管理效率竞争。区域政府的管理效率是其行政管理活动、速度、质量、效能的总体反映。它包括宏观效率、微观效率、组织效率、个人效率四类。就行政的合规性而言，区域政府在管理效率竞争中应遵循合法性标准、利益标准和质量标准；就行政的效率性而言，区域政府应符合数量标准、时间标准、速度标准和预算标准。区域政府的管理效率竞争本质上是组织制度、主体责任、服务意识、工作技能和技术平台的竞争，发达的区域政府运用"并联

engaging parallel and integrated modes of service.

Regional government competition is mainly manifested in the nine areas of specific competition as described above, and is essentially to solve the following problems during the process of allocating urban resources: What policies on operational resources (industrial economy) should be adopted to invigorate the enterprises? What policies on non-operational resources (livelihood economy) should be adopted to create a sound environment? On quasi-operational resources (urban economy) what forms of participation to take, what rules and regulations to abide by, and what policies to be made to fulfill sustainable regional growth? Therefore, the essence of regional government competition is the competition in the effective allocation of the three categories of resources. Its emphasis lies with the allocation of quasi-operational resources, that is, the competition in narrowly defined urban economy with infrastructure investment and construction as its main entity.

4. "Voting by Foot" to Select Regional Governments

Scale effects, cluster effects and neighborhood effects of urban economic development can be formed by regional government competition.

The scale effects of urban economy refer to the effects of "1 + 1 > 2" produced by the organic combination of various factors of production after the total economic volume of the region has reached a certain scale and level. That is, the growth in the scale of urban economy brings about the elevation of economic benefits and comprehensive social benefits. Speaking from the level of regional government, the factors determining the scale of regional economy lie mainly in the policy arrangements and supporting measures on the development and usage of the three types of urban resources. In other words, what policies should be adopted to plan, guide, coordinate, support, supervise and manage the operational resources (industrial economy) to invigorate the enterprises? What policies on non-operational resources (livelihood economy) should be adopted to attain fairness, justice, guarantee and promotion, to optimize the investment environment? What policies on quasi-operational resources (urban economy) should be adopted to promote sustainable development? The specific forms as described in the previous section on the nine aspects ultimately determine the scale effects of the region. That is to say, regional government competition determines the scale effect of

式""一体化"的服务模式，已经在实践中开创了管理效率竞争之先河。

　　区域政府竞争主要表现为上述九个方面的具体竞争，其实质是要在配置城市资源的过程中解决以下问题：对可经营性资源（产业经济），应采取什么政策以增强企业活力？对非经营性资源（民生经济），应采取什么政策以创造良好环境？对准经营性资源（城市经济），应采取什么参与方式、遵循什么规则、配套什么政策以实现本区域可持续增长？可见，区域政府竞争的实质是有效配置三类资源的竞争，其重点是配置准经营性资源，即以基础设施投资建设为主体的狭义城市经济的竞争。

四、"用脚投票"选择区域政府

　　区域政府竞争能形成城市经济发展的规模效应、集聚效应和邻里效应。

　　城市经济的规模效应指该区域的经济总量达到一定规模和水平后，各生产要素的有机结合产生了"1+1>2"的效应，即城市经济的规模增长带来了经济效益和社会综合效益的提高。决定区域经济规模大小的因素，从区域政府层面来说，主要在于其对城市三类资源开发运用的政策安排和措施配套上，即：对可经营性资源（产业经济）采取什么政策来规划、引导、调节、扶持、监督、管理，以增强企业活力；对非经营性资源（民生经济）采取什么政策实现公平、公正、保障、提升，以优化投资环境；对准经营性资源（城市经济）采取什么政策，以促进可持续发展。其具体形式就是上一节所述的九个方面，它们最终决定着该区域的规模效应。也就是说，

the urban infrastructure, the scale effect of population and the scale effects it brings to entrepreneurship and employment, the scale effect of science and technology, the scale effect of capital, the scale effect of industry, the scale effects of the degree of market openness and trade, as well as the effects of policies and organizational management, and others. Regional government competition can form and strengthen the positive scale effects of urban economy.

The cluster effects of urban economy refer to the economic effect and comprehensive social effect produced by the spatial concentration of various economic resources and activities in the region, as well as the centripetal force resulting from that concentration, which makes various economic resources and activities congregate in this region. It is the basic factor for the continual expansion and development of urban economy. The cluster effects of urban economy include the cluster effects of economy, culture, talents, science and technology, capital, transportation infrastructure, organization management, policy measures, and others. For example, the cluster effects of industries include: firstly, the formation of vertical industrial clusters to promote scientific and technological innovation; secondly, the extension of industrial chains to form a virtuous cycle of "resources → products → wastes → resources → products", and their comprehensive use; thirdly, the attainment of energy conservation and emission reduction, ecological and environmental protection, as well as the organic combination of economic benefits and comprehensive social benefits. The cluster effects of industries bring cost advantages and promote division of labor and cooperation. Enterprises in the region share the advantages of industrial brands, thus, the scale of enterprise investment can continue to expand, the level of strategic management can continue to improve, and the social service system can improve day by day. The development of industrial clusters further promotes the transformation of regional economic growth mode. The advantageous cluster of talents, land, capital, technology, management, services, and others forms radiation effects, accelerates the process of industrialization, urbanization and informatization, pushes for the effective utilization of various resources in the region, and promotes the sustainable development of the economy. To enhance the cluster effects of urban economy, regional governments should take the initiatives in the nine major forms of competitions.

The neighborhood effects of urban economy mean the characteristics of the regional environment can influence the mentality and choice of behavior of people. When people are generally expecting to build

区域政府竞争决定着该区域的城市基础设施规模效应，人口规模效应及其带来的创业、就业规模效应，科技规模效应，资金规模效应，产业规模效应，市场开放度和贸易规模效应，以及政策效应和组织管理效应，等等。区域政府竞争能够形成并加强城市经济的正规模效应。

城市经济的集聚效应指该区域的各类经济资源和经济活动在空间上集中产生的经济效果和社会综合效果，以及由此产生的各类经济资源、经济活动向这一区域凝聚的向心力。它是城市经济得以不断扩大发展的基本因素。城市经济的集聚效应包括经济、文化、人才、科技、资金、交通基础设施和组织管理、政策措施等集聚效应。比如产业集聚效应包括：一是形成了垂直产业集群，促进了科技创新；二是延伸了产业链，形成了"资源→产品→废弃物→资源→产品"的良性循环、综合利用；三是实现了节能减排、生态环保，以及经济效益与社会综合效益的有机结合。产业集聚效应带来了成本优势，促进了分工与合作，区域内的企业共同享有产业品牌优势，因此企业的投资规模能不断扩大，战略管理水平不断提升，社会化服务体系日益健全；产业集聚发展更进一步促进了区域经济增长方式的转变，人才、土地、资金、技术、管理、服务等集聚优势形成辐射效应，加速工业化、城镇化、信息化进程，推动区域内各类资源的有效利用，促进经济可持续发展。区域政府要增强城市经济的集聚效应，应在九大竞争形式上赢得主动性。

城市经济的邻里效应指区域环境的特点可以影响人们的思想和行为选择。当人们普遍期望建立一个和谐、舒适、便利的环境，并

a harmonious, comfortable and convenient environment, striving to attain greatest rewards at the lowest cost in economic activities, the influence of regional environment will promote the transmission and exchange of the mood and economic behavior. That is what we call the neighborhood effects. Needless to say, neighborhood effects can be beneficial or detrimental, benign or malignant, positive or negative. The regional environment and comprehensive social development level will also directly affect the neighborhood effects, which include regional economy, culture, talents, science and technology, capital, transportation infrastructure and the organizational efficiency and policy effectiveness of regional governments. Regional government competition is objectively conducive to guiding beneficial, positive and benign neighborhood effects into play.

Due to the existence of regional government competition, in an open social and economic system, there arises investors' choice of where their factors of production should flow, that is, the problems of "voting by foot"[1]. Investors' choices in the flow of people, money and materials will prompt regional governments to provide a better public environment and public services. "Voting by foot" is to choose cities and regions, which in essence is to choose regional governments, regional environment, regional services and others. Regional governments' planning, guidance, support, coordination, supervision and management of the industrial economy, safeguard of the fairness and justice of livelihood economy and its effective promotion, investment and construction of the software and hardware urban infrastructure and intelligent cities, as well as the nine aspects of regional competition in the three types of economy described earlier, can effectively enhance the attractiveness of the regional brands.

力图在经济活动中以最小的代价换取最大的报酬时，区域环境的熏陶会促进这种情绪和经济行为的传递交流，这就是邻里效应。当然邻里效应包含有益的和有害的、良性的和恶性的、积极的和消极的。区域环境和社会综合发展水平也将直接影响邻里效应，这包括区域的经济、文化、人才、科技、资金、交通基础设施以及区域政府的组织效率、政策效率等。区域政府竞争在客观上有利于引导有益的、积极的、良性的邻里效应发挥作用。

因为区域政府竞争的存在，在开放型的社会经济体系中，就产生了投资者的生产要素流向选择即"用脚投票"[1]问题。投资者在人、财、物流动上的选择将促使区域政府提供更优越的公共环境和公共服务。用脚投票是在选择城市、选择区域，实质则是选择区域政府、区域环境、区域服务等。区域政府对产业经济的规划、引导、扶助、协调、监督和管理，维护民生经济的公平公正、促其有效提升，对城市基础设施软硬件乃至智能城市开发运用的投资建设，以及对此三类经济开展前述九个方面的区域竞争，均能够有效提升区域品牌的吸引力。

CHAPTER 6　MODERN MARKET ECONOMY

1. The Horizontal System of Modern Market

After the systematic analyses earlier, the purpose of this chapter is to further clarify that in the horizontal market system, not only are there market subjects in industrial economy—enterprises, there are also market subjects in urban economy—regional governments, as well as market subjects in international economy who provide quasi-operational resources, that is, public goods, including market subjects responsible for the development of space resources in space economy and marine resources in marine economy—governments or enterprises. So to speak, firstly, the market exists not only in industrial economy, but also in other economic forms. Secondly, in the horizontal market system (including industrial economy, urban economy, and international economy such as space economy, marine economy, and others), there are dual competitors—enterprises and governments. And finally, industrial economy is the fundamental field of market economy, whereas urban economy and international economy (including space, deep-sea and other resources that develop through the times) are generative fields of market economy; they are mutually independent and yet, interrelated, and belong to the competition systems of different levels in modern market economy. The multi-level market competition systems collectively constitute modern market economy.

Traditional market theory, also known as firm equilibrium theory, specifically studies how firms determine the price and output of their products in different types of markets. As a result, four basic market types can be distinguished: perfectly competitive market, monopolistic competitive market, oligopolistic market and perfectly monopolistic market. Hence, traditional market theory analyses the market, firms and industries; cost, income and output; and even firm equilibrium in the perfectly competitive market, perfectly monopolistic market, monopolistic competitive market and oligopolistic market. As was known from earlier discussions, firstly, traditional market theory focuses mainly on industrial economy, or rather, the theory itself is clarified in industrial economy. Secondly, Adam Smith's *Wealth of Nations*, being the pioneering work of economics and market economy theory, is undoubtedly a great work. However, limited by the times, after

🔠 现代市场经济

一、现代市场横向体系

在前面的系列分析之后，本章节的目的是要进一步阐明，市场横向体系中，不仅有产业经济中的市场主体——企业，而且有城市经济中的市场主体——区域政府，还有国际经济中提供准经营性资源即公共物品的市场主体，包括在太空经济中开发太空资源和在海洋经济中开发海洋资源的主体——政府或企业。这就是说：首先，市场不仅仅存在于产业经济中，而且存在于其他经济形态中；其次，市场横向体系（包括产业经济、城市经济、国际经济如太空经济、海洋经济等）中存在双重竞争主体——企业和政府；最后，产业经济是市场经济的基础领域，城市经济和国际经济（包括随着时代发展而生的太空资源、深海资源等）是市场经济的生成性领域，二者相互独立又相互联系，分属现代市场经济中不同层面的竞争体系。多层面的市场竞争体系共同构成了现代市场经济。

传统的市场理论又被称为厂商均衡理论，专门研究在不同类型的市场上厂商如何决定其产品的价格和产量。于是就有了四种基本市场类型的划分：完全竞争市场、垄断竞争市场、寡头垄断市场和完全垄断市场。由此，传统市场理论分析了市场、厂商与行业，成本、收益与产量，乃至完全竞争市场、完全垄断市场、垄断竞争市场和寡头垄断市场的厂商均衡，等等。综合此前的论述可知，首先，传统的市场理论主要聚焦于产业经济，或者说是在产业经济中阐述其理论的。其次，亚当·斯密的《国富论》作为经济学和市场经济理论的开山之作，无疑是部伟大的著作，但由于时代的局限

criticizing mercantilism and physiocracy, Adam Smith mainly based on industrial economy to investigate commodity, price, supply and demand, competition and market, and failed to discuss the economic operations of new generative resources and fields in new generative economics. Thirdly, in order to deal with the massive unemployment of British workers in the 1920s and the Great Depression of the United States and even the world economy in the early 1930s, Keynes attempted to lever a new field, urban economy, that is, the investment and construction of infrastructure, to stimulate effective demand. However, confined by the market theory in industrial economy, he failed to explain the effects of governments in their participation and intervention in the investment and construction of urban infrastructure. Finally, as discussed earlier, the contradiction between practice and theory as reflected by market failure or government failure, in essence, is not a problem of the market, but a problem of traditional market theory; not a problem of the imperfection of market theory rooted in industrial economy, but a self-contradictory situation that results inevitably from confining to this theory to define, explain and analyze the economic operation in the field of new generative resources.

Urban economic theory, in the narrow sense, mainly investigates why the government, as provider of public goods, and maintainer of market rules, becomes a participant in the investment and a competitor in the projects during the process of investment, construction, operation and management of the software and hardware urban infrastructure, and even intelligent cities; as infrastructure, why some of the public goods become operational projects in the market system and promote the development of the regional economy. In this theory, urban economy possesses market entities, projects, prices and supply-demand relations different from industrial economy. In addition, being an important field in the horizontal market system, the urban economy formed by generative resources is playing increasingly important roles both in practice and in theory.

There are also topics on the development of international economic resources (such as deep-sea economic resources, space economic resources), which are also generative resources. On the one hand, these new generative resources expand the scope of the market to be explored and their allocation needs to be optimized; on the other hand, we need to enrich market theory and improve market rules in accordance

性，亚当·斯密在批判了重商主义和重农学派之后，主要着笔于产业经济来研究商品、价格、供求、竞争与市场，而未能涉及新生成性资源和新生成性经济领域的经济运行问题。再次，凯恩斯为应对上世纪 20 年代的英国工人大失业和 30 年代初的美国乃至世界经济大萧条，试图撬动城市经济即基础设施投资建设这一新的领域来拉动有效需求，但又囿于产业经济中的市场理论，而难以解释政府在参与、干预城市基础设施投资建设中的作用。最后，如前所述，市场失灵或政府失灵反映出的实践与理论的矛盾，其实质不是市场的问题，而是传统市场理论的问题，不是植根于产业经济的市场理论不完善的问题，而是囿于这一理论去界定、解释、分析新生成性资源领域的经济运行，必然会出现自相矛盾的状况。

狭义城市经济理论主要研究的是：在城市基础设施软硬件乃至智能城市的投资、建设、运营和管理过程中，作为公共物品提供者的政府，为什么既是市场规则的维护者，又变成了投资的参与者、项目的竞争者？在作为基础设施的公共物品中，为什么有一部分变成了市场体系里的可经营性项目，推动着区域经济的发展？在这一理论中，城市经济拥有与产业经济不同的市场主体、项目、价格和供求关系。而作为市场横向体系中的一个重要领域，由生成性资源形成的城市经济正在实践和理论的双重层面发挥出越来越重要的作用。

接下来，还有同属生成性资源的国际经济资源（如深海经济资源、太空经济资源）开发等课题。一方面，这些新的生成性资源扩大了市场的范围，需要我们去开拓并优化配置；另一方面，我们需要根据这些新情况去充实市场理论，完善市场规则。近来，不断有

with these new situations. There have been constant media reports recently that it is an opportune time now to conduct "aerospace" as a big business.[1] Reportedly, China Rocket shall develop commercial launch services, sub-orbital flight experience and space resource utilization. For example, on commercial launch services, the company will provide space satellite networks, space lifts, space shuttles, space special vehicles and others. On sub-orbital flights, the company will provide various products and services such as ground weightless simulation, 360-degree VR experience, sub-orbital space travel and others in accordance with the ages, physical conditions and interests of tourists. Backed by the powerful Chinese aerospace industry, with the US space exploration technology company (Space X) as its benchmark, China Rocket plans to gradually inject assets, introduce strategic investors, and promote the advent of commercialization era of Chinese rockets. Major powers have already begun competing in this field where returns on investment have always been high. Under these circumstances, how should "aerospace economics" be conceived? How should it develop? How effective is it? Aerospace economy faces this problem, and even more so for space economy in a broader sense. These new circumstances are constantly broadening the fields of the market on the one hand, and on the other, calling for the interpretation of the investors and rules of the game that are different from those in industrial economy.

2. The Vertical System of Modern Market

The traditional market system can be looked at mainly from four levels. Firstly, in terms of entities in circulation, the traditional market is composed of the commodity market and the factors of production market; secondly, in terms of spatial scope, it is composed of different regional markets at all levels of various scopes; thirdly, in terms of institutional settings, it is composed of various market organizations and market intermediary organizations; and lastly, in terms of specific methods, it consists of the spot market, forward market and future market.

In contrast, the modern market system emphasizes the systematicity of market structure, especially the systematicity of functional structure. The market functional structure is firstly the interests adjustment system, secondly the competition system, and thirdly the information dissemination system. Therefore, the vertical system of modern market should include at least the following six aspects:

媒体报道：是时候把航天当一门大生意来做了。[1] 据悉，中国长征火箭公司将打造商业发射服务、亚轨道飞行体验、空间资源利用三大业务板块。比如发射服务方面，该公司将推出太空星网、太空顺风车、太空班车、太空专车等。亚轨道飞行方面，该公司将针对游客的年龄、身体状况以及兴趣的不同，推出地面失重模拟训练、360度全方位 VR 体验、亚轨道太空遨游等不同的产品和服务。中国长征火箭公司背靠强大的中国航天工业，对标美国太空探索技术公司，计划逐步注入资产，引入战略投资者，助推中国火箭商业化时代的来临。在这个投资回报率一直很高的领域，大国之间已经展开了竞争。在这种情况下，"航天经济学"应如何立意？如何发展？成效几何？航天经济面临着这个问题，更广义的太空经济更是如此，这类新情况一方面不断扩展着市场领域，另一方面又呼唤着对与产业经济不同的投资主体和游戏规则的解读。

二、现代市场纵向体系

传统市场体系主要包括四个层面的含义：首先，从流通对象来看，传统市场由商品市场和生产要素市场构成；其次，从空间范围来看，由不同区域范围的各级地域性市场构成；再次，从机构设置来看，由各种市场组织以及市场中介组织构成；最后，从具体方式来看，由现货交易市场、远期交易市场和期货交易市场构成。

与之相比，现代市场体系则强调市场构成的体系性，尤其是功能结构的体系性，即市场功能结构首先是利益调节体系，其次是竞争体系，再次是信息传播体系。因此，现代市场纵向体系至少应该包括以下六个方面内容：

(1) The market factor system: It is composed of various types of markets (including the commodity market, factors market and financial market, etc.), and the most basic elements in various types of markets, namely price, supply and demand, competition, and others.

(2) The market organization system: It is the concentration of the main entities or organizers of market factors and market activities, including various types of market entities (such as the retail market, wholesale market, talent market, labor market, financial market, and others), various market intermediaries (including consultation, training, information, accounting, law, property rights, asset valuation and other service agencies), and market management organizations (such as various chambers of commerce and industry associations).

(3) The market legal system: Market economy has the characteristics of property rights economy, contract economy and normative economy. Therefore, the system of laws and regulations regulating market value orientation, transaction behavior, contract behavior and property rights behavior as a whole constitutes the market legal system. It includes market-related legislation, law enforcement, justice, legal education, etc.

(4) The market supervision system: It is a system of policies implementation based on the market legal system, which meets the needs of the market economy, including the supervision and management of institutions, businesses, markets, implementation of policies and regulations, and others.

(5) The market environment system: It mainly includes the three aspects of foundation of real economy, corporate governance structure and social credit system. What is important to this system is to establish and improve the market credit system, regulate trust relations, credit instruments, credit intermediaries and other relevant credit elements by law, and establish the social credit governance mechanism, with the improvement of the market credit guarantee mechanism as a starting point.

(6) The market infrastructure: It is a complete market facility system including various hardware and software. Among them, market service networks, supporting facilities and technologies, various market payment and settlement systems, science and technology information systems and others, are the infrastructure necessary for a mature market economy.

The vertical system of modern market and its six subsystems have the following characteristics:

第一，市场要素体系。它既由各类市场（包括商品市场、要素市场和金融市场等）构成，又由各类市场的最基本元素即价格、供求和竞争等构成。

第二，市场组织体系。它是市场要素与市场活动的主体或组织者的集中地，包括各种类型的市场实体（比如零售市场、批发市场、人才市场、劳务市场、金融市场等）、各类市场中介机构（包括咨询、培训、信息、会计、法律、产权、资产评估等服务机构）以及市场管理组织（比如各种商会、行业协会等）。

第三，市场法制体系。市场经济具有产权经济、契约经济和规范经济的特点，因此，规范市场价值导向、交易行为、契约行为和产权行为等的法律法规的整体就构成了市场法制体系。它包括市场相关的立法、执法、司法和法制教育等。

第四，市场监管体系。它是建立在市场法律体系基础上的、符合市场经济需要的政策执行体系，包括对机构、业务、市场、政策法规执行等的监管。

第五，市场环境体系。它主要包括实体经济基础、企业治理结构和社会信用体系等三大方面。对这一体系而言，重要的是建立健全市场信用体系，以法律制度规范、约束信托关系、信用工具、信用中介和其他相关信用要素，以及以完善市场信用保障机制为起点建立社会信用治理机制。

第六，市场基础设施。它是包含各类软硬件的完整的市场设施系统。其中，市场服务网络、配套设备及技术、各类市场支付清算体系、科技信息系统等，是成熟市场经济必备的基础设施。

现代市场纵向体系及其六个子体系具有如下特点：

(1) The formation of the vertical system of modern market is a gradual historical process. During the early development of market economy, the US mainstream accepted the laissez-faire economic concept, the market factor and market organization systems were developed and promoted, and objection against government intervention in the economy prevailed. In 1890, the United States Congress promulgated the Sherman Antitrust Act, the first anti-monopoly law in American history, prohibiting monopolistic agreements and monopolistic behavior. In 1914, the United States promulgated the Federal Trade Commission Act and the Clayton Antitrust Act to supplement and improve the Sherman Act. Since then, the anti-monopoly system and regulatory practice in the United States have undergone nearly a hundred years of evolution and improvement, and the whole market has formed a pattern of dynamic coexistence of monopoly and competition, development and regulation. Since the 1990s, the information communication and network technology in the United States have developed explosively, the capacity to drive market innovation, and infrastructure upgrades have become the main manifestations of market competition. At the same time, the anti-monopoly objectives of the US government are no longer restricted to simple prevention of market monopoly and price manipulation; technology monopoly that is not for patent protection and network oligopoly are also part of them. During this period, the market environment system and market infrastructure of the United States have been further improved and developed through the improvements of infrastructure like market registration, settlement, trusteeship and backup, improvements in the abilities to handle major disasters and technical failures, enhancements in market information system, improvements in the construction of the credit system, sharing of market supervision data, etc. All these have pushed the market system to a modern stage, and market competition has leaped into a stage promoted by total factors and systematic participation.

(2) The six aspects of the vertical system of modern market are unified. On the one hand, the six market subsystems are interconnected and interactive, organically integrated into a mature market economy system. During the operation of the market economy in practice, any missing subsystem will lead to market deficiencies in that area, causing economic losses to the nation. During the development of market economy across the world, such typical cases are common throughout. On the other hand, within the six market subsystems, factors are also interconnected, interactive and organically unified with each other. For

第一，现代市场纵向体系的形成，是个渐进的历史过程。在早期的市场经济发展中，美国主流认可自由放任的经济理念，市场要素体系与市场组织体系得到发展和提升，反对政府干预经济的理念盛行。1890年，美国国会颁布美国历史上第一部反垄断法《谢尔曼法》，禁止垄断协议和独占行为。1914年，美国颁布《联邦贸易委员会法》和《克莱顿法》，对《谢尔曼法》进行补充和完善。此后美国的反垄断制度和监管实践经历了近百年的演进与完善，整个市场形成了垄断与竞争、发展与监管动态并存的格局。20世纪90年代开始，美国信息通信、网络技术爆发式发展，市场创新驱动能力和基础设施升级换代成为市场竞争的主要表现。与此同时，美国政府反垄断的目标不再局限于简单防止市场独占、操纵价格等行为，专利保护以外的技术垄断和网络寡头垄断也被纳入了打击范围。这一时期，通过完善市场登记、结算、托管和备份等基础设施建设，提高应对重大灾难与技术故障的能力，提升市场信息系统，完善信用体系建设，实施市场监管数据信息共享，等等，美国的市场环境体系和市场基础设施得到了进一步提高与发展。这一切将市场体系推向现代高度，市场竞争发展到了全要素推动和系统参与的飞跃阶段。

第二，现代市场纵向体系的六个方面是统一的。一方面，六个市场子系统相互联系、相互作用，有机结合为一个成熟的市场经济体系。在市场经济实际运行中，缺少哪一个子系统，都会导致市场在那一方面产生缺陷，进而造成国家经济的损失。在世界各国市场经济的发展过程中，这样的典型案例比比皆是。另一方面，在六个

example, in the market factor system, apart from the interconnections of various commodity markets, factor markets and financial markets, in the factor markets, the standardization and development of land markets, gradual establishment of a unified urban and rural labor market, active development of the technology markets, vigorous enhancement of property rights (including technological property rights) trading markets, etc. are all important measures to mutually improve and collectively perfect a modern market system.

(3) The six aspects of the vertical system of modern market are orderly; only an orderly market system is efficient. For example, in an orderly pricing mechanism of commodities, factors and projects, during the formation of the investment price of commodities, factors and projects (resources or generative resources), the market should fully demonstrate its basic role in resource allocation, and set prices according to the supply-demand relationship, and the status of the scarcity of resources and resource generation reflected in the market, thereby promoting the orderly operation of the modern market system. The orderly competition mechanism of commodities, factors and projects is another example. Competition is an inevitable product of market economy, and also a prerequisite of realizing market economy. Only through competition can the prices of commodities, factors and projects fluctuate in the market, and resources be allocated to the most efficient enterprises, regions or phases, thereby realizing the survival of the fittest market entities. Market segmentation, blockade and monopoly are all barriers that must be removed from the modern market system. The orderly opening mechanism of commodities, factors and projects is a further example. In the open modern market system, commodities, factors and projects are open to investors from different regions, industries, home and abroad, all of whom can enter out of own's accord, choose supply and demand at free will, and invest and develop independently. However, this kind of opening must be gradual,

safe, stable and orderly. This shows once again that the six aspects of the vertical system of modern market are mutually independent and yet mutually restrictive; as an example, competition and supervision of the market, freedom and the rule of law, etc., are complete systems of unity of opposites.

(4) The functions of the six aspects of the vertical modern market system are fragile. The reasons are as follows. Firstly, incomplete

市场子系统内，各个要素之间也是相互联系、相互作用、有机统一的。比如在市场要素体系中，除了各类商品市场、要素市场、金融市场互相联系、互相作用外，在要素市场之中，规范和发展土地市场，逐步建立城乡统一的劳动力市场，积极发展技术市场，努力提升产权（包括技术产权）交易市场，等等，都是相互促进、共同完善现代市场体系的重要举措。

第三，现代市场纵向体系的六个方面是有序的，有序的市场体系才有效率。比如商品、要素、项目的价格机制的有序，即在商品、要素、（资源性或生成资源性）项目投资价格的形成过程中，应充分发挥市场在资源配置中的基础性作用，根据市场反映的供求关系、资源稀缺和资源生成状况来定价，从而推动现代市场体系有序运转。再比如商品、要素、项目的竞争机制的有序。竞争是市场经济的必然产物，也是实现市场经济的必然要求。只有通过竞争，商品、要素、项目的价格才会产生市场波动，资源才能被配置到最有效率的企业、区域或环节中，从而实现市场主体的优胜劣汰。分割市场、封锁市场、垄断市场，都是现代市场体系必须要扫除的障碍。又比如商品、要素、项目的开放机制的有序。现代市场体系是开放的，商品、要素、项目对不同区域、行业、国内外投资者都是开放的，各方可以自主进入，自由选择供求，自主投资开发；但这种开放又必定是渐进的、安全的、稳定有序的。这又再次表明，现代市场纵向体系的六个方面既相互独立又相互制约，比如市场的竞争与监管，自由与法治，等等，是对立统一的完整系统。

第四，现代市场纵向体系六个方面的功能是脆弱的。其原因在

understanding: As the market subjects (namely, participants in the commodity market, factor market and project market) have their own demands for interests, during the operation of the market in practice, they tend to focus only on freedom, competition and demand, instead of the rule of law, supervision and balances, resulting in biases in the functions of the six aspects of the vertical system of modern market. Secondly, the untimeliness of policies: Various investors are the main participants of the market, while regional governments across the world are the main supervisors of the market. However, over the historical interactions of the unity of opposites between the government and market, due to the influence of traditional market economy theory, the government is usually inactive, lagging, or when faced with world economic crisis, makes up by "patching and filling holes", rendering the six aspects of the vertical system of modern market unable to fully function. Thirdly, the impact of economic globalization: In the global market system where there is imperfection in legislation, joint law enforcement and coordinated supervision measures, there exist many problems such as vacuum in regulations, regulatory arbitrages, market speculations, and cross-border market development, as well as counterfeiting, fraud and theft. Hence, the improvement of the modern market system and the effective functioning of the six aspects is still a long and arduous process.

(5) The six aspects of the vertical system of modern market are influencing or will soon influence all fields of the horizontal system of modern market. That is to say, the modern market system, which is gradually becoming complete over the course of history, will play a role not only in industrial economy, which is the economic foundation across the world, but also in urban economy and international economy (including deep-sea economy and space economy) gradually with the development and utilization of various generative resources. Different fields and different types of commodity economy, factor economy and

project economy have produced different participants, which require the continuous improvement and perfection of the functions of the six aspects of the vertical system of modern market, which in turn requires the continuous improvement and perfection of contemporary economic theories, in particular, modern market theory.

于：首先，认识上的不完整。由于市场主体（即商品市场、要素市场、项目市场的参与主体）有自己的利益要求，所以在实际的市场运行中，它们往往只讲自由、竞争和需求，避讲法治、监管和均衡，这导致现代市场纵向体系六个方面的功能出现偏颇。其次，政策上的不及时。市场的参与主要依靠各类投资者，市场的监管主要依靠各国区域政府。但在政府与市场既对立又统一的历史互动中，由于传统市场经济理论的影响，政府往往是无为的，或滞后的，或在面临世界经济大危机时采用"补丁填洞"的方式弥补，等等，这使得现代市场纵向体系六个方面的功能无法全部发挥。再次，经济全球化的冲击。在立法、联合执法、协同监管措施还不完善的全球市场体系中，存在大量监管真空、监管套利、市场投机、不同市场跨界发展，以及制假、欺诈、偷骗等问题，因此现代市场体系的健全及六个方面功能的有效发挥，还需要一个漫长的过程。

第五，现代市场纵向体系的六个方面职能，正在或即将作用于现代市场横向体系的各个领域。也就是说，在历史进程中逐渐完整的现代市场体系，不仅会在作为各国经济基础的产业经济中发挥作用，而且伴随着各类生成性资源的开发和利用，也会逐渐在城市经济、国际经济（包括深海经济和太空经济）中发挥作用。不同领域、不同类型的商品经济、要素经济和项目经济，产生了不同的参与主体，它们需要现代市场纵向体系六个方面的功能不断提升、完善。而这又需要当代经济理论，尤其是现代市场理论的不断提升与完善。

3. Efficient Market Division

The concept of an efficient market was first proposed by Eugene Fama in 1970. Fama believed that when the prices of securities can fully reflect the information available to investors, the securities market is an efficient market, where investors can only expect the normal return rate corresponding to the investment risk no matter what securities are chosen randomly.

Fama then put forward the three-level theory of efficient market, that is, according to the types of information available to investors, efficient market can be divided into three levels: weak efficient market, semi-strong efficient market and strong efficient market. In the weak efficient market, all the information of past prices is already fully reflected in the current prices, so technical analysis analyzing the information of historical prices by means of moving average and candlestick charts is ineffective. Besides information of previous prices in the securities market, the semi-strong efficient market also includes all the public information available in the news media, such as the annual and quarterly reports from the companies issuing securities; basic analysis relying on public information such as the financial statements of enterprises is also ineffective. The information in the strong efficient market includes not only all public information, but also all insider information, such as internal information held by senior managers in enterprises. If the strong efficient market holds water, all the above information would already be fully reflected in the current prices, then even investors holding insider information cannot continuously earn abnormal returns.

As a result, Fama put forward the premise for efficient market, that the Efficient Market Hypothesis presumes a perfect market. Firstly, there is no friction in the whole market, that is, there is no transaction costs and taxes; all assets can be completely separated and traded without restrictive provisions. Secondly, the whole market is fully competitive, and all market participants are price takers. Thirdly, there is no information cost. Finally, all market participants receive information at the same time, and all of them are rational and pursue maximum utility.

However, in reality, these assumptions are very difficult to hold. The presence of market frictions indicates that a completely efficient market is impossible. Investors must also consider transaction costs, opportunity

三、有效市场划分

有效市场的概念最初是由尤金·法马在 1970 年提出的。法马认为，当证券价格能够充分反映投资者可获得的信息时，证券市场就是有效市场，即在有效市场中，无论随机选择何种证券，投资者都只能期待与投资风险相当的正常收益率。

接着，法马提出了有效市场的三层次理论，即根据投资者可以获得的信息种类，将有效市场分成了三个层次：弱形式有效市场，半强形式有效市场和强形式有效市场。弱形式有效市场中，以往价格的所有信息已经完全反映在当前的价格之中，所以利用移动平均线和 K 线图等手段分析历史价格信息的技术分析法是无效的。除了证券市场以往的价格信息之外，半强形式有效市场中包含的信息还包括发行证券企业的年度报告、季度报告等在新闻媒体中可以获得的所有公开信息，依靠企业的财务报表等公开信息进行的基础分析法也是无效的。强形式有效市场中的信息既包括所有的公开信息，也包括所有的内幕信息，例如企业内部高级管理人员所掌握的内部信息。如果强形式有效市场假说成立，上述所有的信息都已经完全反映在当前的价格之中，那么，即便是掌握内幕信息的投资者也无法持续获取非正常收益。

于是，法马提出了有效市场的前提假设，即市场有效性假设是以一个完美的市场为前提的：首先，整个市场没有摩擦，即不存在交易成本和税收；所有资产完全可分割、可交易；没有限制性规定。其次，整个市场是充分竞争的，所有市场参与者都是价格的接受者。再次，信息成本为零。最后，所有市场参与者同时接受信息，所有市场参与者都是理性的，并且追求效用最大化。

然而，在现实生活中，这些假设条件是很难成立的。市场摩擦的存在表明不可能存在一个完全有效的市场，投资者进行投资也都

costs, taxes and other costs. All these make the premise of an efficient market difficult to be achieved and the Efficient Market Hypothesis difficult to apply in practice.

Here I won't comment on whether it is reasonable of Fama to define the strength of an efficient market with the amount of transaction information carried by prices. What I do agree with is his methodology of dividing modern market into strong efficient market, semi-strong efficient market and weak efficient market. I think that this methodology of division can be further transplanted from the securities market to the whole modern market economy. Based on the differences in the growth and maturity levels of their market systems across the world, and the achievement of their functions of the six subsystems of the vertical system of modern market, efficient market can be divided into three levels: Markets in which only exist market factor system and market organization system belong to weak efficient markets. Such was the case in the market development of the United States from its founding in 1776 to 1890. On the basis of market factor system and market organization system, if a nation gradually establishes and improves the market legal system and market supervision system, it belongs to the semi-strong efficient market. The market development of the United States from 1890 to 1990 went with this type. On the basis of semi-strong efficient market, only when a nation establishes and improves the market environment system and market infrastructure can it belong to the strong efficient market. The market development and growth of the United States since the 1990s was in accordance with this trend.

The division into "strong", "semi-strong" and "weak" efficient markets based on the degree of maturity and completeness of the six subsystems of the vertical system of modern market is an extension of and reference to the methodology employed by Fama in dividing efficient markets. Not only can it reflect the original picture and genuine progress of the history of market economy across the world, it can also define clearly the different market types, guide the practice of market economy across the world, as well as evaluate its effectiveness scientifically. Constructing modern market systems and improving market functions play important roles in promoting economic development, urban construction and social livelihood, thus nations across the world are actively exploring and striving for breakthroughs in this field.

必须考虑交易成本、机会成本、税收和其他费用，等等。这些都使有效市场的前提难以达到，有效市场假设难以运用到实际中。

在此，我暂且不去评论，法马以价格所承载的交易信息量为标准来界定有效市场的强弱是否合理。我赞成的是他将现代市场分为"强式有效市场""半强式有效市场"与"弱式有效市场"的方法论。我认为可以将这种划分从证券市场移植到整个现代市场经济中，即针对世界各国市场体系发育和成熟程度的不同，按现代市场纵向体系六个子系统功能实现的状况来划分三个层次的有效市场：只存在市场要素体系和市场组织体系的市场，属于弱式有效市场。美国 1776 年建国至 1890 年之间的市场发展状况属于此列。在具备市场要素体系和市场组织体系的基础上，一国市场如果又逐步建立健全了市场法制体系和市场监管体系，则属于"半强式有效市场"。美国 1890 年至 1990 年期间的市场发展状况应该属此类型。在半强式有效市场的基础上，一国市场只有建立并完善了市场环境体系与市场基础设施时，才属于"强式有效市场"。美国上世纪 90 年代开始的市场发展和成长过程，正是按照这一趋势前进的。

按照现代市场纵向体系六个子系统的成熟与完善程度来划分"强式""半强式""弱式"有效市场，是对法马划分有效市场的方法论的延伸和借鉴，它既能反映世界各国市场经济历史的本来面目与真实进程，又便于清晰界定不同市场类型、指导各国市场经济实践并对其效果进行科学评估。构建现代市场体系，完善市场功能，对促进经济发展、城市建设和社会民生具有重要作用，因此世界各国都在此领域积极探索，力求突破。

4. Re-Understanding Market Failure

"Market failure" is a concept that originates from neoclassical economics, so current analysis of market failure mainly focuses on the field of industrial economy. Through the theoretical analysis of the functional structure of the six aspects of the vertical system of modern market in this chapter, and the case study analyzing the historical process of the growth and development of the modern market system in the United States, we can see that firstly, the improvement of market rules lags far behind the historical progress. During the early economic development after its founding in 1776, the mainstream United States concurred with the concept of laissez-faire. The United States at this stage was mainly establishing and improving the market factor system and market organization system. After 1890, the United States promulgated the first anti-monopoly law; particularly after the Great Depression and the world economic crisis in 1929-1933, the market legal system and market supervision system of the United States were gradually improved. Since the 1990s, faced with mixed operations and the explosive development of network technology, information and communication means, the market environment system and market infrastructure of the United States were gradually improved. As can be seen, the integrity and order of the functions of six aspects in the vertical system of modern market, as well as the formation of the complete market mechanism and market rules, have lagged far behind the actual historical progress of the market economy in the United States over the past two hundred years. The complete market function of the six aspects of the vertical system of modern market, both in theory and practice, has not yet been fully recognized and utilized till this day, which cannot but objectively lead to market failure. Among such lags in market rules, the lag in market legal and supervision systems is particularly prominent. It can be said that during the development of the United States from a fully competitive market to a monopolistic competitive market, to an oligopolistic market, and then to a fully monopolistic market, the legal and supervision systems of the United States have been taking a "crisis-oriented" "upgrading by patches" path of "patching and filling holes". Till this day, as the monopolistic competitive market in the United States develops towards the oligopolistic market, there still exist many disputes both in theory and practice on how to effectively regulate the oligopoly market by law. Being important parts of the vertical system of modern market, the legal and supervision systems are indispensable links in a complete market mechanism. Legal supervision measures like "patching

四、重新认识市场失灵

市场失灵是源自新古典经济学的概念，因此当前对市场失灵的分析也主要集中在产业经济领域。通过此章对现代市场纵向体系六个方面功能结构的理论分析，以及通过美国现代市场体系成长发育的历史进程的案例分析，我们可以看到：首先，市场规则的完善远远滞后于历史进程。在 1776 年建国后早期的经济发展中，美国主流认同自由放任理念，此阶段美国主要是建立与完善市场要素体系和市场组织体系。1890 年后，美国颁布第一部反垄断法，尤其在 1929—1933 年美国大萧条和世界经济大危机之后，美国的市场法制体系和市场监管体系才得以逐渐完善。20 世纪 90 年代开始，面对混业经营和网络技术、信息通信手段的爆发式发展，美国的市场环境体系和市场基础设施才逐步得到提升。可见，现代市场纵向体系六个方面功能的完整和有序，乃至完善的市场机制、市场规则的形成，在这两百多年间，是远远落后于美国市场经济的实际历史进程的。在理论与实践上，现代市场纵向体系六个方面融为一体的完整市场功能，至今还没被充分地认识和运用，这不能不在客观上导致市场失灵。这类市场规则的滞后性之中，市场法制与监管系统的滞后是尤为突出的。可以说，在美国从完全竞争市场到垄断竞争市场，到寡头垄断市场，再向完全垄断市场发展的过程中，美国的法制与监管系统一直在走一条"危机导向""补丁升级"的"补丁填洞"之路。直至今日，当美国由垄断竞争市场走向寡头垄断市场的时候，如何对寡头垄断市场实行有效的法制监管，仍然存在理论和实践上的重重争议。法制与监管作为现代市场纵向体系的重要部

and filling holes" of the United States are unable to create an open, fair and just market environment for various kinds of investors, which will also inevitably lead to market failure. Secondly, the realization of social public demand has always lagged behind the satisfaction of the interests of market subjects (that is, manufacturers or other investors). The market produces competition, and competition promotes equilibrium; but in reality, this equilibrium is mainly firm equilibrium, that is, the firm's short- or long-term equilibrium in product and price, cost and benefit, and supply and demand. The balance between social public demand and the interests of firms is basically non-existent. Social public interests are mainly guaranteed by the secondary distributions of governments across the world. The market subjects' protection of their interests may cause barriers, which will also lead to market failure. Due to the above reasons, it can be said that the fragility of the modern market economy system and market failure have become normal.

In reality, there always exist disputes on whether the industrial economy needs the government to formulate industrial policies to "plan, guide, support, coordinate, supervise and manage". The consensus is that in areas where the market fails to function, the government is required to play an active role. Such are areas of market failures. For example, Joseph Stiglitz, 2001 Nobel Prize winner in Economics, put forward "Creating a learning society" in 2014, focusing on the latest discoveries of market failure in economics. His views were that firstly, innovative activities (whether imitative or autonomous) have strong positive externalities, even become public goods of the whole industry in some cases, and result in limited incentives for enterprises. Secondly, information search and dissemination are also public goods in nature, so it is difficult to ensure their full provisions by relying solely on market mechanism. Finally, in the initial developmental stages of emerging industries, there exists a situation of insufficient market or even a total lack of market, which involves not only the market of their own products, but also the market of related inputs. Hence, in order to promote the development of emerging industries, non-market forces are required to play an active role to encourage innovation, provide information and foster markets; government intervention is the most important non-market force with significant effects. Therefore, professor Stiglitz suggested that government intervention may make up for market shortage and rectify market failure specifically in the following ways: (1) industrial

分，是完整市场机制不可或缺的环节，而类似美国的"补丁填洞"的法制监管办法，无法为各类投资者创造公开、公平、公正的市场环境，这也必然会导致市场失灵。其次，社会公众需求的实现始终滞后于市场主体（即厂商或其他投资主体）利益的满足。市场产生竞争，竞争促进均衡，但在现实中，这一均衡主要是厂商均衡，即厂商在产品与价格、成本与收益、供给与需求三个层次上的短期或长期均衡。而社会公众需求与厂商利益的均衡在其中是基本缺位的，社会公众的利益主要靠各国政府的二次分配来保障，市场主体维护其利益的行为，可能对此造成障碍，这也会导致市场失灵。由于上述原因，可以说，现代市场经济体系的脆弱与市场失灵已成为常态。

现实中，围绕产业经济是否需要政府制定产业政策来"规划、引导；扶持、调节；监督、管理"，始终存在争议。共识是：市场发挥不了作用的地方，需要政府来发挥积极的作用，这样的地方就是市场失灵之处。比如，2001年诺贝尔经济学奖获得者约瑟夫·斯蒂格利茨在2014年提出了"学习型社会理论"，着重阐释了经济学关于市场失灵的最新发现。他认为：首先，创新活动（无论是模仿性的还是自主性的）具有很强的正外部性，以致在某些情况下成为全行业的公共物品，造成企业的行动激励受限。其次，信息搜寻和扩散也具有公共物品的性质，因此，单纯依靠市场机制的运作难以保证其被充分提供。最后，新兴产业在初期发展阶段存在市场不足甚至市场缺失的情形，这不仅涉及其自身产品的市场，也涉及相关投入品的市场，因此，为推动新兴产业的发展，需要非市场力量在鼓励创新、提供信息和培育市场方面发挥一定的积极作用，而政府干预就是最为重要而又效果显著的非市场力量。因此，斯蒂格利茨教授提出，政府干预有可能弥补市场不足，矫正市场失灵，其具体方式如下：一是产业政策与贸易政策，它们将有助于在产业范围内

and trade policies, which will help promote knowledge accumulation and dissemination within the industry; (2) fiscal and financial policies, which are the prerequisites for the implementation of industrial policies; (3) investment policies: Through subsidies, governments promote the production and proliferation of knowledge; (4) the construction of intellectual property rights system, which provides positive incentives to the individuals who discover, produce and proliferate knowledge. Thus, in order to promote the development of a "learning society", industrial policies are indispensable.[2] Relevant professors of Peking University have also acknowledged the necessities of industrial policies, and put forward five optimum conditions for the exploration and implementation of industrial policies: (1) Industrial policies must conform to the market and follow the trends. (2) Encourage competition. This is consistent with the Theory of Industrial Policy and Competition proposed by Philippe Aghion, master of the new endogenous economic growth theory. (3) Intervene cautiously. The government is not the pilot in developers' fantasy, but should be a down-to-earth servant, and the key to becoming a good servant is to accurately pinpoint the areas that need service. (4) There must be an exit mechanism, and there is a need for political economics to study the industrial policy exit mechanism. (5) Establish evaluation systems. The establishment of a reasonable policy evaluation system and accountability system is in itself a difficult problem and topic in political economics.[3] As seen, Stiglitz and other scholars still believe that the government and the market are isolated from each other, and that market failures and policy measures to remedy market failures still exist mainly in the area of industrial economy. It should be said that this view represents the mainstream opinion on market failure held by the world's economists today.

However, I hold the view that the various theoretical and practical problems in the economic development of the world today are not problems of the market or market economy, but due to a lack of modern market theory and the imperfection of the modern market economy. Developments in reality require a new economic system. As previously analyzed, the horizontal system of modern market includes the field of industrial resources, the field of urban resources which is being continuously developed, and the field of international resources (such as space resources and deep-sea resources, etc.), which is to be developed; the vertical system of modern market includes six major subsystems, namely, the market factor system, the market organization

促进知识积累和扩散。二是财政和金融政策，它是产业政策实施所需的抓手。三是投资政策，政府通过补贴促进知识的生产和扩散。四是知识产权制度建设，它为知识发明者、生产者和扩散者提供正向激励。因此，为促进"学习型社会"的发展，产业政策是不可或缺的。[2] 北京大学的相关教授也承认产业政策的必要性，并提出着力探究实施产业政策的五大最优条件：一是产业政策必须顺应市场，顺势而为。二是鼓励竞争。这一点与新内生经济增长理论大师阿吉翁提出的"产业政策与竞争政策相结合"理论是一致的。三是谨慎干预，即政府不是发展主义者所幻想的领航员，而应该成为脚踏实地的服务生，要做好服务生，关键在于精准地抓住服务点。四是要有退出机制，需要研究产业政策退出机制的政治经济学。五是建立评估制度。当然，合理的政策评估体制和问责制度的建立，本身又是一个政治经济学的难题和课题。[3] 可见，斯蒂格利茨等学者仍然认为：第一，政府与市场是相隔离的。第二，市场失灵以及弥补市场失灵的政策措施仍主要存在于产业经济领域。应该说，这一观点代表了当今世界经济学界对市场失灵的主流看法。

但我认为，当今世界各国经济发展中出现的各种理论与实践问题，不是市场或市场经济的问题，而是缺少现代市场理论、现代市场经济还不够完善的问题，现实的发展需要一种新的经济学体系。在此之前，我分析了现代市场横向体系包括产业资源领域、正在被持续开发的城市资源领域和将要开发的国际资源（如太空资源和深海资源等）领域，现代市场纵向体系则包括市场要素体系、市场组

system, the market legal system, the market supervision system, the market environment system, and the market infrastructure. Horizontal and vertical systems integrate into a complete modern market system; the full realization of the functions of the six subsystems leads to the formation of a complete modern market mechanism. Henceforth, within this modern market system structure, there exist three types of market failures. The first is "defective market mechanism" failure. It is mainly embodied in the presently vigorously discussed industrial economy. As described previously, the effective attainment of the functions of the six aspects of the vertical system of modern market requires integrity and order. If defects and deficiencies exist in their functions, the fragility of the modern market system will manifest, and the biases of the development of the six subsystems will also lead to different fragilities. This type of market failure often manifests itself at various stages of economic development across the world. The second is "void in market mechanism" failure. This often occurs in the investment, development and construction of new generative resources. Traditional economic theory lacks the concepts of "resource generation" and "generative resources", and hence has difficulties dealing with the development and operation of urban economy with the investment and construction of infrastructure as the main content. Theories on industrial economy fall into contradictions here, blame the government instead for intervening in the market, and lead to a lack of guidance by economic theories on the investment, development and construction of new generative resources (including space economy, ocean economy and others, which will be developed vigorously in the future) across the world. The market operation mechanism is absent here. The third is "market mechanism barrier" failure. As is known from above, whether industrial economy or the investment and development economy of resource generation, they must adhere to the modern market mechanism, that is, the six subsystems of the vertical system of modern market should fully function. However, as the subjects in industrial economy or the subjects in the investment and development of resource generation are driven by interests, man-made barriers that violate market rules are easily caused, thereby hindering the openness, fairness and justice of the market.

Various fields in the horizontal system of modern market need to adhere to the rules of the six subsystems of the vertical system of modern market. Within the commodity, factor and project markets, the price, supply and demand, competition, and other mechanisms exert their

织体系、市场法制体系、市场监管体系、市场环境体系、市场基础设施等六大子系统。横向与纵向结合，形成完整的现代市场体系，六大子系统功能的充分实现，形成完整的现代市场机制。因此，在这一现代市场体系结构内，存在三种市场失灵：一是"市场机制缺陷性"失灵。它主要体现在当前大家热议的产业经济中。如前所述，现代市场纵向体系六个方面功能的有效实现需要整体性和有序性，如果其功能存在缺陷或缺失，现代市场体系的脆弱性就会显现，而六个子系统发展的偏颇也会导致不同的脆弱性。此种市场失灵在世界各国经济发展的不同阶段时常显现。二是"市场机制空白性"失灵。此种情形常出现在新生成性资源领域的投资、开发、建设中。传统经济学理论里缺乏"资源生成""生成性资源"的概念，因此难以处理以基础设施投资建设为主体的城市经济的开发运用，产业经济理论在这里陷入矛盾之中，反而责怪政府干预了市场，这使各国的新生成性资源领域（包括以后会大力发展的太空经济、海洋经济等领域）的投资、开发、建设缺乏市场理论的指导，市场运行机制在其中缺位。三是"市场机制障碍性"失灵。由上可知，不管是产业经济，还是资源生成领域的投资开发经济，都需遵循现代市场机制，即现代市场纵向体系六个子系统要充分发挥其功能作用。然而，产业经济主体或资源生成领域的投资开发主体由于受利益驱动，容易制造与市场规则相违背的人为性障碍，从而妨碍市场的公开、公平、公正。

现代市场横向体系的各个领域都需遵循现代市场纵向体系六大子系统的规则，在商品、要素、项目市场中，让价格、供求、竞争等机制发挥作用，让竞争主体在这六大功能结构中服从市场规则，

influences, so that competitors obey market rules in the structure of the six major functions and principles of market allocation of resources, to fulfill market openness, fairness and justice. Henceforth, only by pinpointing the types of market failure can the right remedies be prescribed, effects of market allocation of resources fully exerted, and functions of governments better effected at the same time.

遵循市场配置资源原则，实现市场的公开、公平、公正。因此，我们只有弄清楚市场失灵的类型，才能对症下药，有的放矢，有效应对，才能真正发挥市场配置资源的作用，同时更好地发挥政府作用。

CHAPTER 7　MATURE EFFECTIVE GOVERNMENTS

1. The Types of Effective Governments

Through the analysis of the modern market economy in Chapter 6, we can figure out three levels of implications behind the "market". Firstly, the rational core of the market—market rules, in the field of industrial economy or resource generation, as "an invisible hand", widely play a role in the operating mechanism of commodities, factors, project prices, supply and demand, competition and others. Secondly, the market as a platform—The market in terms of circulation includes all kinds of tangible regional markets and intangible network markets, as well as all kinds of commodities, factors, projects, talents, technology and funds (including foreign exchange and others) that are circulated and traded in them, the production, circulation, transaction and consumption of which are constantly cycling under the guidance of the "invisible hand". Thirdly, the operation conditions of the market—The six subsystems of the vertical system of modern market are the basic conditions for the complete and orderly operation of the market, which guarantee the open, fair and just operation of market rules. Of course, if the functions and structures of these six subsystems are not complete in a certain field or at a certain stage, the market can still work, and market rules can still function; but the deficiencies of a certain subsystem will bring about fragility in the market, and lead to economic crisis and even worldwide economic depression caused by market failure, and eventually the market will be destroyed or even rebuilt.

Based on the degree of maturity and completeness of the six subsystems of the vertical modern market system, the market economy that consists only of the market factor system and market organization system is called "weak efficient market"; based on this, the market economy that gradually improves its market legal system and market supervision system is called "semi-strong efficient market"; the market economy that further establishes and improves its market environment system and market infrastructure is called "strong efficient market". What needs to be clarified in this chapter is the theory of the three types of effective governments that corresponds to the theory of the three types of efficient markets. There also exist three types of effective governments:

魏 成熟有为政府

一、有为政府的类型

通过第六章对现代市场经济的分析，我们可以总结出"市场"背后隐含的三个层次含义：一是市场的合理内核——市场规则，在产业经济或资源生成领域里，市场规则作为"一只看不见的手"，在商品、要素、项目的价格、供求、竞争等运行机制中广泛发挥作用。二是市场的空间平台——流通意义上的市场，包括各类有形的区域市场和无形的网络市场，以及在这有形与无形市场中流通交易的各类商品、要素、项目、人才、技术、资金（包括外汇等）等，它们的生产、流通、交易、消费在"看不见的手"的指引下不断循环。三是市场的运作条件——市场体系，即现代市场纵向体系的六个子系统是市场完整、有序运行的基础条件，它保障了市场规则的公开、公平、公正运行。当然，如果在某一领域或某一阶段，这六个子系统的功能、结构不健全，市场仍能运转，市场规则仍能发挥作用，但市场体系某一子系统的缺陷会带来市场的脆弱性，并导向市场失灵引发的经济危机甚至世界性经济大萧条，最终市场被破坏甚至被推倒重来。

根据现代市场纵向体系六个子系统的成熟与完善程度，我们把只存在市场要素体系和市场组织体系的市场经济，称为"弱式有效市场"；把在此基础上又逐步健全了市场法制体系和市场监管体系的市场经济，称为"半强式有效市场"；把进一步建立、完善了市场环境体系与市场基础设施的市场经济，称为"强式有效市场"。而我们在此章节需阐明的，主要是与"有效市场三层次"理论相对

"weak effective government", "semi-strong effective government" and "strong effective government".

In Chapter 3, we talk about the three kinds of resources that exist in the real economic operation across the world—operational resources, non-operational resources and quasi-operational resources. As discussed in Chapter 4, for operational resources corresponding to the industrial economy in reality, governments should follow the principles of "planning and guidance; support and coordination; supervision and management" to make policies; for non-operational resources corresponding to the livelihood economy in reality, governments should follow the principles of "general underpinning, fairness and justice, and effective promotion" to make policies; for quasi-operational resources corresponding to urban economy (in its narrow sense) in reality, governments should follow the principles of "participating in market competition, maintaining market order, and following market rules" to make policies. In Chapter 5, we talk about government's competition in broad and narrow senses. In a broad sense, governments promote the competitions of operational resources through supporting policies, which can invigorate the industrial economy and make it develop coordinately, thereby elevating the level of the industrial economy of the region. By promoting the competitions of non-operational resources through supporting policies, governments can promote the growth of livelihood economy, maintain social stability, and optimize the investment and development environment of the region. By promoting the competitions of quasi-operational resources through supporting policies, governments can push the investment, development and construction of urban economy, and promote the comprehensive and sustainable development of the social economy of the region.

Corresponding to the above analysis, we can divide effective governments into three categories. The first category is governments that are only concerned with the allocation of non-operational resources (that is, social public welfare resources related to the livelihood) and the related policies, which could be called weak effective government. This category of governments confine their functions to the basic social public welfare guarantee, and have neither a clear understanding of nor actions on the allocation of operational resources and related policies, and have neither a clear definition of nor measures on the participation in the competition of quasi-operational resources and related policies. The second category is governments that are only concerned with the allocation of non-operational resources and operational resources and the

应的"有为政府三类型"理论，即有为政府也存在"弱式有为政府""半强式有为政府"和"强式有为政府"三种类型。

在第三章《资源稀缺与资源生成》中，我们谈到世界各国的现实经济运行中存在三类资源——可经营性资源、非经营性资源和准经营性资源。在第四章《政府双重属性》中，我们谈到可经营性资源对应现实中的产业经济，政府应采取"规划、引导；扶持、调节；监督、管理"的原则去配套政策；非经营性资源对应现实中的民生经济，政府应采取"基本托底、公平公正、有效提升"的原则去配套政策；准经营性资源对应现实中的城市经济（狭义范畴），政府应采取"参与市场竞争，维护市场秩序，遵循市场规则"的原则去配套政策。在第五章《区域政府竞争》中，我们谈到政府存在广义范畴竞争和狭义范畴竞争：广义范畴竞争中，政府通过配套政策推动可经营性资源竞争，可提高产业经济活力，使其协调发展，从而提升本区域产业经济发展水平；政府通过配套政策推动非经营性资源竞争，可促进民生经济增长，维护社会稳定，优化本区域的投资发展环境；政府通过配套政策推动准经营性资源竞争，可推进城市经济投资、开发、建设，促进本区域社会经济全面可持续发展。

与上述分析相对应，我们可以把有为政府也划分为三类：第一类，只关注非经营性资源（即与社会民生相关的社会公益资源）的调配及相关政策配套的政府，可称之为"弱式有为政府"。这类政府将自身职能只局限于基本的社会公益保障，而对可经营性资源的调配和配套政策问题认识不清，无所作为，对准经营性资源竞争的参与和配套政策问题界定不清，举措不明。第二类，只关注非经营性资源和可经营性资源的调配及相关政策配套的政府，可称之为

related policies, which could be called semi-strong effective governments. In addition to performing basic public functions such as social security, this category of governments also look at the state of market operation. When the operation of the market is failing, this category of governments can use policy measures to mobilize effective demand or effective supply, implement macro-control and intervention to prevent the economy from falling into excessive depression and causing heavy losses and damage. At the same time, such governments can formulate economic strategies, plan and guide the industrial layout, support and adjust production and operation, and supervise market competition under the principles of openness, fairness and justice, regulate and control prices, control the unemployment rate, so as to promote the dynamic equilibrium between aggregate supply and aggregate demand. However, their understanding of quasi-operational resources is vague, leading to unclear definitions and policies, inadequate measures and poor results. The third category is governments that not only pay attention to the allocations of non-operational resources and operational resources and related policies, but also participate in and promote the allocations of quasi-operational resources and related policies, which could be called strong effective governments. This category of governments exert guidance, regulation, forewarning and other functions during economic development, and by relying on market mechanism and using measures on planning, investment, consumption, price, taxation, interest rate, exchange rate, law, and others, bring about value, institutional, organizational and technological innovations. Through the effective allocation of operational resources, such governments improve the economic development environment; through the effective allocation of non-operational resources, they enhance the vitality and coordination of economic development; through the effective allocation of quasi-operational resources, they form the leading edge to promote the comprehensive, scientific and sustainable development of the social economy. The strong effective government mode is the route to success for nations in their competition in the global market system.

2. Government Foresighted Leading (GFL)

In my opinion, the strong effective government should lead with foresight. Enterprises do the things they should do, whilst governments do the things enterprises cannot do or cannot do well. Neither of them can be absent nor vacant. Government foresighted leading (GFL) is to adhere to market rules and rely on market forces, to guide, regulate and

"半强式有为政府"。这类政府除履行社会保障等基本公共职能外，对市场运行状态也予以关注。在市场运行失灵时，这类政府能运用政策措施，调动有效需求或有效供给，进行宏观调控和干预，防止经济陷入过度低迷，带来重大损失与破坏；同时，这类政府能够制定经济战略，规划、引导产业布局，扶持、调节生产经营，以公开、公平、公正原则监管市场竞争，调控物价，控制失业率，以促进总供给与总需求的动态平衡。但其对准经营性资源仍认识模糊，界定不清，政策不明，措施不力，效果不佳。第三类，不仅关注非经营性资源和可经营性资源的调配与政策配套，而且参与、推动准经营性资源的调配和政策配套的政府，被称之为"强式有为政府"。这类政府在经济发展中发挥着导向、调节、预警等作用，依靠市场机制，以规划、投资、消费、价格、税收、利率、汇率、法律等手段，开展理念、制度、组织和技术创新。其通过有效调配可经营性资源，提升经济发展环境；通过有效调配非经营性资源，提升经济发展活力与协调性；通过有效调配准经营性资源，形成领先优势，促进社会经济全面、科学、可持续发展。强式有为政府模式是各国参与全球市场体系竞争的制胜路径。

二、政府超前引领

我认为，强式有为政府应该做好超前引领。企业做企业该做的事，政府则做企业做不了、做不好的事。二者都不能缺位、虚位。政府的超前引领，就是遵循市场规则，依靠市场力量，做好产业经

forewarn the industrial economy, to allocate, participate in and maintain the order of the urban economy, and to guarantee, underpin and elevate the livelihood economy. This requires the government to utilize measures of planning, investment, consumption, price, taxation, interest rate, exchange rate, law and others to bring about policy, value, institutional, organizational and technological innovations, to effectively promote supply-side or demand-side structural reform, form the leading edge in economic growth, and promote scientific and sustainable development.

As can be seen, the prerequisite for government foresighted leading is to rely on market mechanism, that is, the market decides the allocation of resources. The principle behind government foresighted leading is that the governments guide, regulate and forewarn the industrial economy; allocate, participate in and maintain order of the urban economy; and guarantee, underpin and promote the livelihood economy. The means of government foresighted leading include planning, investment, consumption, price, taxation, interest rate, exchange rate, law and others, and bringing about value, institutional, organizational and technological innovations herewith. The purpose of government foresighted leading is to promote structural reform on the supply-side or the demand-side, to form the leading edge for economic growth, and to attain scientific and sustainable development.

In theory, the essential differences between government foresighted leading and Keynesian government intervention are: Firstly, the behavior occasions are different. Government foresighted leading is mainly manifested in top-level designing, planning and layout setting in advance, as opposed to Keynesian mid- and post-intervention, and the policy effects are also different. Secondly, the regulation emphasis and policy measures are different. The emphasis of Keynesianism is on the demand-side, whereas the emphasis of government foresighted leading is on the guidance, adjustment and supervision of industrial resources, urban resources and livelihood resources; Keynesianism mainly uses fiscal policies to intervene in the economy, whereas the policy measures of government foresighted leading are all-rounded and applied throughout the whole process, and constantly innovating and developing. Thirdly, and more importantly, the government's functions are different. The theory on government foresighted leading suggests that governments are one of the subjects in market competition, the mature market economy is "strong effective government plus strong efficient market", and the governments' competition in the market economy cannot be neglected; whereas Keynesianism endeavors to exert the effects of government

济的引导、调节、预警，城市经济的调配、参与、维序，民生经济的保障、托底、提升。这需要政府运用规划、投资、消费、价格、税收、利率、汇率、法律等手段，进行政策、理念、制度、组织、技术创新，有效推动供给侧或需求侧结构性改革，形成经济增长的领先优势，推动科学、可持续发展。

由此可见，政府超前引领的前提是依靠市场机制，即市场决定资源配置。政府超前引领的原则是政府对产业经济发挥引导、调节、预警作用，对城市经济发挥调配、参与、维序作用，对民生经济发挥保障、托底、提升作用。政府超前引领的手段是规划、投资、消费、价格、税收、利率、汇率、法律等，并以此开展理念、制度、组织、技术创新。政府超前引领的目的是推动供给侧或需求侧结构性改革，形成经济增长的领先优势，实现科学、可持续发展。

在理论上，政府超前引领与凯恩斯主义政府干预的本质区别是：第一，行为节点不同。政府超前引领主要体现为事前的顶层设计、规划、布局，与凯恩斯主义的事中、事后干预不同，产生的政策效果也不一样。第二，调节侧重点、政策手段不同。凯恩斯主义的侧重点在于需求侧，而政府超前引领的侧重点在于政府对产业资源、城市资源、民生资源的引导、调节和监督；凯恩斯主义主要运用财政政策干预经济，政府超前引领的政策手段则是全方位、全过程的，且在不断创新发展。第三，也是更重要的是，政府的职能角色不同。超前引领理论提出，政府是市场竞争主体之一，成熟的市场经济是"强式有为政府＋强式有效市场"，政府在市场经济中的竞争作用不可忽视；而凯恩斯主义在实践中试图发挥政府干预的

intervention in practice, and yet in theory, excludes the government from the market. This incomplete market theory and government economic behavior rendered Keynesian theory and its practice limited. Fourthly, the operation modes are different. The main characteristics of classical economics and neoclassical economics are the market (the invisible hand) and a focus on supply (commodity, price, supply regulation). The main characteristics of Keynesian economics are government intervention and a focus on demand (driven by a troika of investment, consumption, and exports). Whereas the theory on government foresighted leading is related to classical and neoclassical economics and Keynesian economics, there are also differences. Its mode of operation is that governments' lead (intervention) integrates with emphasis on supply, which not only ensures the economic principle that the market decides the allocation of resources, but also requires governments to exert their effects of guidance, adjustment and supervision during the process.

On the practical level, most nations in the world are at the critical period of economic transition, social transformation or exploring and overcoming the "Middle Income Trap"; promoting industrial transformation and urban upgrading through government foresighted leading has become one of the development routes explored by nations across the world. With my experience of serving as secretary of the CPC Municipal Committee and mayor in Foshan City of Guangdong Province around 2010 as an example, the following discussions attempt to explore the specific measures taken by the government leading with foresight.

In 2009, Foshan City, with an area of 3,797.72 square kilometers, a resident population of 6.8747 million and a regional GDP of RMB 485.288 billion yuan, ranked 11th amongst large and medium-sized cities in China, with a per capita GDP of RMB 72,167 yuan (about USD 11,000 in that year). Its industrial development entered the late stage of industrialization and the early stage of post-industrialization. Under the new situation of industrial transformation, accelerated urbanization and enhanced internationalization, a very urgent problem for Foshan was how to accelerate industrial transformation and urban upgrading. Keeping in mind the realities, the Foshan Municipal Government conducted in-depth investigation, piloted and experimented five ways to promote industrial transformation and urban upgrading with various policies.

(1) "Double transfer" and "vacating cage to change birds": The Foshan Municipal Government actively implemented the "double transfer" (that

作用，但在理论上仍然把政府置于市场之外，这种不彻底的市场理论和政府经济行为导致了凯恩斯主义理论及其实践的局限性。第四，运行模式不同。古典经济学和新古典经济学最主要的特征是市场（看不见的手）、侧重供给（商品、价格、供给调节），凯恩斯主义经济学的最主要特征是政府干预、侧重需求（投资、消费、出口三驾马车拉动）。而政府超前引领理论与古典、新古典经济学和凯恩斯主义经济学既有联系又有区别，其运行模式是，政府引领（干预）与侧重供给相结合，既秉持市场决定资源配置的经济原则，又要求政府在其中发挥引导、调节、监督的作用。

在实践层面，当前世界各国多数正处于经济转轨、社会转型或探索跨越"中等收入陷阱"的关键时期，通过政府超前引领促进产业转型、城市升级，成为世界各国探讨的发展路径之一。以2010年前后我在广东省佛山市任市委书记、市长的经历为例，下文尝试探讨政府超前引领的具体举措。

2009年，佛山市面积3797.72平方公里、常住人口687.47万人，地区生产总值4852.88亿元人民币，在中国大中城市中排名第11位，人均国内生产总值为72167元人民币（当年约1.1万美元），产业发展进入工业化后期和后工业化初期。在产业转型、城市化加速、国际化程度提升的新形势下，如何加快产业转型和城市升级，对佛山来说是十分迫切的问题。佛山市政府结合实际，深入调研，先行先试，探索出运用政策措施促进产业转型、城市升级的五种路径。

第一，"双转移"和"腾笼换鸟"。佛山市政府积极实施"双转移"（即产业转移和劳动力转移）战略，运用银行贷款、政府贴息、

is, industry transfer and labor force transfer) strategy, using bank loans, government discounts and financial guarantees to promote the "three batches" policy, realizing the "vacating cage to change birds" policy, and leading industries to accelerate their transformation. The specific measures of the so-called "three batches" are as follows:

Firstly, to close or transfer a batch of industries: The government accelerated the elimination of outdated production capacities, shut down or renovated more than 1,200 high-pollution and high-energy-consumption enterprises in ceramics, cement, bleaching and dyeing, aluminum profile casting, glass and other industries, among whom 649 enterprises with high energy consumption and pollution were directly closed down. At the same time, the government guided the transfer of labor-intensive enterprises to less developed areas. In recent years, around 460 projects of Foshan City were transferred to industrial parks in some mountainous cities of Guangdong Province, which not only made room for the industrial transformation and upgrading of Foshan, but also provided the impetus for the economic development of the areas accepting these projects.

Secondly, to upgrade a batch of industries: The government promoted the integration of informatization and industrialization, and the match between service industries and manufacturing industries, and promoted the transformation of traditional industries into heavy, innovative and high-end industries. Take the ceramic industry as an example. In 2007, there were more than 400 manufacturing enterprises in Foshan; after three years of transformation and upgrading, all of the 50 enterprises retained achieved clean production and reengineering of their production process, thereby developing from production bases to multi-functional bases that entail headquarters and exhibition, R&D, logistics and information centers, etc. During these three years, ceramic output in Foshan City decreased by 40%, but output value and tax revenue increased by 33%, energy consumption decreased by 25%, and sulphur dioxide emissions decreased by 20%.

Thirdly, to cultivate a batch of industries: Through inviting and selecting investment, the government focused on optoelectronics, new materials, and modern service industries, cultivated new medicine, environmental protection and electric vehicle industries, and fostered the rapid formation of new energy (solar photovoltaic), new light source (liquid crystal displays) and other emerging industries. These measures have effectively reduced the proportion of traditional industries, and Foshan has become a national demonstration area for new industrialization industries and electronic information (photoelectric display) industries. At the same time, through the "Three-Outmoded

金融担保等政策措施，推进"三个一批"政策，实现"腾笼换鸟"，引领产业加快转型。所谓"三个一批"，具体举措如下：

一是关转一批，即政府加快淘汰落后产能，关停或整治了污染大、能耗高的陶瓷、水泥、漂染、铝型材熔铸、玻璃等行业累计1200多家企业，其中直接关停高能耗、高污染企业649家。同时，政府引导劳动密集型企业向后发地区转移，近年，佛山市约有460个项目转移到广东省一些山区市的产业园区，既为佛山的产业转型升级腾出了发展空间，又为转入地的经济发展注入了动力。

二是提升一批，即政府促进信息化与工业化融合，服务业与制造业配套，推动传统产业向重型化、创新化、高端化转型。以陶瓷产业为例，2007年佛山全市有400多家生产企业，经过三年改造提升，保留的50家企业全部实现清洁生产和生产工艺再造，从生产基地发展为多功能基地，包含总部和会展、研发、物流及信息中心等。这三年期间，佛山市陶瓷产量减少40%，但产值、税收增长33%，能耗下降25%，二氧化硫排放量减少20%。

三是培植一批，即政府通过招商选资，主攻光电、新材料产业和现代服务业，培育了新医药、环保、电动汽车产业，促进了新能源（太阳能光伏）、新光源（液晶显示器）等一批新兴产业的迅速成型。这些举措有效降低了传统产业的比重，佛山市也成为国家新型工业化产业示范基地和国家级电子信息（光电显示）产业示范基地。同时，借助"三旧"（旧城镇、旧厂房、旧村居）改造，佛山

Transformation" (outmoded towns, outmoded factories, outmoded villages), Foshan developed new cities, new industries and new communities, which not only improved the efficiency of land use, but also promoted industrial transformation, urban transformation and environmental reconstruction.

(2) Introducing large projects and promoting industrial upgrading: During the promotion of industrial transformation and urban upgrading, the Foshan Municipal Government paid attention to attracting investment, adopted policy measures to promote financial investment (such as private equity investment, venture investment and others), focused on leading projects in strategic emerging industries, advanced manufacturing industries and modern service industries, and through investing in and introducing large projects of international standards, quickly cultivated new industrial clusters and seized the strategic commanding heights in industrial development. Examples are as follows. Through the introduction of the Qimei electronic flat panel display module project, manufacturers of upstream parts such as chips, panels, molds, and plastics, and downstream TV manufacturers will be attracted to invest, forming a complete industrial chain of LCD flat panel displays, and inspiring the upgrading of household appliances industry in Foshan. The introduction of the IRICO OLCD project inspired the development of the third generation of display industry. The introduction of FAW-Volkswagen project inspired the whole auto parts manufacturing industry to develop into industrial clusters and complete industrial chains.

During this period, Foshan ushered in 87 investment projects from 47 of the Fortune Global 500 enterprises, and 167 investment projects from 99 of the top 500 enterprises in China, formed a batch of key enterprises with leading status in their respective industries in China, which played a leading role in technology, standards and brands, and effectively elevated the industrial structure and urban development standards of Foshan City.

(3) Promoting scientific and technological progress and independent innovation: During this period, there were more than 347,000 enterprises registered in the industrial and commercial administrative bureau of Foshan, of which more than 100,000 were industrial enterprises, but only more than 2,200 enterprises had an output value of more than RMB 100 million yuan, while more than 99% were small and medium-sized enterprises with an output value of less than RMB 100 million yuan. In view of the industrial structure, the Foshan Municipal Government promoted the integrated development of finance, science and technology, and industry, constantly innovated and formulated guidance and

发展新城市、新产业、新社区，既提高了土地利用效率，又促进了产业转型、城市转型和环境再造。

第二，引进大项目、促进产业升级。佛山市政府在推进产业转型、城市升级的过程中，注重招商引资，采用政策措施推动金融投资（如私募股权投资、风险投资等），重点瞄准战略性新兴产业、先进制造业、现代服务业的龙头项目，通过投资、引进具备国际水平的大项目，迅速培育新的产业集群，抢占产业发展的战略制高点。如通过引进奇美电子平板显示模组项目，吸引芯片、面板、模具、塑料等上游配套厂商以及下游的电视整机厂商前来投资，形成液晶平板显示器的完整产业链，带动佛山市家电产业升级；通过引进彩虹有机液晶显示屏项目，带动第三代显示器产业发展；通过引进一汽大众项目，带动整个汽车配件制造业向产业集群和完整的产业链条发展。

这一时期，佛山市引进了世界500强企业中47家的投资项目87个，国内500强企业中99家的投资项目167个，形成了一批在国内同行业中具备龙头地位的骨干企业，在技术、标准和品牌上均有引领示范作用，这有效提升了佛山市的产业结构和城市发展水平。

第三，推动科技进步、自主创新。这一时期，佛山市有工商登记注册企业34.7万多家，其中工业企业超过10万家，但亿元以上产值企业只有2200多家，亿元以下产值的中小企业占了99%以上。鉴于这种产业结构状况，佛山市政府促进金融、科技、产业融合发展，不断创新，制定了夯实基础、创造品牌、注册专利、制定标准、输出品牌的引导和激励政策，鼓励和支持企业自主打造行业

incentive policies of foundation consolidation, brand creation, patent registration, standard formulation, and brand exports, encouraged and supported enterprises to independently establish industry standards, national standards, and even international standards, form their own core technologies, and based on their own brands, patents and standards, entrust other enterprises to make OEM products for Foshan enterprises.

During this period, the Foshan Municipal Government spent RMB 1 billion yuan annually as direct incentives in guiding enterprises to strengthen scientific and technological investment and independent innovation. In 2008, this measure led enterprises to invest more than RMB 22 billion yuan, achieved an increase of 47%; in 2009, in spite of the influence of the international financial crisis, this measure still led enterprises to invest more than RMB 30.8 billion yuan, achieving an increase of 39%. Through such policy measures, the Foshan Municipal Government promoted scientific and technological progress and independent innovation, and took the lead in industrial transformation and urban upgrading. Foshan was awarded one of the "Top 10 Cities to Build Innovation-oriented Country", "Chinese Brand Economic City" and "Capital of Chinese Brands", and the only model city of national famous trademark and famous brand amongst prefecture-level cities in Guangdong Province. In around 2012, Foshan accumulated 130,000 patent applications and 86,000 patent authorizations, both ranking first amongst China's prefecture-level cities; and 42 Famous Trademarks of China and 65 China Top Brand products, ranking fourth amongst China's large and medium-sized cities.

(4) Using financial policies and constructing industrial leading positions: By the strength of capital and financial policy measures, the Foshan Municipal Government promoted the effective integration of enterprises and capital markets to get bigger and stronger. Internally, Foshan implemented three financial development plans: Firstly, through the "463" Plan[1] to promote the public listing of enterprises, the number

of listed enterprises in Foshan increased from 13 in 2007 to 26 in 2010, and a listing echelon comprising 102 enterprises was formed. At the same time, governmental support for mergers and acquisitions also promoted the industrial transformation and upgrading. Secondly, through cultivating equity investment funds, small and medium-sized enterprise guarantee funds, funds for talents, etc., the effective match between industry and finance was promoted. During this period, Foshan had 15 funds, and equity investment funds amounted to about RMB 1.2 billion yuan, amongst which the guiding funds by local governments amounted to RMB 126 million yuan and drove about RMB 1.1 billion

标准、国家标准乃至国际标准，形成自己的核心技术，以自身的品牌、专利、标准为依托，委托其他企业为佛山企业做贴牌生产。

这一时期，佛山市政府每年拿出 10 亿元资金，通过直接奖励的方式引导企业加强科技投入、自主创新。2008 年，这一举措带动企业投入 220 多亿元，增长 47%；2009 年，在国际金融危机的影响下，仍然带动企业投资 308 多亿元，增长 39%。通过这类政策措施，佛山市政府推动科技进步、自主创新，引领产业转型、城市升级，使佛山成为"建设创新型国家十强市""中国品牌经济城市"和"中国品牌之都"，成为广东省地级市中唯一的国家驰名商标和著名品牌示范城市。2010 年前后，佛山累计专利申请量达到 13 万件，专利授权量 8.6 万件，均位居中国地级市第一，拥有中国驰名商标 42 件、中国名牌产品 65 个，在中国大中城市中排名第四位。

第四，运用金融政策，建设产业高地。佛山市政府借助资本力量和金融政策手段，促进企业与资本市场有效结合，做大做强。对内，佛山实施了三项金融发展计划：一是通过推动企业上市的"463"计划[1]，使佛山的上市企业从 2007 年的 13 家增加到 2010 年的 26 家，并形成了由 102 家企业组成的上市梯队。同时，政府支持企业并购也促进了产业转型升级。二是通过培育股权投资基金、中小企业担保基金、人才基金等，推动实业与金融的有效对接。这一时期，佛山共有各类基金 15 支，股权投资基金规模约 12 亿元，其中地方政府投入的引导资金为 1.26 亿元，带动民间资本约 11 亿

yuan of private capital. Enterprises' listing on SME and GEM boards were accelerated, with 45 enterprises ready to file applications and more than 30 getting pre-listing tutoring or ready to reorganize. Thirdly, through financial innovation, such as the development of rural banks, micro-loan companies, and others, financial support was provided for industrial transformation and upgrading.

Externally, capitalizing on the opportunity of establishing Foshan as the only model city of industrial cluster and effective capital market operation in China by the United Nations Industrial Development Organization, Foshan actively attracted foreign banks into the Guangdong Hi-tech Service Zone for Financial Institutions located in Foshan. During this period, 28 projects signed contract of entry, and total investment amounted to RMB 6,579 million yuan. Since the "Supplement VI to the Mainland and Hong Kong Closer Economic Partnership Arrangement (CEPA)"[2] took effect in October 2009, four Hong Kong-funded banks have been stationed in Foshan. These measures guaranteed strong support from the capital market for the transformation and upgrading of enterprises, assisted enterprises to establish a management mechanism in line with international standards, and in particular, enabled private enterprises to establish a modern enterprise system, achieve transformation, and become more vigorous, with private enterprises contributing 61.8% to the economic growth of the entire city.

(5) Promoting the integration of informatization, industrialization, urbanization and internationalization as well as the construction of intelligent Foshan: Following closely the global wave of the information technology revolution and construction of intelligent cities, the Foshan Municipal Government promoted the integration of informatization, industrialization, urbanization and internationalization and the construction of intelligent Foshan through financial policy means, and led the future development of the city. This became a strategic breakthrough in the industrial transformation and upgrading throughout

the "12th Five-Year Plan" period of Foshan City. The specific measures are as follows:

Firstly, integrate informatization with industrialization, to vigorously cultivate technology associated with informatization such as photoelectric display and radio frequency identification, as well as emerging industries such as the Internet of Things, industrial design and service outsourcing, and to transform and upgrade traditional industries. For example, there were more than 1,700 furniture enterprises in Longjiang Town, Shunde District, but only a few of these had an output value exceeding RMB 100 million yuan. The Wision Group adopted three-dimensional visual effect technology, provided personalized

元，加快了企业在中小板、创业板的上市步伐，准备申报的企业有 45 家，辅导改制或拟改制的企业有 30 多家。三是通过金融创新，如发展村镇银行、小额贷款公司等，为产业转型、升级发展提供金融支撑。

对外，借助联合国工业发展组织将佛山确立为中国唯一的产业集群与资本市场有效运作示范城市的契机，佛山市积极引入外来银行进驻位于佛山的广东省金融高新技术服务区。这一时期有 28 个项目签约进驻，总投资 65.79 亿元。仅 2009 年 10 月开始实施《〈内地与香港关于建立更紧密经贸关系的安排〉补充协议六》[2]以来，就有四家港资银行进驻佛山。这些举措使企业的转型升级获得资本市场的有力支持，同时帮助企业建立起与国际接轨的管理机制，尤其使民营企业建立起现代企业制度，实现转型发展，形成新的活力。民营经济对全市经济增长的贡献率达到 61.8%。

第五，推动"四化融合，智慧佛山"建设。佛山市政府紧跟全球信息技术革命和建设智慧城市的浪潮，通过金融政策手段，推动"四化融合，智慧佛山"建设，引领城市未来发展，这成为贯穿佛山市"十二五"时期产业转型升级的战略突破口。其具体举措如下：

一是促进信息化与工业化融合，大力培育与信息化相关联的光电显示、射频识别技术，以及物联网、工业设计、服务外包等新兴产业，改造、提升传统产业。如顺德区龙江镇有 1700 多家家具企业，产值超亿元的企业才几家，而维尚集团采用三维视觉效果技

customization, changed the sales mode of "stocks awaiting purchase" of traditional furniture enterprises, and changed the buyers' market into the sellers' market. Within a mere two or three years, the scale of sales exceeded RMB 300 million yuan. For another example, the Midea Group used the Internet of Things technology to transform and upgrade household appliances to intelligent appliances, replaced traditional appliances and brought about a new revolution in the household appliance industry.

Secondly, integrate informatization with urbanization, to actively explore and promote the integration of telecommunication network, television network and the Internet, and develop intelligent services and management systems such as intelligent transportation, intelligent public order, intelligent urban management, intelligent education, intelligent medical treatment, intelligent culture, intelligent commerce, intelligent government affairs, and others, so as to form the ubiquitous "U Foshan" to attain the three major leaps from management to service, from governance to operation, from partial application to integrated service, turning Foshan into an intelligent city conducive to living, commerce and development.

Thirdly, integrate informatization with internationalization. On the micro level, the government guides enterprises to build internationalized R&D, production, sales and service systems based on information technology such as the Internet of Things, the Internet, radio frequency identification and others, and to improve their capability to exploit the international market, e.g., to turn Foshan into an international purchasing center for ceramics and household appliances based on the Internet of Things. On the macro level, through the construction of cross-departmental, cross-sectoral, and cross-regional "electronic ports", that is, customs clearance information platform, the government provided enterprises with "one-stop" customs clearance services such as electronic payment, logistics distribution, electronic customs declaration, electronic inspection, and others, paving the "highway" for enterprises to enter the international market.

During the first half of 2010, Foshan's regional GDP amounted to RMB 265.1 billion yuan, with an increase of 13.8%. The proportion of advanced manufacturing industries, high-tech industries and modern service industries was increasing continuously, gradually possessing the excellent structure of a modern industrial system and forming the development trend of advanced cities. The practice of Foshan City has proven that government foresighted leading by effectively using policy

术，提供个性化定制，改变传统家具企业"以货待购"的销售模式，变买方市场为卖方市场，仅两三年销售规模就超过了 3 亿元。又如美的集团用物联网技术将家用电器改造提升为智能家电，取代了传统家电，带来了家电产业的新革命。

二是促进信息化与城镇化融合，积极探索推进电信网、电视网、互联网三网融合，发展智能交通、智能治安、智能城管、智能教育、智能医疗、智能文化、智能商务、智能政务等智能服务和管理体系，形成无处不在的"U佛山"，促进城市实现从管理到服务、从治理到运营、从局部应用到一体化服务的三大跨越，使佛山市成为宜居、宜商、宜发展的智慧家园。

三是促进信息化与国际化融合。在微观层面，政府引导企业以物联网、互联网和射频识别等信息技术为依托，建立国际化的研发、生产、销售和服务体系，提高开拓国际市场的能力，如依托物联网把佛山打造成为陶瓷、家电的国际采购中心。在宏观层面，政府通过建设跨部门、跨行业、跨地区的"电子口岸"即大通关信息平台，为企业提供电子支付、物流配送、电子报关、电子报检等"一站式"通关服务，为企业进入国际市场铺就了"高速公路"。

2010 年上半年，佛山市地区生产总值达 2651 亿元，增速 13.8%，且先进制造业、高新技术产业和现代服务业比重不断提高，逐渐具备现代产业体系的优良结构，形成向先进城市发展的趋势。佛山市的实践证明，政府有效运用政策措施进行超前引领，

measures is a victorious route to promote the transformation of local industries and urban upgrading, and can strongly promote the scientific and sustainable development of regional economy.[3]

3. Innovation is Competitiveness

For social and economic development, strong effective government should lead with foresight; government foresighted leading is the key to regional competition and development. Competition needs innovation; innovation is competitiveness, and sustainable innovation is sustainable competitiveness. Government innovation is the core of regional government competition across the world. As observed from the innovation level, government needs value innovation, organizational innovation, institutional innovation, and technological innovation.

First of all, "value foresighted leading" is an important competitiveness when regional economic development is at the factor-driven stage. At this stage, economic growth across the world depends mainly on the input of production factors such as labor force, land and other natural resources. This is a simple expansion in quantity and competition for resources and prices, and is prone to excessive plundering of production factors, low productivity, lagging technology, resource exhaustion, brain drain, intensification of social contradictions and other problems. Hence, at this stage, the thoughts, directions and modes of development are decisive. Advanced values determine the future setups and trends of the region. The value innovation of the regional government becomes the focus of regional competition, and this includes the overall grasp and control of the three types of regional resources, the positioning of future development strategies for the region, the overall planning of the future development mode of the region, and solutions to the development mode and development motive at the level of top-level design. Hence, when regional economic development is at the factor-driven stage, sound value foresighted leading, and the coordinated, green and open development of the three types of resources will promote the stable and coordinated growth of the regional economy.

Secondly, "organizational foresighted leading" is the key to competition when regional economic development is at the investment-driven stage. When regional development is at the investment-driven stage, the main means of regional competition across the world are to expand the scale of investment to stimulate economic growth. On one

是促进地方产业转型、城市升级的制胜路径，能够有力促进区域经济的科学、可持续发展。[3]

三、创新就是竞争力

对于社会经济发展，强式有为政府需要超前引领；政府超前引领是区域竞争与发展的关键。而竞争需要创新，创新就是竞争力，持续的创新就是持续的竞争力，政府创新是世界各国区域政府竞争的核心。从创新层次上来看，政府需要理念创新、组织创新、制度创新和技术创新。

首先，"理念超前引领"是区域经济发展处于要素驱动阶段时的重要竞争力。当区域发展处于要素驱动阶段时，世界各国的经济增长均主要依靠劳动力、土地和其他自然资源等生产要素的投入来实现。这是一种数量上的简单扩张，以拼资源、拼价格为主，容易产生过分掠夺生产要素、生产效率低下、技术滞后、资源枯竭、人才流失、社会矛盾激化等问题。因此，在这一阶段，发展的思路、方向和方式具有决定意义。先进理念决定着区域未来的格局与走向。区域政府的理念创新成为区域竞争焦点，这包括对区域三类资源的整体把握和调控，对区域未来发展战略的定位和发展模式的全面规划，以及在顶层设计层面解决好发展方式、发展动力等问题。因此，在区域经济发展处于要素驱动阶段时，做好理念上的超前引领，坚持三类资源的协调、绿色、开放式发展，将推动该区域经济的稳定、协调增长。

其次，"组织超前引领"是区域经济发展处于投资驱动阶段时竞争的关键。当区域发展处于投资驱动阶段时，世界各国区域竞争的主要手段都是扩大投资规模，以刺激经济增长。一方面，因为投

hand, due to the existence of the investment multiplier effect, investment can promote economic expansion by multiple times, which is also proven by Keynes' effective demand theory. Hence, investment is an important means to increase effective demand and GDP. During periods of regional economic downturn, in particular, governments can reverse the trend of economic decline by increasing investment to help turn the economy around. However, on the other hand, simple pursuit of the short-term effects of stimulation through investment is prone to "investment hunger" and "investment dependence", and will cause a series of symptoms such as economic ups and downs, backward technological innovation abilities, and others. Hence, at the investment-driven stage of regional economic development, innovation in organizational management becomes the key, that is, the government needs to regulate the investment and management of the three types of regional resources, strengthen rapid response capabilities of the organization, get closer to the market, serve the enterprises, develop network structure and matrix structure, reduce management levels, so as to effectively enhance the effects of investment with greater efficiency and flexibility. Hence, when regional economic development is at the investment-driven stage, sound organizational foresighted leading is the key to the stable and orderly development of the regional economy, and to winning in regional competition.

Thirdly, "institutional and technological foresighted leading" are the winning points in competition when regional economic development is at the innovation-driven stage. The innovation-driven stage is the most explosive stage of economic development, when both the allocation of the three types of resources and social economic development have started the leap from quantitative change to qualitative change and the growth in social economy has achieved a breakthrough in the entire process and in all the factors. At this stage, technological innovation is the core driving force, whilst institutional innovation is the fundamental guarantee of technological innovation. Technological innovation expedites new formats, new products, new industries and new models; institutional innovation guarantees and promotes the integration and innovation of science and technology, finance and industries; together, they make possible the sustainability of innovation-driven models. Henceforth at this stage, sound technological and institutional foresighted leading becomes important means of regional competition.

Finally, "comprehensive foresighted leading" is the inevitable choice in competition when regional economic development is at the wealth-driven stage. If regional economy development across the world truly

资乘数效应的存在，投资能够促进经济成倍扩张，凯恩斯的有效需求理论也证明了这一点。因此，投资是提高有效需求、提升国内生产总值的重要手段，尤其是在区域经济低迷时期，政府可以通过加大投资力度来扭转经济下滑的态势，使经济走出低谷。但另一方面，如果片面追求投资的短期刺激效果，容易形成"投资饥渴""投资依赖"，出现经济大起大落、技术创新能力落后等一系列症状。因此，在区域经济发展的投资驱动阶段，组织管理创新成为关键，即政府需要规范对区域三类资源的投资、管理，强化组织快速反应的能力，贴近市场，服务企业，发展网络结构和矩阵结构，减少管理层级，以更高的效率和更强的灵活性，有效提升投资效果。因此，在区域经济发展处于投资驱动阶段时，做好组织管理层面的超前引领，是区域经济稳定有序发展、赢得区域间竞争的关键。

再次，"制度与技术超前引领"是区域经济发展处于创新驱动阶段时的竞争制胜点。创新驱动阶段是经济发展最具爆发力的阶段，无论是三类资源的配置还是社会经济的发展均开始了从量变到质变的飞跃，社会经济的增长实现了全过程、全要素的突破。在这一阶段，技术创新是核心驱动力，制度创新则是技术创新的根本保障。技术创新催生新业态、新产品、新产业、新模式；制度创新保障和促进科技、金融、产业的融合与创新：它们共同构成了创新驱动模式的可持续性。因此在这一阶段，做好技术与制度的超前引领成为区域竞争的重要手段。

最后，"全面超前引领"是区域经济发展处于财富驱动阶段时竞争的必然选择。如果世界各国区域经济的发展确实沿着要素驱

follows the tracks of factor-driven, investment-driven, innovation-driven and wealth-driven, then at the wealth-driven stage, individual creativity will be brought into full play, people's work and life will be fully balanced, the three major industries will change rapidly with each passing day, the entire society's consciousness of resources and environment will become stronger and stronger, and new economic development models and personal growth models will be constantly brought forth, and these require governments not only to carry out value innovation, technological innovation, organizational innovation, and institutional innovation, but also to realize comprehensive foresighted leading, scientific and orderly allocation of the three types of regional resources, so as to ensure the long-term advantages in regional competition. As economic development at this stage is flexible, rapid and diverse, it requires governmental systems, policies and measures to coordinate with it. Only in this way, can regional governments grasp the pulse of the wealth-driven era, take leads in the value orientation, and maintain the economic vitality. Hence, at this stage, sustained innovation and foresighted leading in all aspects, in the entire process, and in all factors will be an inevitable choice for regional competition.

4. Government Failure Revisited

As mentioned earlier, in *The Wealth of Nations*, Adam Smith proposed the theories of "the invisible hand" and "the government as night watchman", which were carried forward by classical economics and neoclassical economics. Faced with the British economic depression, unemployment of workers and the great economic crisis of 1929-1933 in the United States and even the world, Keynes put forward a series of propositions and specific measures on state intervention in the economy. Since then, government's intervention in and regulation of the economy has become an important policy of Western nations, and has been further expanded by post-Keynesianism. At the end of the 1970s, the economy of Western nations fell into stagflation; the Phillips curve could not explain the stagflation phenomenon of increased unemployment, economic stagnation and high inflation rates existing simultaneously. The concept of "government failure" spontaneously emerged and became the focus of mainstream economic research.

According to traditional economics, government failure, also known as government defeat or government defect, refers to the situation that individual demand for public goods is not well satisfied, while the public sector tends to waste and abuse resources when providing public goods,

动、投资驱动、创新驱动和财富驱动的轨迹前行,那么在财富驱动阶段,个人创造性将充分发挥,人的工作生活将获得全面平衡,三大产业的发展将日新月异,社会整体的资源和环境意识将越来越强,新的经济发展模式和个人成长模式将不断推陈出新。而这不仅需要政府进行理念创新、组织创新、技术创新和制度创新,而且需要实现全面超前引领,科学、有序地配置区域三类资源,以保障区域竞争的长久优势。因为这一阶段的经济发展是灵活、迅捷、多样的,它要求政府的制度、政策、措施与其相协调,只有如此,区域政府才能把握住财富驱动时代的脉搏,引领价值导向,保持经济活力的延续。因此在这一阶段,做好全方位、全过程、全要素的持续创新和超前引领将是区域竞争的必然选择。

四、重新认识政府失灵

如前所述,亚当·斯密在《国富论》中提出"看不见的手"和"守夜人政府"理论,被古典经济学、新古典经济学发扬光大。凯恩斯面对英国经济萧条、工人失业和 1929—1933 年美国乃至世界的经济大危机,提出了国家干预经济的系列主张与具体措施,从此政府对经济的干预调节成了西方国家的重要政策,并被后凯恩斯主义扩大化。上世纪 70 年代末,西方国家经济陷入滞胀,菲利普斯曲线难以解释失业增加、经济停滞不前和高通胀率并存的滞胀现象,"政府失灵"的概念油然而生,并开始成为主流经济学研究的焦点问题。

政府失灵,又称政府失败或政府缺陷,按传统的经济学观点,是指个人对公共物品的需求得不到很好地满足,公共部门在提供公

resulting in excessive or inefficient public expenditure, and lack of efficiency in governmental activities or intervention measures. Or in other words, the government makes decisions that reduce or fail to improve economic efficiency. Its main manifestations include: Firstly, due to the constraints of competency and other objective factors, government's intervention in economic activities cannot meet expectations. Secondly, government's intervention in economic activities meets expectations, but its inefficiency or high costs rendered resources inadequately or ineffectively utilized. Thirdly, government's intervention in economic activities meets expectations with a rather high efficiency, but it brings about unexpected adverse side effects. Fourthly, some externalities or international economic and trade problems cannot be solved by a single government, such as pollution from nuclear use, international trade disputes, and others. The main reasons for government failure include: firstly, the deficiencies in public decision-making lead to the inefficiency of public policies or even deviation from public objectives; secondly, the inefficient public policy implementation results in policy failure; thirdly, the uncertainty of public policies themselves results in intervention failure; fourthly, government failure caused by rent-seeking; and lastly, government failure is caused by defects inherent in the process of governmental regulation of the economy.

I will not comment here on the accuracies of the above views, or whether they are complete; instead, based on the practice of effective allocation of the three types of resources across the world, I shall attempt to analyze and evaluate the roles of regional governments in resource allocation and economic development.

The three types of resources exist in each nation or region, and how these resources are allocated defines the type of effective government. As mentioned above, for non-operational resources (livelihood economy), government's policies should follow the principles of "fairness and justice, general underpinning and effective promotion"; for operational resources (industrial economy), government's policies should embody the principles of "planning and guidance; support and coordination; supervision and management"; for quasi-operational resources (urban economy, and even space economy, marine economy, and others), government's policies should follow the principles of "acting as not only competitors, but also allocators and supervisors". In the process of allocating the three types

共物品时趋向于浪费和滥用资源，致使公共支出规模过大或者效率降低，政府的活动或干预措施缺乏效率，或者说，政府作出了降低经济效率的决策或不能实施改善经济效率的决策。传统经济学认为其主要表现形式包括：第一，由于行为能力和其他客观因素制约，政府干预经济活动达不到预期目标。第二，政府干预经济活动达到了预期目标，但效率低下，或者说成本昂贵，导致资源并未得到充分有效的利用。第三，政府干预经济活动达到了预期目标，也有较高的效率，但都带来不利的、事先未曾预料到的副作用。第四，某些外部性问题或国际性经济贸易问题，一国政府无能力解决，如核利用中的污染问题、国际贸易纠纷问题等。传统经济学认为政府失灵的主要原因包括：第一，公共决策过程中的缺陷导致公共政策低效甚至偏离公共目标；第二，公共政策执行的低效率引起了政策失灵；第三，公共政策自身的不确定性导致干预失灵；第四，寻租造成了政府失灵；第五，政府在调控经济的过程中所固有的缺陷导致了政府失灵；等等。

在此，我不去评论上述观点正确或完善与否，而是尝试从实践出发，通过各国对三类资源的有效配置来分析、评估区域政府在资源配置、经济发展中扮演的角色和发挥的作用。

每个国家或区域都存在三类资源，而如何配置这三类资源则界定了有为政府的类型。如前所述，对非经营性资源（民生经济），政府的配套政策应遵循"公平公正、基本托底、有效提升"原则；对可经营性资源（产业经济），政府的配套政策应体现"规划、引导；扶持、调节；监督、管理"原则；对准经营性资源（城市经济乃至太空经济、海洋经济等），政府的配套政策应遵循"既是竞争参与者，又是调配、监督者"的原则。也就是说，国家或区域政府

of resources, national or regional governments should make policies according to the different characteristics of the various resources in order to promote the balanced and rapid development of social economy. Such policies or government actions, are what is expected of effective governments. On this basis, according to the degree of perfection of the above-mentioned supporting policies, effective governments can be further categorized into weak effective government, semi-strong effective government and strong effective government.

Governments should be effective in the market economy, nevertheless, there exist in reality, three types of government failures: (1) The type of "inadequate livelihood economy": Such governments regard livelihood economy as a burden, without any general underpinning or effective promotion, nor consideration of the important effects that a fair and just foundation of livelihood has on building an investment environment that is stable, harmonious, and conducive to commerce, living, business and tourism. This type of government failure arises from governmental "lack of knowledge". (2) The type of "lack of industrial polices": This includes not only the lack of "planning, guidance and support" policies on the industrial economy, but also the lack of "coordination, supervision and management" policies on it. If regional governments are deficient in policies in both aspects as mentioned above, or only emphasize on one of the aspects, circumstances will arise where discipline is lacking or intervention is inappropriate. This type of government failure arises from governmental "misunderstanding". (3) The type of "void urban construction": For example, there are very few or even no policies and measures to promote regional economic growth through urban construction (investment in and construction of software and hardware infrastructure, and even the development and operation of intelligent cities). Or some infrastructure investment and development does exist, but the scale is small and the layout is scattered; the government neither participates as one of the competitors nor acts as the main regulator to fully exert its regulatory effects. Or the government does participate in the competition, but does not adhere to the market rules. Instead it aims only for administrative performances, invests without regard to returns, focuses only on construction and neglects management, and considers only public welfare and neglects benefits. This will result in massive wastage of urban infrastructure, low-quality operation of urban construction, disorderly operation of urban management, etc. This type

在配置三类资源的过程中，应根据各类资源的不同特点，配套相匹配的政策，促进社会经济的均衡、高速发展，而这类政策亦即政府行为，就是有为政府的应有之义。在此基础上，根据上述政府配套政策的完善与否，有为政府又可划分为弱式有为政府、半强式有为政府和强式有为政府。

政府在市场经济中应有所作为，然而在现实中存在三种政府失灵：一是"民生经济不足型"政府失灵。此类政府把民生经济当作一种负担，既没有基本托底，又没有有效提升，更没有考虑到公平、公正的民生基础对营造稳定、和谐、宜商、宜居、宜业、宜游的投资环境的重要作用。此类政府失灵是政府"缺知型"的失灵。二是"产业政策缺失型"政府失灵。它既包括对产业经济的"规划、引导、扶持"政策的缺失，又包括对产业经济的"调节、监督、管理"政策的缺失。区域政府如果缺乏上述两方面的政策，或者只偏重其中一类政策，就会出现放任自流或干预失当的状况。此类政府失灵是政府"错知型"的失灵。三是"城市建设空白型"政府失灵。比如缺少或几乎没有通过城市建设（基础设施软硬件的投资建设乃至智能城市的开发运营）促进区域经济增长的政策措施。或者存在某些基础设施的投资建设，但规模小，布局分散，政府既没有作为主体之一参与竞争，又没有作为主要监管者在其中发挥调节作用。又或者，政府参与竞争，但没有遵循市场规则，而是为了行政政绩，只负责投入，不在乎收益，只注重建设，不重视经营，只考虑公益性，而忽视效益性，这造成了城市基础设施大量耗损、城市建设低质运作、城市管理无序运行等问题。此类政府失灵是政

of government failure arises from governmental "ignorance".

Regional governments across the world have dual quasi-macro and quasi-micro attributes, so do governments in the integration of the global economy. Together with enterprises, they become the dual competitors in the market economic system. Governments need to face the problem of how to lead with foresight through value, technological, organizational and institutional innovations, avoid or reduce market failures, thereby accomplishing the best mode of "effective government plus efficient market" in the modern market economy. We should foster the organic combination of effective government and efficient market, and boost the overall, scientific and sustainable development of the global economy.

府"无知型"的失灵。

　　世界各国的区域政府均具有准宏观和准微观的双重属性（世界各国政府在全球经济一体化运行中同样具有此双重属性），在市场经济体系中与企业一起成为双重竞争主体。政府如何通过理念、组织、技术和制度创新，做到超前引领，避免或减少政府失灵，从而形成现代市场经济中"有为政府＋有效市场"的最佳模式，是世界各国政府都需要面对的课题。我们应促进有为政府与有效市场的有机结合，助力全球经济全面、科学、可持续发展。

CHAPTER 8 THE CHOICES OF EFFECTIVE GOVERNMENT AND EFFICIENT MARKET MODES

1. Potential Economic Growth Rate and Real Economic Growth Rate

The vertical modern market system includes six aspects: market factor system, market organization system, market legal system, market supervision system, market environment system and market infrastructure. Economic resources across the world can be divided into three categories: operational resources, non-operational resources and quasi-operational resources. The different ways of matching the two result in different combination modes for effective government and efficient market in the market economy.

In order to clarify these different combination modes, the two indicators of potential economic growth rate and real economic growth rate ought to be analyzed first.

Potential economic growth rate refers to the highest growth rate of aggregate goods and services produced by a nation in the modern market system, or in other words, the highest economic growth rate that a nation can attain under the condition that various resources are allocated optimally. This includes two connotations. Firstly, the market is efficient, that is, the basic market functions (including market factor system and market organization system), the basic market order (including market legal system and market supervision system), and the foundation of the market environment (including market environment system and market infrastructure) in the modern market system are sound. Secondly, the government is effective, that is, operational resources, non-operational resources and quasi-operational resources can be effectively allocated, and matched with policies and systems by the government. As can be seen, potential economic growth rate is the growth rate that the government of a nation can achieve when it makes the best use of the three types of resources under a sound modern market system, and is the growth rate realized under the mode of "strong effective government plus strong efficient market".

The real economic growth rate is the percentage change in the value of a nation's Gross National Product (GNP) during a specific period of time, as compared to an earlier period. The GNP measured at current market prices of the end-period is the nominal economic growth rate, whereas the GNP measured at constant market prices of the base-period

删 有为政府与有效市场模式的选择

一、潜在经济增长率与现实经济增长率

现代市场纵向体系包括市场要素体系、市场组织体系、市场法制体系、市场监管体系、市场环境体系和市场基础设施六大方面；各国经济资源分为可经营性资源、非经营性资源和准经营性资源三大类：二者的不同匹配方式产生了有为政府与有效市场在市场经济中的不同组合模式。

为了厘清这些不同的组合模式，让我们先来分析潜在经济增长率与现实经济增长率两大指标。

潜在经济增长率，是指在现代市场体系中一国所生产的总的产品和劳务的最高增长率，或者说在各种资源得到最优配置的条件下，一国所能达到的最高经济增长率。这包括两方面内涵：一是市场有效，即现代市场体系中的市场基本功能（包括市场要素体系和市场组织体系）、市场基本秩序（包括市场法制体系和市场监管体系）与市场环境基础（包括市场环境体系和市场基础设施）是健全的；二是政府有为，即一国政府对可经营性资源、非经营性资源和准经营性资源能够有效调配、配套政策和制度。可见，潜在经济增长率是在现代市场体系健全的条件下，一国政府对三类资源最大限度地充分利用时所能实现的增长率，是"强式有为政府＋强式有效市场"模式下实现的增长率。

现实经济增长率或实际经济增长率，是指一国末期国民生产总值与基期国民生产总值的比较。以末期现行价格计算末期国民生产总值，属名义经济增长率，以基期价格（即不变价格）计算末期国

is the real economic growth rate. The real economic growth rate reflects the rate of real economic growth; it is a dynamic indicator of changes in the level of economic development in a nation within a certain period of time.

Due to differences in the degree of market development and government capabilities across the world, there exists the mode of "weak effective government plus weak efficient market", such as in most middle- or low-income nations, and the mode of "semi-strong effective government plus strong efficient market", such as in the United States today, and also the mode of "strong effective government plus semi-strong efficient market", such as in China at present, which still needs to further improve its market competition order, market credit system and market infrastructure. There exists a certain gap between the real economic growth rate in all these nations and the potential economic growth rate under the mode of "strong effective government and strong efficient market".

This gap is where the potential of economic growth across the world lies. The series of economic measures taken to bridge this gap are where the vitality of economic development across the world lies, and the series of policies or systems made to bridge this gap are where innovation for economic development across the world lies. A mature market economy equates strong effective government plus strong efficient market, which is the highest form of combination of governments and market, the best mode concluded from economic practice through constant exploration, and also the only route to the realization of the potential economic growth rate across the world.

In the real economy, situations often arise where aggregate social demand is less than aggregate social supply, or aggregate social demand is greater than aggregate social supply. We can start from the modes of effective government and efficient market, the six subsystems of the vertical market system, and the government's allocation of the three types of resources, to find the root causes of problems, and put forward the direction and basic route to their solution.

2. Washington Consensus and the Middle Income Trap

At the end of the 1980s, the world economy slipped into recession and economic growth rates across the world shrank, with inadequate impetus for economic growth, weak demand, and decreasing population growth rate. The economic globalization encountered twists and

民生产总值，属实际经济增长率。实际经济增长率即为实际经济增长速度，它是反映一个国家一定时期内经济发展水平变化程度的动态指标。

由于各国市场发展程度和政府能力状况不一，现今世界存在"弱式有为政府＋弱式有效市场"的模式，比如大多数中低收入水平的国家；也存在"半强式有为政府＋强式有效市场"的模式，比如现在的美国；还存在"强式有为政府＋半强式有效市场"的模式，比如目前仍然需要进一步完善市场竞争秩序、市场信用体系和市场基础设施的中国；所有这些国家的实际经济增长率与"强式有为政府＋强式有效市场"模式下的潜在经济增长率相比，都存在一定的差距。

这一差距就是各国经济增长的潜力所在，针对这一差距采取的系列经济措施就是各国经济发展的活力所在，针对这一差距所配套的系列政策或制度就是各国经济发展的创新力所在。成熟的市场经济＝强式有为政府＋强式有效市场，它是政府与市场结合的最高级模式，是由各国在经济实践中不断探索总结出的最佳模式，也是实现各国潜在经济增长率的必由之路。

在现实经济中，经常出现社会总需求小于社会总供给，或者社会总需求大于社会总供给的状况。我们可以从"有为政府＋有效市场"的组合模式入手，从市场纵向体系的六个子系统和政府调配三类资源的状况中找到问题的根源，提出解决问题的方向与基本路径。

二、华盛顿共识与中等收入陷阱

上个世纪 80 年代末，世界经济陷入衰退，各国经济增长率萎缩，经济增长动力不足，需求不振，人口增长率下降，经济全球化

turns, the financial market was turbulent, and international trade and investment remained in a slump.... Faced with such situations, in 1989, the American Institute for International Economics invited the International Monetary Fund, the World Bank, the Inter-American Development Bank, and others, to seminars in Washington D.C., and formed the so-called "Washington Consensus". The Consensus is a set of ten policy measures: (1) fiscal policy discipline, with avoidance of large fiscal deficits and inflation rates, to stabilize macro economy; (2) redirection of public spending toward broad-based provision of key pro-growth, pro-poor services like primary education, primary health care and infrastructure investment; (3) tax reform, broadening the tax base and adopting moderate marginal tax rates; (4) interest rates that are market determined; (5) competitive exchange rates; (6) trade liberalization and opening up markets; (7) liberalization of inward foreign direct investment; (8) privatization of state enterprises; (9) deregulation; (10) legal security for property rights.

The core of the Washington Consensus is "minimal state and expedited privatization and liberalization". In theory, it advocates the implementation of a perfectly free market economy model to minimize the roles played by governments, and believes that as long as the market can allocate resources freely, economic growth can be attained. In terms of policies, its measures mainly include expediting the liberalization of the market, and domestic and foreign trade, expediting the privatization of state-owned enterprises, as well as reducing fiscal deficits, strictly restricting loans and issuance of currencies in order to achieve macroeconomic stability.

The original purpose of the Washington Consensus was to provide economic reform measures and countermeasures for Latin American countries that were mired in debt crisis, and to provide political and economic theoretical basis for Eastern European countries in transition. It should be said that during specific stages, the ten policy measures of the Washington Consensus did have certain effectiveness on stimulating the economic development of various nations. Nevertheless, these not only neglected the importance of improving the six subsystems of the market system, but also neglected the importance of governments across the world allocating the three types of economic resources, hence, falling into the "weak effective government plus weak efficient market" mode. In this mode, the government has basically no regulatory effects on the economy, the market development is not complete, the legal system

遇到波折，金融市场动荡，国际贸易和投资持续低迷……。面对这些状况，1989 年，美国国际经济研究所邀请国际货币基金组织、世界银行、美洲开发银行等在华盛顿召开研讨会，形成所谓"华盛顿共识"。该共识被概括为十条政策措施：第一，加强财政纪律，压缩财政赤字，降低通货膨胀率，稳定宏观经济形势。第二，把政府开支的重点转向经济效益高的领域和有利于改善收入分配的领域（如文教卫生和基础设施）。第三，开展税制改革，降低边际税率，扩大税基。第四，利率市场化。第五，采用一种具有竞争力的汇率制度。第六，贸易自由化，开放市场。第七，放松对外资的限制。第八，国有企业私有化。第九，放松政府的管制。第十，保护私人财产权。

华盛顿共识的核心是"主张政府的角色最小化，快速私有化和自由化"。在理论上，其主张实行完全的自由市场经济模式，最大限度减少政府的作用；认为只要市场能够自由配置资源，就能够实现经济增长。在政策上，其举措主要包括市场和内外贸易的快速自由化，国有企业的快速私有化，以及减少财政赤字、严格限制贷款和货币发行以实现宏观经济稳定化。

华盛顿共识的初衷是为陷入债务危机的拉美国家提供经济改革的方案和对策，并为东欧国家转轨提供政治经济上的理论依据。应该说，在特定阶段内，华盛顿共识的十项政策措施对刺激各国经济发展具有一定的有效性。但它既忽视了完善市场体系六个子系统建设的重要性，更忽视了各国政府调配三类经济资源的重要性，因此落入"弱式有为政府＋弱式有效市场"的模式——政府对经济基本没起到调控作用，市场发育也不健全，法制欠缺，秩序混乱，市场

is lacking, disorder prevails, and the market competition mechanism is often impeded. Such theoretical propositions, policy measures and modes will certainly not endure and fall into dilemma.

In 2006, the World Bank put forward the concept of "middle-income trap": Those middle-income economies, that is, the emerging markets, during the process of reaching high-income levels, after breaking through the "poverty trap" of per capita GDP of USD 1,000, would rapidly move to the "take-off stage" of USD 1,000 to USD 3,000 (per capita GDP). However, when the per capita GDP reaches about USD 3,000, the contradictions that have been accumulating during the rapid development will erupt all at once, and the renewal of mechanism and systems of these economies will reach a bottleneck. Contradictions are difficult to overcome, and the economic growth slows down or falls into stagnation, that is, the stage of middle-income trap.

At this stage, these countries are facing two dilemmas: On the one hand, the costs of resources, raw materials, labor force, capital, and management remain high. On the other hand, they have difficulties innovating due to lack of core cutting-edge technologies, and are stuck in the middle and low ends of the industrial chain without competitiveness. The decline or stagnation of economic growth leads to further employment difficulties, shortage of social public services, fragile financial system, polarization between the rich and poor, rampant corruption, lack of faith, social unrest and other issues. Consequently, these countries hover in the middle-income stage for long periods, unable to become high-income economies.

Latin American countries that adhered to the Washington Consensus to promote economic reform have also become typical examples of countries caught in the middle-income trap. Argentina's per capita GDP already exceeded USD 1,000 in 1964, and rose to over USD 8,000 by the late 1990s; however, it fell to over USD 2,000 in 2002, and then rose again to over USD 12,000 in 2014. Mexico's per capita GDP already reached

USD 1,000 in 1973, but in 2016 was just over USD 8,000. After forty years it was still classified as an upper middle class country. Many countries in Latin America are similar, failing to cross the USD 15,000 (per capita GDP) threshold for developed countries despite their repeated efforts over the past twenty or thirty years and a lot of ups and downs.

竞争机制也常被阻断。这种理论主张、政策措施和模式肯定是没有持久生命力的，必然会陷入困境。

2006 年，世界银行提出"中等收入陷阱"概念：那些中等收入经济体即新兴市场国家在跻身高收入国家的进程中，突破人均国内生产总值 1000 美元的"贫困陷阱"后，很快会奔向 1000 美元至 3000 美元的"起飞阶段"；但人均国内生产总值达到 3000 美元左右时，快速发展中积聚的矛盾会集中爆发，这些经济体自身的体制与机制更新陷入瓶颈，难以克服矛盾，落入经济增长的回落或停滞期，即中等收入陷阱阶段。

在这一阶段，这些国家面临两方面的困境：一方面，资源、原材料、劳动力、资金和管理等成本居高不下。另一方面，它们又缺乏核心的尖端技术，难以创新，处于产业链条的中低端，缺乏竞争力。由此而来的经济增长的回落或停滞进一步导致就业困难、社会公共服务短缺、金融体系脆弱、贫富分化、腐败多发、信仰缺失、社会动荡等。于是这些国家长期在中等收入阶段徘徊，迟迟不能进入高收入国家行列。

遵循华盛顿共识推进经济改革的拉美国家也成了陷入中等收入陷阱的典型代表。阿根廷 1964 年的人均国内生产总值就已超过 1000 美元，在上世纪 90 年代末上升到了 8000 多美元，但 2002 年又下降到了 2000 多美元，2014 年又回升到了 12,000 多美元。墨西哥 1973 年人均国内生产总值已达到 1000 美元，而 2016 年人均国内生产总值仍然只有 8000 多美元，40 多年后还属于中等偏上国家。拉美地区许多国家都与之类似，虽然经过二三十年的努力，几经反复，但一直没能跨过 15,000 美元的发达国家门槛。

We can use Argentina as a typical case to analyze the "nidus" of stagnation in Latin American countries. Firstly, there were huge fluctuations in the real economic growth rate. During the 45 years from 1963 to 2008, Argentina's per capita GDP grew at an average annual rate of only 1.4% and saw negative growth for 16 years. In 1963, Argentina's per capita GDP was USD 842, which already reached the level of middle- and high-income countries at that time, but after 45 years, it only grew to USD 8,236, still at the same level. Secondly, the technology engine was weak. In terms of the proportion of R&D expenditure in GDP, Argentina's was 0.41% in 2003, ranked beyond top 40 in the world. In terms of R&D personnel, in 2006, there were only 1.1 R&D personnel in every 1,000 people in Argentina. In terms of labor quality, in 2007, the proportion of labor force with college education and above in Argentina was 29.5%, with no obvious advantage. Thirdly, it suffered severe polarization between the rich and the poor, and prominent social conflicts. In terms of Gini Coefficient, Argentina was around 0.45 in the mid-1980s, close to 0.5 in the late 1990s and 0.51 in 2007. Problems of inequitable distribution are reflected not only in property income, but also in wage grade. Coupled with underdeveloped urban infrastructure and public services, Argentina's public security worsened continuously, and social conflicts were prominent. Finally, government management was ineffective. There was long-term instability in Argentina's macro economy, exchange rates fluctuated sharply, inflation rates remained high, fiscal deficit was common, and problems accumulated in the supply side. However, the legal and economic measures of the government's macro-economic management were weak, "treating the symptoms but not the disease", which resulted in widespread economic dislocation and social imbalance.

It can be said that the Washington Consensus and "shock therapy" it advocated have both failed, for the following reasons: Firstly, the efficient market is a market with full competition, orderly legal supervision and sound social credit. The Washington Consensus only focused on the competition and elevation of the basic functions of the market, that is, the market factor system and market organization system, but ignored the improvements of the basic order in the market, that is, the market legal system and market supervision system, as well as the developments and improvements of the market environment foundation (including the market environment system and market infrastructure). As a result,

我们可以以阿根廷这个典型案例来剖析拉美国家发展停滞的"病灶"：首先，现实经济增长率起伏大。阿根廷在 1963 年至 2008 年的 45 年间，其人均国内生产总值年均增长率仅为 1.4%，有 16 年人均国内生产总值负增长。1963 年，阿根廷人均国内生产总值为 842 美元，已达到当时的中高收入国家水平，但到 45 年后的 2008 年，其人均国内生产总值仅增长到 8236 美元，仍为中高收入国家水平。其次，科技引擎薄弱。从研发费用支出占国内生产总值比重来看，2003 年阿根廷为 0.41%，在世界排名 40 位以后；从研发人才来看，2006 年阿根廷每千人中的研发人员只有 1.1 人；从劳动力素质看，2007 年阿根廷劳动力中具有大学以上教育程度的比重为 29.5%，优势不明显。再次，贫富分化严重，社会矛盾突出。从基尼系数上看，阿根廷在 20 世纪 80 年代中期就是 0.45 左右，到 90 年代末接近 0.5，2007 年达到 0.51。分配不公问题不仅体现在财产性收入中，而且也体现在工资档次上。再加上城市基础设施和公共服务滞后，阿根廷治安不断恶化，社会矛盾突出。最后，政府管理不得法。阿根廷宏观经济长期不稳定，汇率大起大落，通货膨胀居高不下，财政逆差司空见惯，供给侧问题成堆。但政府在宏观管理的法律手段、经济手段上都很软弱，"头痛医头、脚痛医脚"，因此造成普遍的经济失调、社会失衡。

可以说，华盛顿共识及其提倡的"休克疗法"都失败了，这是因为：首先，有效市场是市场充分竞争、法制监管有序、社会信用健全的市场。华盛顿共识只侧重市场基本功能即市场要素体系和市场组织体系的竞争与提升，却忽略了市场基本秩序即市场法制体系和市场监管体系的健全，以及市场环境基础（包括市场环境体系和市场基础设施）的发展与完善。因此，华盛顿共识中的市场经济是

the market economy in the Washington Consensus was a free market economy, rather than a modern market economy with sound systems. Moreover, effective governments are governments which abide by market rules, maintain market order and participate in market competition. The Washington Consensus only recognized the guarantee of non-operational resources (social public goods) by various governments across the world, utterly ignored that governments need to "plan, guide and support" besides the responsibilities to "coordinate, supervise and manage" the competition in operational resources (industrial resources), and even neglected the necessity of governments to participate besides promoting the construction of quasi-operational resources (urban resources). Only governments that have effective policies to support the allocation of the three types of resources are strong effective governments in the mature market economy. Henceforth, the "deregulation" in the Washington Consensus was essentially anarchism, and had obvious defects compared with the theory that modern mature market economy equals strong effective government plus strong efficient market. Furthermore, for the real economic growth rate to approach or reach the potential economic growth rate, apart from improving the modern market systems, the most important task at hand is to strengthen governmental capacities, including institutional arrangements and institutional construction, transformation of development mode, etc. This was void in the Washington Consensus. To strengthen the capacities, governments not only need to abide by the rules of the market economy, but also need to control its development and take part in the competition. This requires a sound institutional environment and transformation of the mode of development. The so-called institutional environment construction includes not only improving the legislation, law enforcement and judicial systems related to the market economy, and popularizing related legal education, but also setting the subjects, contents and modes of supervision, supervising effectively the institutions, businesses, and execution of policies and regulations as the market economy requires, and establishing social and institutional norms conducive to the reform and development of government organizations. The transformation of the mode of development means that we should transform from Adam Smith's mode of "market (the invisible hand) plus focus on supply (regulation of commodity, price and supply)" or Keynes' mode of "government intervention plus focus on demand (the troika of investment, consumption and export)" to a modern mature market economic mode of "government leading (intervention) plus focus on

自由市场经济而非体系健全的现代市场经济。其次，有为政府是遵守市场规则、维护市场秩序、参与市场竞争的政府。华盛顿共识只承认各国政府对非经营性资源即社会公共物品的保障，而完全忽视了各国政府对可经营性资源即产业资源领域的竞争除了有"调节、监督、管理"的责任，还有"规划、引导、扶持"的必要，更忽视了各国政府对准经营性资源即城市资源除了有推动建设的责任，也有参与竞争的必要。只有为三类资源的调配配套有效政策的政府，才是成熟市场经济中的强式有为政府。因此华盛顿共识中的"放松政府管制"实质上是无政府主义的，它与"现代成熟市场经济 = 强式有为政府 + 强式有效市场"理论比较，具有明显缺陷。再次，各国的现实经济增长率要接近或达到潜在经济增长率，除了要完善现代市场体系外，当前重中之重的是要加强政府能力建设，包括制度安排与制度建设、发展模式转换等。这在华盛顿共识中是空白的。要加强能力建设，各国政府既需要遵循市场经济规则，又需要驾驭市场经济发展，参与市场经济竞争。这需要建设良好的制度环境，转换发展模式。所谓制度环境建设，既包括健全市场经济相关的立法、执法、司法体系，做好相关法制教育，又包括按照市场经济要求，构建监管的主体、内容和方式，对机构、业务、政策法规执行情况等实施有效监管，还包括建立有利于政府组织改革、发展的社会和制度规范等。所谓发展模式转换，是说应当从亚当·斯密的"市场（看不见的手）+ 侧重供给（商品、价格、供给调节）"模式，或者凯恩斯的"政府干预 + 侧重需求（投资、消费、出口三驾马车

supply (supply-side structural new engine)", that is, a "strong effective government plus strong efficient market" development mode. The government should lead foresightedly in all aspects in the entire process of market economic activities.

3. The Combination and Assessment of "Effective Government Plus Efficient Market" Mode

The relationship between governments and markets has always been one of the core disputed issues in economics, the focus being on the effects governments have on resource allocations in the market economy and their influence on economic growth, urban constructions and social livelihood.

A brief recap on the views of various economic schools as discussed above: Firstly, the mercantilism in the early stage of capitalism advocated government's intervention in economic life, prohibition of gold and silver outflows, and increases in gold and silver inflow. The main idea was that the growth of a nation's strength is based upon trade surplus, that is, when exports exceed imports, wealth can be obtained. Henceforth, it advocated that it is best if agriculture, commerce and manufacturing are regulated by governments, develop foreign trade monopoly, protect the domestic market through high tariff rates and other trade restrictions, and use the raw materials and markets from colonies for the manufacturing industry. This theory motivated the rapid development of early capitalism. Secondly, after the rise of classical economics, the market allocated the resources became the mainstream view. Adam Smith's economic liberalism and Ricardo's theory of comparative cost limited governments' functions to very small areas, their objective was merely the assurance of effective market operation. Thirdly, Keynesianism, which rose in the 1930s, advocated governmental use of expansionary economic policies to promote economic growth through increasing demand; the government should not only ensure market operation, it should also ensure supply and demand equilibrium in the economic system by interfering in the economy through monetary policies and fiscal policies. Fourthly, in the 1970s and 1980s, economists such as M. Friedman and A. B. Laffer suggested that the government should not participate in economic activities directly, etc., to solve economic crisis by improving supply, ...

拉动）模式，转换到"政府引领（干预）+ 侧重供给（供给侧结构性新引擎）"的现代成熟市场经济发展模式上来，即转换到"强式有为政府 + 强式有效市场"的发展模式上来。政府超前引领应作用于市场经济活动的全方位和全过程。

三、"有为政府 + 有效市场"模式组合及评价

政府与市场的关系一直以来都是经济学争论的核心问题之一，其焦点便是政府在市场经济资源配置中的作用及其对经济增长、城市建设、社会民生的影响。

简单回顾一下前文论述过的各经济流派观点：首先，资本主义早期的重商主义主张国家干预经济生活，禁止金银输出，增加金银输入。其主要理念是一国国力的增长基于贸易顺差，即出口额大于进口额时就能获取财富。因此它主张最好由政府来管制农业、商业和制造业，发展对外贸易垄断，通过高关税率及其他贸易限制来保护本国市场，并利用殖民地为母国的制造业提供原料和市场。此理论为早期资本主义的快速发展注入了动力。其次，古典经济学兴起后，用市场来配置资源成为主流观点。亚当·斯密的经济自由主义和李嘉图的比较成本理论，都将政府限定在一个极小的职能范围内，其职能目标也完全是为了保障市场的有效运行。再次，20 世纪30 年代兴起的凯恩斯主义主张，国家应采用扩张性经济政策，通过增加需求促进经济增长，政府不仅仅要保障市场运行，还要通过货币政策和财政政策来干预经济，以保障经济体系中的供需平衡。最后，20 世纪七八十年代，弗里德曼和拉弗等经济学家又提出政府不直接参与经济活动等办法，以改善供给来解决经济危机……

As we return now to the structure of six functions of the vertical modern market system, faced with the common problems in the contemporary world, namely the effective allocation of the three types of resources, we will discover that the relationship between the government and the market is not a simple relationship of two sides in a contradiction. The division of weak efficient market, semi-strong efficient market and strong efficient market is not only quantifiable, but also real history; the categorization into weak effective government, semi-strong effective government and strong effective government not only reflects the true performance of nations in market economy, but also resolves the current problem on the relationship between government and market. In theory, there exist at least nine modes for the combination of the two.

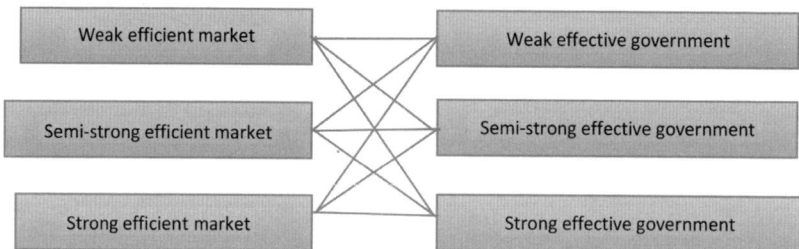

The 1st mode is "weak effective government plus weak efficient market", that is, the government does basically not regulate the economy, the market development is not complete, the market competition mechanism is often impeded, the legal system is inadequate, and disorder exists. This mode is usually prevalent in middle and low-income countries. The 2nd mode is "weak effective government plus semi-strong efficient market". Such a mode is difficult to exist in the real economy because there must be market legal system and market supervision system in semi-strong efficient markets, and it is impossible for weak effective governments to establish these systems. The 3rd mode is "weak effective government plus strong efficient market", which is purely an assumption, and there is no such case in the real world. The 4th mode is "semi-strong effective government plus weak efficient market", under which the government can better allocate non-operational resources, provide basic public goods; at the same time, the government begins to allocate and support operational resources, but is not good at grasping the market development trends, nor can it independently solve the problems arising from market operation. This situation is similar to that in 1978-1984 after China's reform and opening up, and is the operation or regulation mode in the early stages of market economy. The 5th mode

现在，当我们回到现代市场纵向体系的六大功能结构中，面对当代世界各国的共同问题即三种资源的有效配置时，我们会发现，政府与市场的关系不是简单的矛盾双方的关系。弱式有效市场、半强式有效市场和强式有效市场的划分，既是可量化的，更是历史的真实进程；弱式有为政府、半强式有为政府和强式有为政府的界定，既反映了世界各国在市场经济中的真实表现，又可破解当前的政府与市场关系难题。二者的组合在理论上至少存在九种模式：

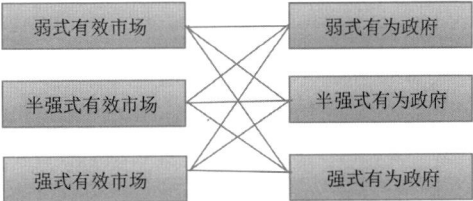

弱式有效市场	弱式有为政府
半强式有效市场	半强式有为政府
强式有效市场	强式有为政府

模式一是"弱式有为政府＋弱式有效市场"，即政府对经济基本没能发挥调控作用，市场发育也不完善，市场竞争机制常被阻断，法制欠缺，秩序混乱，这种模式常见于中低收入国家。模式二是"弱式有为政府＋半强式有效市场"，该模式在现实经济中难以存在，因为半强式有效市场必定存在市场法制体系和市场监管体系，弱式有为政府不可能建立这些体系。模式三是"弱式有为政府＋强式有效市场"，这纯属一种理论假定，现实世界中没有实际案例支撑。模式四是"半强式有为政府＋弱式有效市场"，该模式下，政府在非经营性资源调配上可以较好地履行职责，提供基本的公共物品，同时，政府也开始具备对可经营性资源的调配和扶持能力，但对市场发展趋势把握不好，对市场运行中出现的问题不能自主解决。这种情形类似中国改革开放后的 1978 年至 1984 年的情形，属于市场经济初期的运行或调控模式。模式五是"半强式有为政府＋

is "semi-strong effective government plus semi-strong efficient market", a semi-mature market economy mode. Under this mode, on the one hand, the government can plan and guide the industrial layout, support and regulate production and operation; on the other hand, the government can continuously improve the market supervision mechanism, legal guarantee mechanism, environmental support mechanism, and others. This mode is prevalent in nations in their mid-term development stages of market economy, and is very similar to China's situation before joining the WTO. The 6th mode is "semi-strong effective government plus strong efficient market", very much in line with the current situation in the United States. During the economic development of the United States, the market plays a decisive role in the allocation of resources, whilst the government also plays an important role in the allocation of non-operational resources. However, constrained by system or ideology, the United States has been ambiguous or inconsistent when allocating operational resources and defining and developing quasi-operational resources. Hence, it has difficulties achieving a breakthrough in these two aspects, and its overall economic growth and urban upgrading are lacking in planning, not systematic nor forward-looking. The 7th mode is "strong effective government plus weak efficient market", which is difficult to exist in reality. This is because the functions of strong effective governments are at least aligning with the semi-strong efficient markets. Nations with planned economies do not belong to this mode. The 8th mode is "strong effective government plus semi-strong efficient market", very much akin to current China. China's economic mode is generally regarded as a gradually maturing market economy led by the government. China has made remarkable economic achievements, but it also faces challenges in further improving market competition, market order, market credit and market infrastructure. The 9th mode is "strong effective government plus strong efficient market", the highest or best mode of government and market combination, which is the goal in theory and practice across the world, and an inevitable route to achieve truly mature market economy.

4. Strong Effective Government Plus Strong Efficient Market Equals Mature Market Economy

As mentioned above, strong effective government essentially includes the following: firstly, it can effectively allocate non-operational resources and support them with policies, promote social harmony and stability, enhance and optimize the economic development environment;

半强式有效市场"，属于半成熟市场经济模式，该模式下，一方面政府能够规划、引导产业布局，扶持、调节生产经营，另一方面政府能够不断改善市场监管机制、法律保障机制、环境支撑机制等。此模式常见于处在市场经济中期发展阶段的国家，中国在加入世界贸易组织之前的情况与此非常类似。模式六是"半强式有为政府 + 强式有效市场"，这很符合美国当前的状况。美国经济发展中，市场在配置资源方面具有决定性作用，同时政府也在非经营性资源的调配中发挥着重要作用，但碍于制度或理念的限制，美国在可经营性资源的调配、准经营性资源的界定与开发上存在模糊或言行不一的问题，所以在这两方面美国难有突破，其整体经济增长和城市的提升缺少规划性、系统性和前瞻性。模式七是"强式有为政府 + 弱式有效市场"，这在现实中难以存在。因为强式有为政府的功能作用起码是与半强式有效市场相对应的。计划经济国家不属于此模式。模式八是"强式有为政府 + 半强式有效市场"，这非常类似现阶段的中国。中国经济模式通常被认为是政府主导的逐渐成熟的市场经济，中国取得了世界瞩目的经济成就，但也面临着进一步完善市场竞争、市场秩序、市场信用以及市场基础设施的挑战。模式九是"强式有为政府 + 强式有效市场"，这是政府与市场组合的最高级或最佳模式，是世界各国实践探索和理论突破的目标，也是达到真正成熟的市场经济的必由之路。

四、强式有为政府 + 强式有效市场 = 成熟市场经济

如前所述，强式有为政府包括如下含义：一是能对非经营性资源有效调配并配套政策，促使社会和谐稳定，提升和优化经济发展

secondly, it can effectively allocate operational resources and support them with policies, maintain the openness, fairness and justice of the market, and effectively raise the overall productivity of society; thirdly, it can effectively allocate quasi-operational resources and participate in competition, promote the comprehensive and sustainable development of urban construction and socio-economy. The effectiveness of strong effective government is embodied in the integration of allocating the three types of resources, making policies and attaining the goals. There are three criteria for a strong effective government: firstly, respecting market rules; secondly, maintaining economic order and stabilizing economic development; thirdly, effectively allocating resources and participating in regional competition.

Strong efficient market essentially includes the following: firstly, the completeness of market basic functions (including market factor system and market organization system); secondly, the completeness of market basic order (including market legal system and market supervision system); and thirdly, the completeness of market environment foundation (including market environment system and market infrastructure). The efficiency of a strong efficient market is the overall effects brought about by the six subsystems of the vertical modern market system, embodied in the integration of substantial competition in production, fair market and orderly business operation. There are three criteria for a strong efficient market: firstly, substantial market competition; secondly, orderly legal supervision; and thirdly, sound social credit system.

In reality, strong effective government needs at least three conditions. Firstly, keeping pace with the times, referring mainly to the urgent need for governments to be "ahead" of new technology. Rapid development in science and technology brings new resources, new tools, new industries and new formats, which will shock the existing governmental management system. Advances in science and technology bring about new demands and higher efficiency in production and life, but at the same time, overwhelm the government with new problems. Henceforth, to function properly in economic growth, urban construction, and social livelihood, or in other words, to allocate reasonably non-operational resources, operational resources, and quasi-operational resources, the government's ideologies, policies and measures should all keep pace with the times. Secondly, all-round competition, that is, strong effective government needs to lead foresightedly, using its value, institutional,

环境；二是能对可经营性资源有效调配并配套政策，维护市场的公开、公平、公正，有效提高社会的整体生产效率；三是能对准经营性资源有效调配并参与竞争，推动城市建设和社会经济全面、可持续发展。强式有为政府的有为体现在对三类资源的调配、政策配套、目标实现三者合一之中。强式有为政府的标准有三：一是尊重市场规律；二是维护经济秩序，稳定经济发展；三是有效调配资源，参与区域竞争。

强式有效市场包括如下含义：一是市场基本功能的健全（包括市场要素体系和市场组织体系），二是市场基本秩序的健全（包括市场法制体系和市场监管体系），三是市场环境基础的健全（包括市场环境体系和市场基础设施）。强式有效市场的有效，是现代市场纵向体系六个子系统整体发挥作用，体现在生产充分竞争、市场公平、营商有序三者合一之中。强式有效市场标准有三：一是市场充分竞争，二是法制监管有序，三是社会信用体系健全。

现实中，强式有为政府至少需要具备三个条件：一是与时俱进，主要指政府急需"跑赢"新科技。日新月异的科技发展衍生出新资源、新工具、新产业、新业态，将对原有的政府管理系统产生冲击。新科技带来生产生活的新需求和高效率，同时也带来政府治理应接不暇的新问题。因此，政府要在经济增长、城市建设、社会民生三大职能中，或者说在非经营性资源、可经营性资源、准经营性资源的调配中有所作为，其理念、政策、措施均应与时俱进。二是全方位竞争，即强式有为政府需要超前引领，运用理念、组织、制度和技术创新等方式，在社会民生事业（优化公共物品配置，有效提升经济发展环境）、经济增长（引领、扶持、调节、监管市场主体，有效提升生产效率）和城市建设发展（遵循市场规则，参与项

organizational, technological innovations, etc. to systematically participate in all-round competition throughout the process in all factors in social livelihood undertakings (optimizing the allocation of public goods, effectively elevating the economic development environment), economic growth (leading, supporting, regulating and supervising the market subjects, effectively increasing productivity), and urban construction development (abiding by market rules and participating in construction projects). The so-called all-round competition is based on enterprise competition, but not limited to competition in goods production in its traditional sense, but instead, encompasses the entire process of goal planning, policy making and the final outcome to achieve comprehensive and sustainable socio-economic development of the nation. Thirdly, the disclosure of government affairs, including disclosure of information on decision-making, execution, management, services, results, key items (areas), and others. The openness and transparency of government affairs can guarantee the rights of all sectors in society to know, to participate, to express, and to supervise, and better allocate resources in important areas such as economic growth, urban construction, and social livelihood. Transparent, ruled by law, innovative, service-oriented, clean and honest strong effective governments will stimulate market vitality and social creativity, and thus benefit the world and mankind.

It can be said that the relationships between governments and markets can be analogized to the "Goldbach Conjecture" in economics. The great achievements in economic growth, urban construction, social livelihood by the organic combination of effective governments and efficient markets have already been confirmed by successful cases home and abroad. Here are just three examples for illustration:

The first example is the rapid development of the Pearl River Delta, which is an epitome of the "Chinese Dream". As reported by the Russian journalist Pepe Escobar, Shenzhen in 1979 was just a barren fishing village north to Hong Kong. In the early 1990s, the Pearl River Delta just started to develop into China's largest labor-intensive manufacturing center. And today, the Pearl River Delta, with Guangzhou, Shenzhen, Foshan and Dongguan as its axis, whilst accelerating its development of high-end industries in the value chain and building first-class national manufacturing innovation centers and national science and technology industry innovation centers, is at the same time, building first-class international metropolitan clusters in its urbanization strategies. The fascination with innovation and the promotion of urbanization in the Pearl River Delta are expediting and leading China into a new socio-economic model. The Pearl River Delta in China has accomplished in

目建设）中，全方位、系统性地参与全过程、全要素竞争。所谓全方位竞争，是以企业竞争为基础，但不仅局限于传统概念上的商品生产竞争，而是涵盖了实现一国社会经济全面、可持续发展的目标规划、政策措施和最终成果的全过程。三是政务公开，包括决策、执行、管理、服务、结果和重点事项（领域）信息公开等。政务公开透明能够保障社会各方的知情权、参与权、表达权和监督权，在经济增长、城市建设、社会民生等重要领域提升资源的调配效果。透明、法治、创新、服务和廉洁型的强式有为政府，将有利于激发市场活力和社会创造力，造福于各国，造福于人类。

可以说，政府和市场的关系，堪称经济学上的"哥德巴赫猜想"。而有为政府和有效市场的有机结合所造就的经济增长、城市建设、社会民生方面的巨大成效，已被海内外成功案例所证实。这里仅举三例说明：

第一例是作为"中国梦"缩影的珠三角的腾飞。正如俄罗斯记者佩佩·埃斯科巴尔报道的那样，1979 年的深圳，只是香港北面一个贫瘠的渔村。上世纪 90 年代初，珠江三角洲才起步向中国最大的劳动密集型制造业中心发展。而如今，以广州、深圳、佛山、东莞为轴心的珠三角，在加速向价值链高端产业发展、打造一流的国家制造业创新中心和国家科技产业创新中心的同时，更在城市化策略中构建一流的国际大都市簇群。珠三角对创新的着迷和对城市化的推动，正催生和引领中国走向一个新的社会经济模式。中国的珠三角用短短 20 年的时间完成了西方花费 200 年做到的事情。而改

just 20 years what the West spent 200 years doing. And the driving force behind the re-writing of economic development, urban construction, and social livelihood undertaking in the Pearl River Delta is "market plus government" – the value reconstruction of an innovative market economy idea. The Pearl River Delta is continuously exploring various ways to synergize government and market, and continuously making new breakthroughs in economic growth, urban construction and social livelihood undertakings.

The second example is the "Singapore Consensus", which promotes overall social progress. In 1960, the per capita GDP of China's Hong Kong and Singapore were USD 405 and USD 428 respectively; by 1980, USD 5,700 and USD 4,927 respectively; and by 2013, USD 38,358 and USD 56,389 respectively, with Singapore far exceeding Hong Kong, China. During this period, Singapore successfully realized five economic transformations—establishing labor-intensive industries in the 1960s, establishing economic-intensive industries in the 1970s, shifting to capital-intensive industries in the 1980s, committing to technology-intensive industries in the 1990s, and focusing on knowledge-intensive industries in the 21st century. The government was the main driving force behind. The combination of government and market, and that of economic development policies and social development policies, effectively stroke a balance between efficiency and fairness, development and stability, and promoted economic growth, urban upgrading and overall social progress. What the world has commended as the "Singapore Consensus", was precisely the fruit of "effective government plus efficient market", and is leading the nation to comprehensive and sustainable developments.

The third example is the world-class urban clusters established in the Great Bay Area of Guangdong, Hong Kong and Macao. Speaking of great bay areas, people naturally think of the Tokyo Bay Area, the San Francisco Bay Area and the New York Bay Area. These three bay areas connecting the coastline are all core economic and cultural urban clusters of their nations. The Tokyo Bay Area has the headquarters of

Toyota, Sony, Mitsubishi, and other Fortune Global 500 companies; the San Francisco Bay Area has Apple, Google, Facebook, and other Internet giants; whilst the New York Bay Area has gathered a large number of financial institutions there, becoming the heartland of global finance. The Great Bay Area of Guangdong, Hong Kong and Macao refers to the nine cities that constitute the Pearl River Delta Economic Zone, including Guangzhou, Shenzhen, Zhuhai, Dongguan, Huizhou, Zhongshan, Foshan, Zhaoqing and Jiangmen, as well as the two special administrative regions

写珠三角经济发展、城市建设、社会民生事业格局的推手正是"市场＋政府"——一个创新型市场经济思路的价值重构。珠三角不断探索政府与市场的协同之道，不断取得经济增长、城市建设、社会民生事业的新突破。

第二例是推动社会全面进步的"新加坡共识"。1960 年，中国香港人均本地生产总值、新加坡的人均国内生产总值分别为 405 美元、428 美元，到 1980 年，分别为 5700 美元、4927 美元，而到 2013 年，分别为 38,358 美元、56,389 美元，新加坡已遥遥领先中国香港。在这期间，新加坡成功实现了五次经济转型——60 年代建立劳动密集型产业，70 年代打造资源密集型产业，80 年代转向资本密集型产业，90 年代致力于科技密集型产业，21 世纪主攻知识密集型产业，其背后推手主要都是政府。政府与市场的结合，经济发展政策与社会发展政策的结合，有效地达成了效率与公平、发展与稳定的统一，促进了经济增长、城市提升和社会全面进步。为世人称道的"新加坡共识"正是"有为政府＋有效市场"战略的成果，引领着国家全面、可持续地发展。

第三例是粤港澳大湾区所建立的世界级城市群。说到大湾区，人们自然想起东京湾区、旧金山湾区和纽约湾区。这三个连接海岸线的湾区，都是各自国家的经济、文化核心城市群区域。东京湾区聚集了丰田、索尼、三菱等世界 500 强企业的总部；旧金山湾区聚集了苹果、谷歌、脸书等互联网巨头；纽约湾区则聚集了一大批金融机构，成为全球金融的心脏地带。粤港澳大湾区则是指构成珠三角经济区的九个城市，包括广州、深圳、珠海、东莞、惠州、中山、佛山、肇庆和江门，以及香港和澳门两个特别行政区，粤港澳

of Hong Kong and Macao. The construction of the urban clusters in the Great Bay Area of Guangdong, Hong Kong and Macao, shall set those of Tokyo and New York as a benchmark, and surpass them. In 2016, the GDP of the Guangdong, Hong Kong and Macao Great Bay Area was about USD 1.38 trillion, comparable to that of the ROK, which ranked 11th in the world economy. The ports handling capacity reached 65.2 million TEU (Twenty-foot Equivalent Unit), exceeding the sum of the Tokyo, New York and San Francisco Bay Areas. The passenger throughput at the airports reached 186 million, ranking the highest amongst the bay areas. In 2016, the total value of imports and exports in the Guangdong, Hong Kong and Macao Great Bay Area reached USD 1,796.67 billion, received foreign direct investment USD 102.91 billion, accounting for 5.9% of global FDI inflows. In 2017, China's "Government Work Report" emphasized promoting the construction of the Guangdong, Hong Kong and Macao Great Bay Area, striving to make it a first-class international bay area and world-class urban cluster.

Specific measures include:

(1) Promoting infrastructure interconnectivity and building world-class urban clusters, that is, accelerating the coordinated development of Bay Area ports, airports and rapid transportation networks, and actively constructing infrastructure of the import and export ports;

(2) Accelerating the development of logistics and shipping and establishing world-class shipping clusters, which includes accelerating the construction of free trade ports, vigorously developing the intermodal logistics system, upgrading the Bay Area shipping services, and others;

(3) Promoting scientific and technological innovation, resource sharing and building an international center for scientific and technological innovation: Apart from constructing infrastructure for science and technology in the Bay Area, establishing science and technology transfer mechanism, encouraging the youths to innovate and start their own businesses, and promoting the development of finance

for science and technology, there are also needs to outsource services for science and technology and protect intellectual property cooperatively;

(4) Promoting integrated developments of manufacturing industries and building a "Made in China 2025" demonstration zone, which will promote the coordinated development of manufacturing industrial chains, strengthen industrial informatization, promote international cooperation in production capacity, and encourage the equipment manufacturing industry to enter the international market;

大湾区城市群建设将对标东京和纽约城市群，并超越东京、纽约城市群。2016 年，粤港澳大湾区经济总量约 1.38 万亿美元，与世界经济体排名第 11 的韩国相当；港口集装箱吞吐量达 6520 万标箱，超过东京、纽约、旧金山三大湾区之和；机场旅客吞吐量达 1.86 亿人次，居各湾区之首。2016 年，粤港澳大湾区对外进出口总值达 17,966.7 亿美元；获外商直接投资总额 1029.1 亿美元，占全球外商直接投资流入量的 5.9%。2017 年，中国《政府工作报告》强调推进粤港澳大湾区建设，使其朝国际一流湾区和世界级城市群迈进。具体举措有：

第一，推进基础设施互联互通，建设世界级城市群，既加快湾区港口、机场、快速交通网络协同发展，又积极实施进出口岸基础设施建设。

第二，加快物流航运发展，建立世界级航运群。这包括加快建设自由贸易港，大力发展联运物流体系，提升湾区航运服务功能，等等。

第三，促进科技创新、资源共享，打造国际科技创新中心。除了加强湾区科技基础设施建设、建立科技转移转化机制、鼓励青年创新创业、推动科技金融发展之外，还要大力发展科技服务外包、开展知识产权保护协作。

第四，推动制造业一体化发展，建设"中国制造 2025"示范区。它将推动制造业产业链协同发展、加强工业信息化建设、促进国际产能合作、鼓励装备制造业走向国际市场。

(5) Enhancing innovative developments of the financial industry and establishing an international hub, which includes strengthening finances in shipping, actively innovating finances in science and technology, promoting the integration of industry and finance, accelerating the construction of financial platforms, and promoting the docking of offshore finance and onshore finance;

(6) Strengthening integration in the Bay Area, and creating a circle of quality life suitable for living, business and tourism: The rise of the Guangdong, Hong Kong and Macao Great Bay Area has created a new development pattern, and become the new engine for regional economy, and all these are attributed to the dual function of "effective government plus efficient market". It is in the framework of this strategic planning that the Guangdong, Hong Kong and Macao Great Bay Area has achieved substantial developments.

第五，提升金融业创新发展，建立国际枢纽。这包括培育壮大航运金融、积极创新科技金融、推动产融结合、加快金融平台建设、促进离岸金融与在岸金融对接。

　　第六，强化湾区一体化水平，打造宜居、宜业、宜游的优质生活圈。……粤港澳大湾区的成功崛起，打造了一种新的发展格局，成为区域经济新引擎，而这一切都归功于"有为政府＋有效市场"的双重作用，因为这样的战略规划，粤港澳大湾区才能取得实质的发展成效。

CHAPTER 9   BUILDING UP A NEW ENGINE FOR GLOBAL ECONOMIC DEVELOPMENT

1. Kindleberger Trap and Endogenous Growth Theory

In order to discuss the building of a new engine for global economic development, it is necessary to review two economic theories, the Kindleberger Trap and Endogenous Growth Theory.

As Joseph S. Nye, a well-known US political scientist and professor at Harvard University, wrote in January 2017 in his article "The Kindleberger Trap", "Charles Kindleberger, an intellectual architect of the Marshall Plan who later taught at MIT, argued that the disastrous decade of the 1930s was caused when the US replaced Britain as the largest global power but failed to take on Britain's role in providing global public goods. The result was the collapse of the global system into depression, genocide, and world war."

Professor Nye pointed out, "Small countries have little incentive to pay for such global public goods. Because their small contributions make little difference to whether they benefit or not, it is rational for them to ride for free. But the largest powers can see the effect and feel the benefit of their contributions. So it is rational for the largest countries to lead. When they do not, global public goods are under-produced." In his view, Donald Trump, the President-elect of the United States, should heed lessons drawn from others' mistakes when formulating his policies toward China: the Thucydides Trap that if an established power (such as the United States) becomes too fearful of a rising country (such as China), war will become unavoidable, as well as the Kindleberger Trap—a China that seems too weak rather than too strong.[1]

Nevertheless, if we meticulously examine the situation, China has played a fairly constructive role in the global governance system and has achieved developments in stages from capital supply to institutional construction and then to value innovation. Since 2008, China has begun contributing more capital to global governance, including injecting capital to promote multilateralization of the "Chiang Mai Initiative", to the International Monetary Fund and the World Bank. Moreover, China has been taking part in global governance with regard to institutional construction. As landmarks, China launched the "Belt and Road" Initiative

玖 构建全球经济发展新引擎

一、金德尔伯格陷阱与内生增长理论

为了讨论全球经济发展新引擎的构建问题，我们有必要先回顾一下两个经济学理论——金德尔伯格陷阱与内生增长理论。

金德尔伯格陷阱由美国著名政治学家、哈佛大学教授约瑟夫·E.奈提出。他于2017年撰文指出，马歇尔计划的构建者之一、后执教于麻省理工学院的查尔斯·金德尔伯格认为，20世纪30年代的灾难起源于奉行孤立主义的美国在第一次世界大战后取代英国成为全球最大强权，但又未能像英国一样承担起提供全球公共物品的责任，在全球合作体系中继续搭便车。其结果是全球体系崩溃，陷入萧条、种族灭绝和世界大战。

奈指出，在国际上，小国缺少提供全球公共物品的动力。因为小国贡献太小，对于自己能否受益影响甚微，所以搭便车对它们而言更为合理。但大国能看到自己贡献的效果，也能感受到其所带来的好处。因此大国有理由带头，不然就会有全球公共物品E.不足的问题。

奈认为，美国候任总统唐纳德·特朗普在制定对华政策的时候，应该当心前车之鉴：其一是修昔底德陷阱，即如果一个现存的大国（如美国）视一个崛起的大国（如中国）为威胁，战争将变得不可避免。其二，也是特朗普更需注意的，是金德尔伯格陷阱，即中国在国际上不是展示强大，而是示弱。[1]

然而如果我们仔细研究实际情况的话，中国在全球治理体系中发挥了相当的建设性作用，并实现了从资金供给到制度建设再到理念创新的阶段性发展。从2008年开始，中国开始为全球治理贡献更多资金，包括注资推动"清迈倡议"多边化、注资国际货币基金组织和世界银行。不仅如此，中国也开始在制度建设上为全球治理

and started the Asian Infrastructure Investment Bank in 2013, and in 2014, China put forward the construction of the New Development Bank of BRICs. And since 2016, starting from the Hangzhou Summit of the G20 in particular, China has begun contributing ideas and philosophies to global governance. From capital to institutions and then to philosophies, China is gradually becoming a mature and responsible leading country.

In Kindleberger's view, global public goods included the international trade system, the international monetary system, capital flows, macroeconomic policies and crisis management mechanisms, etc. Joseph E. Stiglitz, Nobel Laureate in Economics and professor at Columbia University, believed on the other hand, that global public goods included five major categories, namely international economic stability, international security, international environment, international humanitarian assistance and knowledge.

At this point, putting aside the political and ideological disputes brought about by the Kindleberger's Trap for the time being, merely from the perspective of economics, there are at least three problems to be solved: Firstly, what are the global public goods? Or in other words, what kind of products can be regarded as global public goods? Secondly, who will provide the global public goods? Thirdly, how are such global public goods to be provided or accepted?

Let's put aside the above-mentioned questions and turn to the Endogenous Growth Theory for a while. Endogenous Growth Theory is a branch of macroeconomic theories that originated in the mid-1980s. Its core idea is that the economy can grow sustainably without relying on external forces, endogenous technological progress being the decisive factor of sustained economic growth. This theory emphasizes incomplete competition and progressive increases in returns.

Since the era of Adam Smith, the debate throughout the entire circle of economics has revolved around the factors driving economic growth for more than 200 years. The eventual consensus is that, for a long period of time, the economic growth of a nation mainly depends on the following three factors. Firstly, the accumulation of productive resources over time; secondly, the utilization efficiency of resource stock with a nation's given technological knowledge; and thirdly, technological progress. However, the most popular neoclassical economic growth theory since the 1960s takes technological progress as an exogenous factor for economic growth,

作出贡献，其标志性事件就是 2013 年中国提出"一带一路"倡议并启动亚洲基础设施投资银行建设，2014 年中国又提出建设金砖国家新开发银行。而从 2016 年开始，特别是以 20 国集团杭州峰会为起点，中国开始在全球治理中贡献思想和理念。从资金到制度再到理念，中国在一步步成为一个成熟的、负责任的大国。

在金德尔伯格看来，全球公共物品包括国际贸易体系、国际货币体系、资本流动、宏观经济政策以及危机管理机制等。诺贝尔经济学奖得主、美国哥伦比亚大学教授斯蒂格利茨则认为，全球公共物品包括国际经济稳定、国际安全、国际环境、国际人道主义援助、知识等五大类。

在此，我们暂且不论金德尔伯格陷阱带来的政治和意识形态争议，仅从经济学角度分析，它至少存在三方面问题需解决：其一，全球公共物品是什么？或者说什么类型的产品才能被视为全球公共物品？其二，谁来提供全球公共物品？其三，以什么方式提供或以什么方式接受此类全球性公共物品？

暂时搁置上述问题，我们再来看内生增长理论。内生增长理论是产生于 20 世纪 80 年代中期的一个宏观经济理论分支。其核心思想是认为经济能够不依赖外力推动而实现持续增长，内生的技术进步是保证经济持续增长的决定因素。该理论强调不完全竞争和收益递增。

自亚当·斯密以来，整个经济学界围绕着驱动经济增长的因素争论了长达 200 多年，最终形成的比较一致的观点是，一个相当长的时期里，一国的经济增长主要取决于下列三个因素：一是随着时间的推移，生产性资源的积累；二是在一国的技术知识既定的情况下，资源存量的使用效率；三是技术进步。但是，上世纪 60 年代

and concludes that long-term economic growth will stop when factor income diminishes. On the other hand, the newly-formed endogenous growth theory in the 1990s holds that the long-term growth rate is dependent on endogenous factors. In other words, the process of labor input includes human capital arising from formal education, training, and on-the-job training; and the process of accumulating material capital includes technological progress arising from R&D, innovation and other activities. Henceforth, this theory internalizes technological progress and other factors, and concludes that due to the technological progress, factor income will progressively increase, thereby long-term growth rate is positive. As a result, the orientation of policies of neoclassical economic growth theory and that of endogenous growth theory differ from each other.

As theories develop, many economists realize that the biggest problem faced by endogenous growth theory is how to conduct empirical analysis. This empirical research is, in fact, to be carried out along two technical routes: one is on differences amongst nations to find evidence of endogenous growth; the other is on economic growth factors based on a nation's long-term data, or on a specific factor independently, such as the effects of opening up policies, taxation, equality, financial progress, education expenditure, innovation and other factors on economic growth.

At this point, I have no intention to introduce too more about the relevant models of endogenous growth theory and its modern development, and the revival of the so-called Neo-Schumpeterism. I just want to reiterate that the traditional economists who study a nation's economic growth factors are at this stage, still confined to the industrial economy as described by Adam Smith, still looking for new driving forces for growth therein, and still believing that technological progress is the deciding factor in endogenous growth.

I do not judge endogenous growth theory. I just want to point out that: (1) The endogenous growth of an economy refers to the sustainable development of a nation's economy. (2) The discussion on endogenous economic growth factors should not always be confined to industrial economy, but should encompass the three economic fields, namely, industrial economy, livelihood economy and urban economy. (3) I do not object to traditional economists looking for impetus in endogenous growth (such as technology, etc.) from the scarcity of resources in

以来最流行的新古典经济增长理论，把技术进步等作为外生因素来解释经济增长，并由此得出当要素收益递减时长期经济增长将停止的结论。而上世纪90年代形成的新经济学即内生增长理论则认为，长期增长率是由内生因素解释的。也就是说，劳动投入过程包含着由正规教育、培训、在职学习等形成的人力资本，物质资本积累过程包含着由研发、创新等活动形成的技术进步，因此该理论把技术进步等要素内化，得出因技术进步的存在，要素收益会递增，因而长期增长率是正的的结论。因此，新古典经济增长理论和内生增长理论的政策导向就出现了分歧。

随着理论的发展，不少经济学家意识到，内生增长理论面临的最大问题就是如何进行实证分析。这种实证研究事实上是沿着两条技术路线进行的：一条是进行国别研究，寻找内生增长的证据；另一条是根据一国的长时段数据，研究经济增长因素，或者单独讨论某个具体因素，如对外开放、税收、平等、金融进步、教育支出、创新等对于经济增长的作用。

在此，我不想更多笔墨去介绍内生增长理论的相关模型、现代发展，以及所谓新熊彼特主义的复兴。我只是想重述，研究一国经济增长因素的传统经济学家，即使在现阶段仍然还局限在亚当·斯密所阐述的产业经济中，仍然在产业经济内寻找增长的新动力，仍然认为技术进步是内生增长的决定因素……

我不想评论内生增长理论的对错与否，只是想指出：第一，经济的内生增长，应该是指一个国家的经济可持续发展。第二，对经济内生增长因素的讨论不能总是局限在产业经济中，而应该涵盖三类经济领域，即产业经济、民生经济、城市经济。第三，我不反对传统经济学家从产业经济的资源稀缺角度去寻找内生增长的动力

industrial economy, but at this stage, we should look more from the resource generation in urban economy. (4) The newly generated resources in the three types of resources, which is mainly, at this moment, the urban economy with investment and construction of the software and hardware infrastructure and even the development and operation of intelligent cities as its main contents, followed by economies in emerging areas of space, deep sea, polar resources and network, are not only social quasi-public goods, but also global quasi-public goods, and even a new economic growth pole or in other words, the new engine for global economic development.

Take international aid, a global public good as an example. It is interrelated with the three types of resources and the three types of economy, and can be divided into social-typed, economic-typed, and environmental-typed. International aid that is associated with the livelihood economy across the world is public welfare-like, and can be called social-typed international aid. International aid that is associated with the industrial economy across the world is commodity like, and can be called economic-typed international aid. International aid that is associated with the urban economy across the world can be called environmental-typed international aid. International disaster relief, relief, poverty alleviation, medical treatment, education and others are supplied to the international community for free through the United Nations and other organizations, and are therefore public welfare-like and social-typed. The related products from the three major industries are commodity-like, and are supplied to the international community through import and export and related institutions, under the guidance of market rules, which is economic-typed international aid. The investment and construction of infrastructure software and hardware between nations, which are aid or business in nature, or both, are environmental-typed international aid. The type to be adopted is determined by the relationship between nations and many other factors.

Thus far, we have discussed the classification and characterization of the three types of resources, the three types of economy and the corresponding government policies, and the classification, characterization and supply of international aid; and this effectively solves the problems of what global public goods are, where they are coming from and going to in the Kindleberger Trap. The newly generated resources based on infrastructure investment and construction are not only globalized quasi-public goods, but also a new engine for national or even global economic development.

（比如技术等），但我们在现阶段更应该从城市经济中的资源生成角度去寻找内生增长的动力。第四，三类资源中的新生成性资源——当前主要是以基础设施软硬件投资建设乃至智能城市开发运营为主体的城市经济，之后还会有太空、深海、极地、网络等新兴领域经济——既是社会准公共物品，又是全球准公共物品，更是世界新的经济增长极，或者说世界经济发展的新引擎。

以国际援助这一全球公共物品为例，它与三类资源、三类经济是相互联系的，也可分为社会型、经济型和环境型三类。与各国民生经济相关联的国际援助，带有公益性，我们可以把它称为社会型国际援助；与各国产业经济相联系的国际援助，带有商品性，我们可以把它称为经济型国际援助；与各国城市经济相联系的国际援助，我们可以把它称为环境型国际援助。比如国际赈灾、救济、扶贫、医疗、教育等，属国际社会公益性质，即为社会型国际援助，是通过联合国等组织机构无偿提供给国际社会的；比如三大产业的相关产品，属国际市场商品性质，是通过国家间的进出口贸易和相关制度安排，按市场规则提供给国际社会的，即为经济型国际援助；再比如国家间的基础设施软硬件投资建设，具有援助性质或商业性质或二者兼有，则属环境型国际援助。至于采取何种方式是根据国与国之间的关系等多种因素来定的。

至此，我们沿着三类资源、三类经济的分类、定性及政府政策的配套方式，延伸到国际援助的分类、定性与供给上来，这将有效解决金德尔伯格陷阱中何为全球公共物品、全球公共物品从何处来又到何处去的问题。以基础设施投资建设为主体的新生成性资源领域，既是全球性准公共物品，又是世界各国乃至全球经济发展的新引擎。

2. The Arrival of the Era of Urbanization-led Economic Growth

There are competitions among countries and cities across the world, including China. Cities are major participants in global competition, the yardstick to measure innovation of major nations, and the window to decode the interactions between markets and governments. Foshan City, Guangdong Province, where I served as Secretary of the CPC Municipal Committee and Mayor, is taking Chengdu, Wuhan, Hangzhou, Nanjing, Qingdao, Changsha, Wuxi, Ningbo, Dalian, Zhengzhou and other domestic cities with similar economic aggregates as benchmarks. These cities are benchmarks for one another, striving to build a "sample pool" of urban innovation, and exploring for sustainable urban economic growth.

Referring to the effective measures taken by other big cities, Foshan has made many plans and arrangements. (1) Being three major manufacturing cities, Wuxi, Ningbo and Foshan should adhere to the real economy and focus on intelligent manufacturing. Foshan, in particular, needs to speed up "Made in China 2025". (2) Drawing on the experience of cultivating new industrial clusters in Chengdu, Wuhan and Nanjing, Foshan should cultivate new economic growth poles in intelligent equipment, new energy vehicles and other fields. (3) Backed by Guangzhou, the "mega city", Foshan needs to link with it to provide intra-city services. (4) Foshan should compete in attracting business, to attract the Fortune Global 500 enterprises. (5) Foshan should innovate financially to dedicatedly serve the real economy. (6) Foshan should take urbanization, industrial and urban integration as the new pivot for urban competition. (7) Regional competition and cooperation has entered the "urban cluster era". Referring to the experience of Wuhan's and Chengdu's building of hub cities—expediting the construction of major transport hubs, Foshan should build three-dimensional transportation and make every effort to promote a new round of infrastructure construction. (8) Foshan should hasten the construction of an intelligent city, to establish a new service system conducive to living, business and tourism and find the new "key" to stimulate urban economic growth.

Following Foshan's example, Beijing-Tianjin-Hebei, the Pearl River Delta and Yangtze River Delta, being China's three major economic growth poles, are all fully implementing urban and rural planning, promoting infrastructure construction, planning industrial layout, protecting environment, and improving the level of public services, to promote regional integration and sustainable development of regional economy. These measures have had remarkable results. At present, the

二、城市化主导的经济增长时代的来临

在世界各国，包括中国，都上演着大国竞争、城市竞秀的宏景。城市，是国家参与全球竞争的主体、丈量大国创新实力的标尺，以及解码市场与政府互动之道的窗口。我曾任市委书记、市长的广东省佛山市，就正对标着国内经济总量类似的成都、武汉、杭州、南京、青岛、长沙、无锡、宁波、大连、郑州等同行者。这些城市互为坐标，努力构建一个城市创新的"样本池"，探索城市经济可持续增长的新路径。

参照其他大城市的有力举措，佛山市作出了诸多规划部署：第一，无锡、宁波、佛山是三座制造业大城市，应坚守实体经济，主攻智能制造，佛山尤其要加速打造"中国制造2025"。第二，参照成都、武汉、南京培育新工业集群的经验，佛山要在智能装备、新能源汽车等领域培育新的经济增长极。第三，背靠"超级城市"广州，佛山要构建与广州相联结的同城服务。第四，佛山应参与招商竞逐，争取世界500强企业入驻。第五，佛山应开展金融创新，全力服务实体经济。第六，佛山应把城镇化发展、产业与城市融合作为城市竞争的新支点。第七，区域的竞争与合作已进入"城市群时代"，参考武汉、成都努力建设枢纽城市——加速建设重大交通枢纽的经验，佛山应建设立体交通，全力推动新一轮基础设施建设。第八，佛山应加快建设智能城市，构建宜居、宜业、宜游的新服务体系，找到激发城市经济增长潜力的新"钥匙"……

从佛山市推而广之，作为中国三大经济增长极的京津冀、珠三角和长三角，都在全面实施城乡规划、推进基础设施建设、规划产业布局、落实环境保护、提升公共服务水平等，以促进区域一体化和区域经济可持续发展。这些举措取得了显著效果，当前三大经济

infrastructure integration of the three economic circles are progressing orderly, the level of labor division and cooperation advanced among regions, newly styled urbanization steadily promoted, and national sponge cities and national utility tunnels constructed orderly. At the same time, other regional urban clusters in China have taken many significant measures with remarkable results in their continuous promotion of regional coordinated developments and cultivation of new economic growth poles.

In addition to regional governments' diligent efforts, the central government has also made great efforts to promote investment and construction of such basic fields as big science projects, national science and technology major projects, and major science and technology platforms. At the same time, the interconnected rural transport infrastructure network is also forming an orderly new structure, and promoting the urban-rural integration. Infrastructure constructions of transportation, municipal administration, energy, water conservancy, information, environmental protection and others are precisely laying solid foundations for cultivating new economic growth points, and will continuously produce massive economic and social effects.

The era of urbanization-led economic growth has arrived. As far as China was concerned, 2013 was a turning point especially, when the situation of "excessive industrialization and backward urbanization" that mainly depends on industrial economy has begun to change, urbanization has become a new momentum for economic growth, and in turn gradually promoted the transformation and upgrading of industrial economy.

3. Community of National Interests

From a worldwide perspective, the global population has been gathering in major cities in the recent more than half a century. The scale of cities and economic efficiency, per capita urban output and urban population size are significantly positively correlated. The larger the scale of cities, the higher the productivity. The United States, Japan, ROK, Singapore, Australia, and Canada, etc., are as such; their economic activities are concentrated in large metropolitan areas, where the economic output of large cities is far greater.

From the perspective of urban development, PPP (public private partnership) is an effective method to integrate government and market. Darrin Grimsey and Mervyn K. Lewis suggested in the book *Public Private Partnership: The Worldwide Revolution in Infrastructure Provision*

圈的基础设施一体化有序推进，地域间分工合作程度提升，新型城镇化稳步推进，国家海绵城市建设、国家地下综合管廊建设等均在有序进行。同时，中国其他区域城市群也在促进区域协调发展、培育新经济增长极方面不断努力，实施了许多成效显著的重大举措。

除了区域政府的努力探索，中央政府也着力推动大科学工程、重大科技专项、重大科技平台等基础领域投资建设。同时，互联互通的农村交通基础设施网络建设，也正在形成有序的新结构，推动城乡一体化的发展。交通基础设施建设、市政基础设施建设、能源基础设施建设、水利基础设施建设、信息基础设施建设、环保基础设施建设等，正为培育新的经济增长点奠定牢固的基础，并将持续产生巨大的经济效应和社会效应。

城市化主导经济增长的时代已经到来。对中国来说，2013 年尤其是一个拐点，那种主要依赖产业经济的"工业化超前、城市化滞后"的状况开始改变，城市化成为经济增长的新动能，并反过来逐步推动着产业经济的转型升级。

三、国家利益共同体

从世界范围看，近半个多世纪，全球人口在向大城市集聚。城市规模和经济效率、人均城市产出与城市人口规模有明显的正相关关系，城市规模越大，生产率越高。美国、日本、韩国、新加坡、澳大利亚、加拿大等都是如此，其经济活动聚集在大的都市圈，大城市的经济产出更大。

从城市发展角度，PPP（政府和社会资本合作）是一种政府与市场结合的有效方式。达霖·格里姆赛与默文·K.刘易斯在《PPP

and Project Finance that the greatest advantage of the PPP method lies in introducing market mechanism into infrastructure investment and financing. Its specific effects include: (1) introducing competition mechanism to promote building government integrity; (2) alleviating the shortage of funds due to the government's lack of money, and accelerating the construction of infrastructure and development of public utilities; (3) giving full play to the initiatives and creativities of foreign and private enterprises, and improving the efficiency in project operation and the quality of services; (4) effectively promoting the completeness of market laws and regulations; (5) promoting technology transfer; (6) training professionals and experts; (7) promoting the development of financial markets; (8) reducing capital expenditures for foreign and private enterprises, and achieving "big projects from small investments"; (9) alleviating the debt burden of investors through off-balance-sheet financing; (10) making use of the limited recourse to allocate risks rationally, strengthen the control of project income, and maintain a high rate of return on investment (compared to full recourse).

In addition, during the process of building the "Belt and Road", China will develop the Industrial Parks represented by the "Silk Road Post Stations" into the major platform to support economy and trade interconnections and industrial development. We will start from constructing core traffic nodes such as seaports, airports and inland waterless ports, and take the Industrial Parks neighboring these ports as the core and main carriers to systematically solve the problems restricting the industrial transfer of host nations caused by weaknesses in the software and hardware. This way China will summarize an effective development mode of PPC (Port Park City). The core of this mode is the development, construction and operation of ports. Through advance management followed by Industrial Parks and development of supporting urban functions, host nations will achieve regional interconnected developments, forming a relatively complete ecological circle of ports, logistics and financial parks. PPC has become a new business card for the circulation of trade and interconnection construction of nations along the "Belt and Road"; international economic cooperation characterized by "infrastructure construction and supporting Industrial Parks" has also become a new mode for international economic growth.

The infrastructure construction is becoming more and more important in economic development. In 2016, KPMG International put forward ten major trends that would change the world of infrastructure

革命——公共服务中的政府和社会资本合作》一书中提出，PPP 方式最大的优点在于将市场机制引入到基础设施的投融资领域，其具体效果包括：第一，引入竞争机制，促进了政府诚信建设；第二，缓解政府财力不足导致的资金短缺困境，加快基础设施建设和公共事业发展；第三，充分发挥外商及民营企业的能动性和创造性，提高项目运营效率和服务质量；第四，有效促进了市场法律法规制度的完善；第五，促进了技术转移；第六，培养了专业人才；第七，促进了金融市场的发展；第八，对外商及民营企业而言，减少资本金支出，实现"小投入做大项目"；第九，利用表外融资的特点，减轻投资者的债务负担；第十，利用有限追索权的特点，合理分配风险，加强对项目收益的控制，保持较高的投资收益率（对比完全追索权）。

此外，中国在"一带一路"建设的过程中，将以"丝路驿站"为代表的产业园区（即以海港、空港、内陆无水港等核心交通节点建设为切入点，以临港的产业园区为核心和主要载体，系统解决制约东道国产业转移的软硬件短板问题）打造成支持经贸互联互通和产业发展的大平台，并在这一过程中总结出卓有成效的 PPC（港口公园式城市）开发模式。这一模式的核心是港口的开发、建设、经营。通过管理先行、产业园区跟进、配套城市功能的开发等，东道国区域将实现联动发展，进而形成一个较为完善的港口、物流、金融园区生态圈。PPC 成为"一带一路"沿线国家商贸流通和互联互通建设的一张新名片，"基础设施建设＋产业园区配套"的国际经济合作也成为国际经济增长的新模式。

基础设施建设在经济发展中的重要性日益提升。2016 年，毕马威国际会计师事务所曾就未来五年世界性基础设施建设提出十大

over the next five years in the world economic development: (1) The macro risk environment has begun to shift. (2) Competition for investment heats up. (3) The investment interest is focusing on the larger benefits to unclog the pipeline. (4) The asset management gets more sophisticated. (5) Technology rockets up the infrastructure agenda. (6) Security has become an important issue in urban construction. (7) The gap between public and private narrows. (8) Through financial innovations, institutions will promote the rapid rise in the investment of infrastructure constructions. (9) The institutional debt market takes off. (10) China and India have been making a leap. KPMG's report was an observation and judgment of global infrastructure construction, revealing the possible route of world economic growth.

"Research Report on Economic Focus of G20 (2016-2017)" also demonstrated the importance of infrastructure constructions, holding that the prominent highlight in the economic operation of the Group of 20 is the investment and construction of infrastructure, which is an important engine driving the recovery of the world economy and its sustainable growth. As the report pointed out: (1) The supply of infrastructure in emerging and developing economies is obviously inadequate with a huge gap, whilst the existing infrastructure in developed economies are gradually aging; hence there is a great demand for infrastructure construction across the world. (2) During a period of global economic downturn and investment inefficiency, strengthening investments in infrastructure, especially promoting and optimizing high-quality investments, will strongly motivate economic growth in the short and long term, and will also create employment and improve productivity. (3) Being a part of the new growth strategy, increasing investments in infrastructure is also the common focus of the G20 and a key issue in the G20 Summit. The G20 Summit held in November 2014 agreed to establish a Global Infrastructure Hub with a four-year mandate, which aims to develop "a knowledge-sharing platform and network between governments, the private sector, development banks and other international organizations. The Hub will foster collaboration among these groups to improve the functioning and financing of infrastructure markets." (4) In October 2014, the World Bank launched Global Infrastructure Facility (GIF) to deliver complex public-private infrastructure projects and encourage more private infrastructure investment. (5) In recent years, the BRICS economic

趋势，即在世界经济发展的大潮中：第一，宏观风险环境已经开始转化。第二，投资竞争加剧。第三，政府将清除基础设施投资的障碍，以促进更大的经济和社会利益。第四，城市设施管理更加多样化。第五，技术变革加速影响基础设施建设。第六，安全成为城市建设的重要议题。第七，基础设施建设存在公私合营的发展空间。第八，各类机构通过金融创新，将推动基础设施建设投资的迅速崛起。第九，基础设施建设将进入负债投资运营时代。第十，中国和印度日益活跃，发展迅速。毕马威的报告是对全球基础设施建设的观察和研判，揭示了世界经济增长的可能路径。

《二十国集团（G20）经济热点分析报告（2016—2017）》也揭示了基础设施建设的重要性，认为二十国集团经济运行的显著亮点是基础设施的投资建设，这是驱动世界经济复苏并可持续增长的重要引擎。报告指出：第一，当前新兴和发展中经济体的基础设施供给明显不足，存在巨大缺口，而发达经济体的现有基础设施又逐步老化，各国都有很大的基础设施建设需求。第二，在全球经济不景气、缺乏投资效率的时期，加强基础设施投资，尤其是推动并优化高质量投资，无论在短期还是长期，都将为经济增长提供强大的动力支持，也有利于创造就业和提高生产力。第三，作为新增长战略的一部分，增加基础设施投资也是二十国集团共同关注的焦点，是二十国集团峰会的重点议题。2014年11月召开的二十国集团领导人峰会同意成立为期四年的全球基础设施中心，致力于为政府、私人部门、开发银行和其他国际组织提供分享知识的平台和网络，促进各方合作，以改善基础设施市场的运行和融资状况。第四，世界银行2014年10月也宣布要建立一个全球基础设施基金，旨在促进复杂的公私合作经营的基础设施项目的实施，同时推动私营部门在基础设施投资中发挥作用。第五，近年来金砖国家经济合作、亚洲

cooperation and regional economic cooperation in Asia have also attached great importance to joint infrastructure constructions with such fruitful collaboration as the BRICS New Development Bank and Asian Infrastructure Investment Bank. (6) According to the estimate of the Global Infrastructure Hub, there will be an investment gap of USD10 trillion to USD20 trillion in the infrastructure investment market by 2030, which will adversely affect the global economic development. Therefore, in 2016, the Global Infrastructure Hub called on governments across the world to re-focus on infrastructure investment, exploit development opportunities with great investment potential, and boost the global economy, etc. As can be predicted, with the profound development of regional or global economic integration, the demand for cross-regional and cross-border interconnected infrastructure will increase day by day, while the global infrastructure construction is ushering in a new round of development opportunities. The rapid growth of infrastructure investments will be an important engine driving the recovery of the world economy and its sustainable growth.[2]

In the 5th chapter of this book, we have analyzed the scale effects, cluster effects and neighborhood effects of urban economic development, which is mainly based on the investment and development of the software and hardware infrastructure, and even on the development and operation of intelligent cities. As the economic growth across the world enters a new stage of urbanization and urban-rural integration, the investment and construction of global infrastructure has condensed all nations into a community of interests. All nations need to invest resources, coordinate with each other, formulate rules and promote accordingly in order to maximize the due important role of the new engine for world economic growth.

4. Building Up a New Engine for Global Economic Development

In 1948, Ragnar Nurkse likened trade to the growth engine of the 19th century to justify the strategy of substituting imports for industrialization. During the financial crisis in 2012-2014, the annual growth rate of global trade was less than 4%, which was far below the average growth rate of about 7% before the crisis. Consequently, World Bank officials once again raised the question on how to "restart" the global trade engine. I believe that the world economy generally develops from the factor-driven stage

区域经济合作也都非常重视基础设施领域的共同建设，并取得了务实合作成果，建立了金砖国家新开发银行、亚洲基础设施投资银行等。第六，据全球基础设施中心预测，到 2030 年，基础设施投资市场将存在 10 万亿至 20 万亿美元的投资缺口，对全球经济发展前景将带来不利影响。因此，2016 年，全球基础设施中心发出倡议，号召各国政府重新把注意力放在基础设施投资领域，开拓极具投资潜力的发展机遇，提振全球经济，等等。可以预见，在区域或全球经济一体化深入发展的情况下，对跨区域、跨国界互联互通的基础设施的需求将日益增长，全球基础设施建设正迎来一轮新的发展机遇。基础设施投资的快速增长，将成为驱动世界经济复苏和可持续增长的重要引擎。[2]

在本书第五章《区域政府竞争》中，我们分析了以基础设施软硬件投资建设乃至智能城市开发运营为主体的城市经济发展具有规模效应、集聚效应和邻里效应。在世界各国经济增长进入城市化发展、城镇化发展、城乡一体化发展的新阶段，全球基础设施投资建设将各个国家凝聚为利益共同体。对于这一世界经济增长的新引擎，各国都需要投入资源、相互协调、制定规则、有序推进，使之发挥出应有的重要作用。

四、构建全球经济发展新引擎

1948 年，拉格纳·纳克斯把贸易比作 19 世纪的增长引擎，借以说明用进口替代工业化战略的合理性。2012—2014 年金融危机爆发期间，全球贸易年增长率不到 4%，远远低于危机前 7% 左右的平均增速，于是，又有世界银行官员提出如何"重启"全球贸易引擎的问题。我认为，世界各国的经济发展基本都遵循从要素驱动阶

to the investment-driven stage, and then to the innovation-driven stage. Many nations, especially those rich in natural resources such as oil, natural gas, minerals and agricultural products, etc., whose economic growth was driven by tangible factors like land and labor force, have reached their extremes with signs of unsustainability.

Henceforth, a new engine is needed to realize economic growth in the new century. In my opinion, in the modern market system made up of "effective government plus efficient market", a new structural engine on the supply side (rather than a "trade engine" on the demand side) will give full play in competition to enterprises in the allocation of industrial resources and to the government in that of urban resources. These new structural engines on the supply side include investment engines, innovation engines and regulation engines that combine tangible and intangible factors, and will have important effects on global economic governance and development.

Building Up a New Engine for Global Investment

Investment-driven growth depends not only on the supply-side allocation and competition of products and industrial resources, but also on the supply-side competitive performance of the government in allocating urban resources and promoting infrastructure construction. It can bring about capital growth to nations, promote technological innovation and deepen market mechanisms' development, as well as increase employment, thereby it has long-term sustainability. In order to build a new engine for global investment, we should take the following measures:

First, to promote the structural reform in the supply side, which includes the following two aspects:

Firstly, promoting new industrialization that is driven by and in turn advances informatization: The new industrialization fully exploits science and technology as well as advantages of human resources with better economic benefits and little environmental pollution by consuming less resources. It encompasses three aspects: (1) Supporting and guiding the transformation and upgrading of traditional industries—Scientific and technological progress can be used to transform those old industries which consume resources and the environment into new recycling industries. Technological transformation can revitalize huge stock assets, optimize and enhance industrial efficiency, stimulate demand, and promote economic growth. (2) Supporting and cultivating strategic

段到投资驱动阶段，再到创新驱动阶段的路径。许多国家，尤其是那些石油、天然气、矿产、农产品等自然资源丰富的经济体，以土地、劳动力等有形要素驱动经济增长，已经发展到了极致并呈现出不可持续性。

因此，要在新世纪实现经济增长，需要新的引擎。我认为，由"有为政府＋有效市场"构成的现代市场体系中，发动供给侧结构性新引擎（而非需求侧"贸易引擎"），将在竞争中充分发挥企业对产业资源、政府对城市资源的配置作用。这类供给侧结构性新引擎包括结合了有形与无形要素的投资引擎、创新引擎和规则引擎，将对全球经济治理与发展起到重要作用。

构建全球投资新引擎

投资驱动型增长，既取决于供给侧产品和产业资源的配置与竞争状况，又取决于供给侧政府调配城市资源和推动基础设施建设的竞争表现。它能给各国带来资本增长，促进技术革新和市场机制深化发展，并增加岗位就业，因而具有长期可持续性。为了构建全球投资新引擎，我们应采取如下措施：

第一，推进供给侧结构性改革，这又包括如下两方面：

首先，推动新型工业化。所谓新型工业化，就是坚持以信息化带动工业化，以工业化促进信息化，就是科技含量高、经济效益好、资源消耗低、环境污染少、人力资源优势得到充分发挥的工业化。它涉及三个方面：一是扶持、引导传统产业改造、提升。科学技术进步在应用领域的落地，能够将消耗资源、环境的旧工业改造为循环发展的新工业。各国扶持、引导企业进行技术改造，能盘活巨大的存量资产，优化、提升产业效益，拉动需求，进而推动经济增长。二是扶持、培植战略性新兴产业和高技术产业。各国应在信

emerging industries and high-tech industries—On the foundation of the information industry, intelligent industries, which are incremental assets, should be developed across the world. Intelligent industry is a new industrial structure with human intelligence, computer network and physical equipment as basic elements, and its growth is of a green development mode. Nations should focus on supporting and nurturing R&D innovation, achievement transformation and industrialization of core and key technologies of enterprises, cultivate dominant industries and leading industries, and build a sound industrial chain and modern service network. (3) With the help of market competition, nations should promote mergers and acquisitions, integration and reorganization of enterprises, eliminate old industries constantly, promote the development of new industries, usher industrialization to a higher level, and enhance the core competitiveness of enterprises. This is one of the important means to realize the effective investment and transfer between new and old forces on the supply side.

Secondly, expediting the modernization of agriculture: It refers to the process and means by which traditional agriculture transforms to modern agriculture. During this process, agriculture has increasingly had at its disposal, modern industries, modern scientific technology and modern economic management techniques. Nations should utilize modern development ideas to combine agricultural development with the building of an ecological civilization and transform the outdated traditional agriculture into eco-agriculture with the advanced productivity of the contemporary world. Specifically, agricultural modernization includes not only the expansion of land management, but also the "modernization of farmers". Nations should guide farmers to overcome ignorance and backwardness and become "educated, skilled and capable" modern farmers. In terms of organizational mode, whether large or small-scale family-run farms, nations should support farmers' cooperative organizations or assist in dispersing farmers to cater to the market, so that they can provide one-stop services in pre-production, mid-production and post-production process, as well as a one-stop operation process from the purchase of the means of production, to storage, processing, transportation, and sales of agricultural products. In addition, nations should promote operations in an appropriate scale, appropriate urbanization, and vocational education in agricultural technology. In a word, agricultural modernization includes advanced production means, scientific production technology, industrialized operation, socialized agricultural services, regional industrial layout, and the overall modernization of agricultural infrastructure, ecological

息工业基础上发展智能工业这种增量资产，智能工业是以人脑智慧、电脑网络和物理设备为基本要素的新型工业结构，它具有绿色发展方式的增长形态。各国应着重扶持、培育企业核心和关键技术的研发创新、成果转化及产业化，应培植优势产业和主导产业，构建完善的产业链和现代化服务网络。三是各国应借助市场竞争，推动企业兼并收购、整合重组，不断淘汰旧工业，推进新型工业发展，将工业化推向更高水平，提升企业的核心竞争力。它是实现供给侧有效投资、新旧动力转换的重要手段之一。

其次，加快农业现代化。农业现代化指从传统农业向现代农业转化的过程和手段。在这一过程中，农业日益被现代化工业、现代化科学技术和现代经济管理方法武装起来。各国应运用现代化发展理念，将农业发展与生态文明建设结合起来，使落后的传统农业转化为符合当代世界先进生产力水平的生态农业。具体而言，农业现代化的内涵既包括土地经营规模的扩大化，又包括"农民的现代化"。各国应引导农民摆脱愚昧、落后状态，成为"有文化、有技术、会经营"的新式农民。以组织方式而言，不管是大农场，还是小规模家庭经营，各国都应扶持农民合作组织或帮助分散农户与市场对接，实现产前、产中、产后服务一条龙，以及购买生产资料、开展农产品储存加工运输和农产品销售的运营一条龙。此外，各国还应促进适度规模经营、适度城镇化，推进农业技术教育职业化等。总之，农业现代化包括农业生产手段先进化、生产技术科学化、经营方式产业化、农业服务社会化、产业布局区域化，以及农

environment, competency of agricultural laborers and farmers' lives. The modernization of agriculture can create a stable social environment for industrialization and urbanization, reduce social costs and prosper the economies across the world.

Second, to increase investments and construction of infrastructure, which includes three aspects:

Firstly, promoting new urbanization—The urbanization is characterized by overall coordinated urban and rural planning, urban and rural integration, industrial interaction, frugality and intensity, ecological livability and harmonious development. It is where large, medium-sized and small cities, small towns, and new rural communities mutually promote and develop coordinately. In developed nations, the urban population generally accounts for more than 80%. As the urban-rural integration accelerates and the city-centered urban pattern are formed across the world, planning and constructing new human-oriented towns, constructing facilities for basic urban public services such as education, medical treatment, culture, sports and others, as well as developing recreational tourism, business logistics, information industry, transportation and others, will provide new growth potential to the world.

Secondly, promoting the modernization of infrastructure—This includes the modernization of energy, transportation, environmental protection, information, irrigation and others. For example, promoting comprehensive urban transportation construction, building convenient regional transportation network; speeding up the construction of sponge cities to enhance the ability of urban disaster prevention and mitigation; building and improving the drainage and waterlogging prevention system to effectively eliminate the risk of urban waterlogging; promoting the treatment of urban black and odious water bodies, to improve the quality of the urban water resource environment; improving regional parkland to share a common green life; building urban utility tunnel for pipelines to operate orderly and efficiently; strengthening urban water supply facilities to guarantee the water supply security; optimizing orderly the urban energy supply to vigorously promote urban energy conservation and emission reduction; enhancing the efficiency of waste and sewage facilities to achieve resource conservation and recycling; enhancing the construction of information infrastructure to promote the development of intelligent cities; etc. The investment in this area has great room and potential, which can effectively promote economic growth across the world.

业基础设施、生态环境、农业劳动者水平和农民生活的全面现代化。农业现代化能为工业化和城市化创造稳定的社会环境，降低社会成本，繁荣各国经济。

第二，加大基础设施投资建设，这包括三方面：

首先，推进新型城镇化，它既是以城乡统筹、城乡一体、产业互动、节约集约、生态宜居、和谐发展为基础特征的城镇化，也是大中小城市、小城镇、新型农村社区协调发展、互促共进的城镇化。发达国家城镇人口一般占80%以上。随着各国城乡一体化进程的加速和以城市为中心的城镇体系的形成，以人为核心的新型城镇的规划与建设，城乡基本公共服务如教育、医疗、文化、体育等设施的建设，以及休闲旅游、商贸物流、信息产业、交通运输的发展等，都将为世界各国提供新的增长潜力。

其次，推进基础设施现代化。它包括能源、交通、环保、信息和农田水利等基础设施的现代化。比如促进城市综合交通建设，构筑区域便捷交通网络；加快推进海绵城市建设，增强城市防灾减灾能力；构建并完善排水防涝体系，有效解决城市内涝风险；推进城市黑臭水体整治，重塑城市水资源环境品质；健全区域公园绿地体系，共享绿色城市生活；构建城市地下综合管廊，统筹管线有序高效运作；加强城市供水设施建设，健全供水安全保障体系；有序优化城市能源供给，大力促进城市节能减排；提升垃圾污水设施效能，实现资源节约循环利用；提升信息基础设施建设，推动智能城市发展；等等。这方面的投资回旋空间大、潜力足，能有效推动各国经济增长。

Moreover, promoting the development and construction of intelligent cities—An intelligent city is a system, also known as a network city, digital city or information city. It is built upon human brain wisdom, computer network, physical equipment and other basic factors, which form intelligent urban management. It includes intelligent infrastructure like intelligent transportation, intelligent electric power, intelligent buildings, intelligent environmental protection, intelligent security; intelligent social life like intelligent medical treatment, intelligent education, and intelligent families; as well as intelligent social productions like intelligent enterprises, intelligent banks, and intelligent stores. Intelligent urban systems can comprehensively raise the modernization level of urban production, life, management and operation, and further open up a new route for economic growth across the world.

Third, to increase the investment in scientific and technological projects, such as the NNMI of the US, which invested USD 1 billion in the first phase and set up 45 manufacturing innovation institutes within 10 years; as well as "Knowledge Transfer Partnership" of the UK, and the Industry 4.0 for intelligent manufacturing based on CPS (Cyber-Physics System) of Germany. These measures can integrate the innovative resources of talents, enterprises and social institutions, guide the directions for industrial R & D, and promote industrial upgrading and development. Investments across the world in big data, cloud computing, the Internet of Things, NBIC (nanotechnology, biotechnology, information technology, cognitive science) and others, will upgrade economies across the world sustainably.

Fourth, to enhance financial support capacities: Nations not only need supporting policies to guide the financial industry to serve the real economy, but also need to promote the integration of finance, science and technology, and industries through the innovation of policies. The reform, innovation and development of the financial system are indispensable for investment in the new economic engine.

Building Up a New Engine for Global Innovation

For a region, a nation, or even the world, as they enter a transitional period of economic development mode, the economic form develops from industrial resources allocation through enterprise competition to urban resources allocation through government competition, and the engine of economic growth develops from a single market mechanism to an "effective government plus efficient market" mechanism. These new circumstances in global economic development would inevitably lead

　　再次，推进智能城市开发建设。智能城市是一个系统，也称为网络城市、数字化城市、信息城市。它由人脑智慧、电脑网络、物理设备等基本要素建构，推动城市管理智能化，具体包括智能交通、智能电力、智能建筑、智能环保、智能安全等基础设施的智能化，智能医疗、智能教育、智能家庭等社会生活的智能化，以及智能企业、智能银行、智能商店等社会生产的智能化。智能城市系统能全面提升城市生产、生活、管理、运行的现代化水平，将进一步为各国开拓新的经济增长点。

　　第三，加大科技项目投入。例如"美国制造业创新网络计划"，首期投入 10 亿美元，十年内建立 45 个制造业创新研究院；再比如英国的"知识转移伙伴计划"，以及基于信息物理系统推动智能制造的德国工业 4.0 战略。这些举措能整合人才、企业、社会机构的创新资源，引领产业研发方向，促进产业提升发展。世界各国对大数据、云计算、物联网等的投入，对 NBIC 即纳米技术、生物技术、信息技术和认知科学等的投入，将促进各国经济的可持续提升。

　　第四，提升金融配套能力。各国既需要配套政策，引领金融行业服务于实体经济，又需要通过政策创新，推进金融、科技、产业三者的融合。投资新引擎离不开金融体系的改革、创新和发展。

构建全球创新新引擎

　　无论是区域还是国家，乃至世界，当其进入经济发展模式的转换时期，经济形式从通过企业竞争配置产业资源发展到通过国家政府竞争配置城市资源，经济增长引擎从单一的市场机制发展到"有为政府＋有效市场"机制，这些全球经济发展的新情况必然导致一系列新问题，比如如何维护全球经济治理体系的公平、公正原则，

to a series of new problems, such as how to maintain the principles of fairness and justice in the global economic governance system, how to protect the interests of developing nations in the global economic order, how to maintain or enhance the degree of openness of the economic system in order to resist protectionism, and how to formulate norms to face challenges in new economic fields (such as the network). In order to combat these challenges, the existing public mechanisms or public goods (including ideological, material, organizational and institutional public goods) that coordinate and govern the global economic order need to be innovated and improved.

Firstly, we should promote the innovations of value public goods, that is, ideas. To begin with, the market should be an efficient market. The vertical modern market system is a complete system composed of six subsystems. Some nations over-emphasized the competition between market factors and market organizations, while neglecting the construction of the legal supervision system and the perfection of the market environment system and market infrastructure, which will deviate from the market principles of openness, fairness and justice. Moreover, the government should be an effective government. Governments across the world should not only plan, guide, support, coordinate, supervise and manage the allocation of operational resources, that is, industrial resources; but also ensure general underpinning and guarantee fairness and justice, and effectively upgrade non-operational resources, that is, social public goods. They should also adjust and compete in the allocation of quasi-operational resources, that is, urban resources. Furthermore, the mature market economic mode pursued across the world should be "strong effective government plus strong efficient market"; in the macro system of market economy, industrial resources should be allocated through enterprise competition, and urban resources through government competition. Governments across the world should play an important role in global economic growth.

Secondly, we should promote the innovations of material public goods, that is, technology. The most typical path for current developments in science and technology is the integration of informatization and industrialization, urbanization and agricultural modernization, to promote the modernization of infrastructure, which in Chinese, is termed "Internet+". Through building intelligent cities which combine tangible and intangible factors, governments provide intelligent public transport, urban management, education, medical treatment, cultural, commercial, government administration, environmental protection, energy and public

如何保护发展中国家在全球经济秩序中的利益，如何维持或提升经济体系的开放程度以抵制保护主义，如何制定规范、应对经济新领域（例如网络领域）的挑战。为了应对这些挑战，现存的协调、治理全球经济秩序的公共机制或公共物品（包括思想性、物质性、组织性和制度性公共物品），就需要予以创新和完善。

第一，推进思想性公共物品即理念的创新。首先，市场应是有效市场。现代市场纵向体系是由六个子系统组成的完整体系。一些国家过分强调市场要素与市场组织的竞争，而忽视法制监管体系的建设、市场环境体系和市场基础设施的健全，这都将偏离公开、公平、公正的市场原则。其次，政府应是有为政府。各国政府不仅应对可经营性资源即产业资源的配置实施规划、引导、扶持、调节、监督和管理，而且应对非经营性资源即社会公共物品基本托底，确保公平公正、有效提升，还应对准经营性资源即城市资源的配置进行调节并参与竞争。再次，世界各国追求的成熟市场经济模式应是"强式有为政府＋强式有效市场"，即在市场经济大系统中，通过企业竞争配置产业资源，通过政府竞争配置城市资源。各国政府应在全球经济增长中发挥重要作用。

第二，推进物质性公共物品即技术的创新。当前科技发展的最典型路径是信息化与工业化、城镇化、农业现代化融合，促进基础设施现代化，用汉语即"互联网+"。政府通过建设结合了有形要素与无形要素的智能城市，向社会提供智能化的公共交通、城管、教育、医疗、文化、商务、政务、环保、能源和治安服务，为社会经

security services to the society; and create a safe, efficient, convenient, green and harmonious development environment for the social economy and livelihood undertakings. These not only benefit people, but also accelerate industrialization transformation, urbanization and internationalization of cities and even nations, thus further promote the rise of emerging nations.

Thirdly, we should promote the innovations of organizational public goods, that is, management. As far as organizational management is concerned, there are similarities between that of a city, and that of a nation or even the world. Traditional urban construction and organizational frameworks, such as "urban sprawl", are prone to traffic lights failure, road congestion, traffic jam, air pollution, inefficiency, and other problems even if there are first, second, third, fourth, and even fifth ring roads. The development of modern cities requires grouped-layouts planned scientifically. Just as network development will reshape the spatial order and global supply chain development will "erase national boundaries", group-based urban development structure can effectively solve the series of problems brought about by traditional urban sprawl. Similar to the urban structure, the organization and management of the world economic order needs to reform from the urban sprawl mode towards the grouped-layout, and continuously innovate and develop; however, this requires corresponding new rules and necessary "infrastructure" investment, so that a rational layout can be formed to promote harmonious and sustainable development of the world.

Fourthly, we should promote the innovations of institutional public goods, that is, rules. The construction of a nation is guided by the triad of conceptual planning, urban and rural planning and land use planning. Within this framework, the specific policies on strategic planning, layout positioning, implementation criteria, policy evaluation, legal protection and others are systematically formulated with multiple layers. Global economic governance is framed by the Charter of the United Nations and the regulatory mechanisms of UNCTAD, the OECD and WTO. Nations around the world strive towards "making globalization bring more opportunities" and "sharing the fruits of economic growth in an all-inclusive manner". The importance of rules in global economic development is evident here. Faced with the current new circumstances, we should innovate thoughts on economic growth and relevant institutional rules, promote the structural reform of fiscal and monetary policies across the world, and maintain the consistency and coordination of economy, labor, employment and social policies. Only with equal

济和民生事业提供安全、高效、便捷、绿色、和谐的发展环境。这不仅能造福民众，还将推动城市乃至国家加快工业化转轨、城市化转型和国际化提升，进而促进新兴国家的崛起。

第三，推进组织性公共物品即管理的创新。就组织管理而言，小到一座城市，大到一个国家乃至世界，都有相通之处。传统的城市建设和组织框架如"摊大饼"，即使有了一环、二环、三环、四环甚至五环道路，仍然还容易发生红绿灯失效、公路堵塞、交通不畅、空气污染、效率低下等问题。现代城市的发展需要科学规划的组团式布局，这就像网络发展会重塑空间秩序、全球供应链发展能"抹掉国界"一样，组团式的城市发展架构能有效解决传统摊大饼式城市管理带来的系列问题。世界经济秩序的组织管理如城市架构一样，需要从摊大饼模式向组团式布局改革并不断创新发展，但这需要相应的新规则和必要的"基础设施"投资，才能形成合理布局，促进世界和谐、可持续发展。

第四，推进制度性公共物品即规则的创新。国家的建设有概念规划、城乡规划和土地规划这三位一体的规划系统作为引领，在这一框架下形成战略规划、布局定位、标准制定、政策评估、法制保障等既体系严谨又层次细分的具体方针。全球经济治理有《联合国宪章》以及联合国贸发会议、经合组织和世贸组织等的规章机制作为框架，世界各国围绕着"让全球化带来更多机遇"和"让经济增长成果普惠共享"而努力，可见规则在全球经济发展中的重要性。面对当前的新形势，我们需要创新经济增长理念和相关制度性规则，促进各国财政、货币的结构性改革，保持经济发展、劳动、就业和社会政策的一致与相互配合。只有需求管理和供给侧改革并

emphasis on demand management and supply-side reform, combination of short-term policies with medium-term and long-term policies, common progress of social economic development and environmental protection, and mutual consultation, establishment and sharing of the global economic governance layout, can the global economy achieve healthy and sustainable growth.

Building Up a New Engine for Global Rules

To build a "Four I's" world economy that is innovative, invigorative, interconnected and inclusive, improvements in the global economic governance system are needed. Corresponding to non-operational resources across the world are the international public goods supply systems; corresponding to operational resources across the world are the international industrial resources allocation systems; and corresponding to quasi-operational resources are the global urban resources allocation systems. They each operate in adherence to the rules which exist objectively. A sound global economic governance system requires corresponding international rules, as follows:

Firstly, the rules on international security order—peace and stability: This is a consensus across the world and the basic guarantee of the international public goods supply system. Nations across the world should strive together to strengthen international security cooperation, protect the purposes and principles of the Charter of the United Nations, maintain the basic criteria for international relations, create a peaceful, stable, just and reasonable international security order, and build a healthy and orderly environment for economic development.

Secondly, the rules on international economic competition—fairness and efficiency: This is the basic criterion for enterprise competition in the industrial resources allocation systems across the world. As an example, the G20 formulated the guiding principles of "promoting trade and investment openness", including reducing tariff and non-tariff barriers to trade, reducing barriers to and restrictions on foreign direct investment, implementing trade facilitation measures to reduce cross-border transaction costs, appropriately reducing border restrictions on trade and investment, promoting broader cross-border coordination, and minimizing discriminatory measures against the third party through multilateral, plurilateral and bilateral agreements, etc. As another example, the guiding principles of "promoting competition and improving the business environment", including strengthening and implementing competition law, reducing administrative and legal barriers for starting enterprises and expanding operations, promoting fair market

重，短期政策与中长期政策结合，社会经济发展与环境保护共进，共商、共建、共享全球经济治理格局，全球经济才能健康、可持续增长。

构建全球规则新引擎

构建创新、活力、联动、包容的"四 I"世界经济，需要完善全球经济治理体系。与各国非经营性资源相对应的是国际公共物品供给体系；与各国可经营性资源相对应的是国际产业资源配置体系；与各国准经营性资源相对应的是世界城市资源配置体系：它们各自遵循客观存在的规则运行。完善的全球经济治理体系需要相应的国际规则，具体包括：

第一，国际安全秩序规则——和平、稳定。这已是世界各国的共识，是国际公共物品供给体系的基本保障。世界各国应共同努力，加强国际安全合作，捍卫《联合国宪章》的宗旨和原则，维护国际关系的基本准则，营造和平、稳定、公正、合理的国际安全秩序，构建健康有序的经济发展环境。

第二，国际经济竞争规则——公平、效率。这是世界各国产业资源配置体系中企业竞争的基本准则。比如 20 国集团制定了"促进贸易和投资开放"指导原则，包括减少关税和非关税贸易壁垒，减少对外国直接投资的壁垒和限制，实施贸易便利化措施以降低跨境交易成本，适当减少贸易和投资的边境限制，促进更广泛的跨境协调，通过多边、诸边和双边协议最小化对第三方的歧视性措施等。再比如"促进竞争并改善商业环境"指导原则，包括强化及落实竞争法律，减少开办企业和扩大经营的行政及法律障碍，促进公

competition, implementing efficient bankruptcy proceedings, reducing restrictive provisions that hinder competition, reducing additional burdens on regulatory compliance, as well as effectively supervising regulatory policies, strengthening the rule of law, improving judicial efficiency, combating corruption, etc. All these are the rules on fairness and efficiency that need to be adhered to when nations guiding and standardizing enterprise competition across the world.

Thirdly, the rules on international common governance—cooperation and win-win situations: This is the basic criterion that must be adhered to by intergovernmental competitions in the urban resources allocation systems. Both tangible and intangible factors exist in urban resources. Amongst these, new urbanization, intelligent city development, and investments in the modernization of infrastructure with energy, transportation, environmental protection, information and water conservancy as the subjects, will be the new engine for economic growth across the world, which can bring about capital expansion, increase in employment, technological innovation, deepening of market, sustainable economic growth, social benefits, environmental improvements, enhancing of national strength and other effects. Due to differences in their pace of urbanization, policies and institutional arrangements, effects and competitiveness of investment-driven growth are different in different nations. However, the competitions between governments should be cooperative and sustainable so as to jointly enhance the global economic governance system and innovate the economic growth mode. The basic principle should be win-win cooperation. Building up an innovative, invigorative, interconnected and inclusive world economic system with win-win cooperation as its core, will promote sustained innovation in the growth mode, enhance the level of global economic governance, and thus benefiting various nations and the world.

平的市场竞争，实施高效的破产程序，减少妨碍竞争的限制性规定，减少额外的监管合规负担，并对监管政策进行有效监督，加强法治，提高司法效率，打击腐败，等等。这些无不是各国在引导、规范企业竞争时需要遵循的公平与效率规则。

第三，国际共同治理规则——合作、共赢。这是城市资源配置体系中政府间竞争所需要遵循的基本准则。城市资源存在着有形和无形两类要素，其中，新型城镇化，智能城市开发，对以能源、交通、环保、信息、水利等为主体的基础设施现代化的投资，将是世界各国经济增长的新引擎，能带来资本扩大、就业增加、技术革新、市场深化、经济可持续增长、社会受益、环境改善、国力提升等效果。由于各国城市化进程、政策举措和制度安排不一，其投资驱动增长的效果与竞争力不一。但政府间的竞争应该是合作竞争，应该是可持续发展的竞争，应该是共同提升全球经济治理体系的竞争和共同创新经济增长方式的竞争。其基本原则应是合作共赢。构建以合作共赢为核心的创新型、活力型、联动型和包容型世界经济体系，将促进增长方式的持续创新，提升全球经济治理水平，进而造福于各国，造福于世界。

APPENDIX   ON MICROECONOMICS, MEZZOECONOMICS, AND MACROECONOMICS

The traditional economics system is classified into microeconomics and macroeconomics. In my opinion though, the modern economics system should be classified into three branches: microeconomics, mezzoeconomics and macroeconomics. They are complementary, each with different focuses, forming a whole that manifests the roles, functions and codes of conduct of enterprises, regional governments and nations (including international economic governance organizations) with respect to resource allocations in the market economy.

1. Microeconomics

Microeconomics, as a branch of modern economics, regards single economic units (single producers, single consumers, single economic activities in the market) as its subject of research.

The fundamental problem in microeconomic research is how to allocate industrial resources. Its basic theory is that supply and demand determine the relative price. Its core idea is that free exchange tends to maximize the utilization of resources, under which case the allocation of resources is considered to be Pareto Optimality. Thus, the main areas of microeconomics encompass consumer choice, firm supply and income distribution, with the price theory as its core; hence, microeconomics, under many circumstances, is also called "price theory and its applications".

Microeconomics, which studies the economic behavior of individuals in the market and the corresponding economic variables, sets off from the scarcity of industrial resources and deems it the code of conduct for individuals to capitalize on the limited resources to the greatest possible extent so as to obtain maximum benefits and examine accordingly the conditions under which individuals maximize their benefits. The codes of conduct in commodity and labor markets are as follows: (1) Consumers choose commodities according to their prices to obtain the maximum utility or satisfaction from the commodities purchased with their limited income. (2) Manufacturers are the suppliers of goods and services, aiming to use minimum costs to produce the most output and obtain maximum profits. (3) The choices made by consumers and manufacturers are manifested through the supply and demand in the market and affect prices, the changes of which, in turn, coordinate the supply and

附录 关于微观、中观、宏观经济学

传统经济学体系划分为微观经济学和宏观经济学。我认为，现代经济学体系应界定为三脉：微观经济学、中观经济学和宏观经济学。它们各有侧重，互为补充，形成一个整体，揭示出企业、区域政府与国家（包括国际经济治理组织）在市场经济资源配置中的角色、作用和行为准则。

一、微观经济学

微观经济学又称个体经济学，是现代经济学的一个分支，是一门主要以单个经济单位（单个生产者、消费者和市场经济活动）作为研究对象的学科。

微观经济学研究的基本问题是如何决定产业资源配置，其基本理论是供求决定相对价格。其中心思想是，自由交换往往使资源得到最充分的利用，在这种情况下的资源配置被认为是帕累托最优。所以微观经济学的主要研究范围包括消费者选择、厂商供给和收入分配。其中心理论是价格理论，因此微观经济学在很多场合又被称为"价格理论及其应用"。

微观经济学研究市场中个体的经济行为以及相应的经济变量。它从产业资源稀缺这个基本概念出发，认为所有个体的行为准则是设法利用有限资源取得最大收益，并由此来考察个体取得最大收益的条件。在商品与劳务市场上存在如下行为准则：首先，消费者根据各种商品的不同价格进行选择，设法用有限的收入从购买的各种商品中获得最大的效用或满足。其次，厂商是各种商品及劳务的供给者，其目的在于用最小的成本，获得最大的产量和最多的利润。最后，消费者和厂商的抉择通过市场的供求关系表现出来，作用于价格，价格的变动反过来协调供求。因此，市场机制的作用、均衡

demand. It follows, therefore, that the effects of market mechanisms, the attainment of equilibrium prices, the optimal allocation of industrial resources, the failure of market mechanisms, the government intervention and others, are the main contents of microeconomic research.

The history of microeconomics can be traced back to Adam Smith's *Wealth of Nations* and Alfred Marshall's *Principles of Economics*. After the 1930s, the British economist Joan Robinson and the American economist Edward Hastings Chamberlin proposed the theory of equilibrium of the firm on the basis of Marshall's theory of equilibrium price. The proposals of the equilibrium price theory, the consumer behavior theory, the producer behavior theory, the equilibrium theory of the firm, welfare economics, and others, eventually defined the microeconomic system. (See Figure 1)

The development of microeconomics thus far, has roughly gone through four stages: the first stage was from the mid-17th century to the mid-19th century, which is the early or embryonic stage of microeconomics; the second stage was from the late 19th century to the early 20th century, which is the stage of neoclassical economics, when the foundation of microeconomics was laid; the third stage was from the 1930s to the 1960s, which is the establishment stage of microeconomics; the fourth stage was from the 1960s to the present day, which is the stage for further development, expansion and evolution of microeconomics.

The new developments in microeconomics in recent years are worth mentioning here:

(1) The new consumption theory, such as revealed preference, consumer choice under risks, "consumption being also household production", and others;

(2) The new theory of the firm, such as the nature of the firm, maximization models, principal-agent problem, internal organizational efficiency, non-optimizing theories, etc.;

(3) The non-equilibrium theory: Through investigating the real social

economy, especially that of developing nations, this theory reveals that over a given period of time, the economies of most developing nations, even of some developed nations, are in a state of non-equilibrium, which is an important question on, supplement to, and development of the equilibrium theory.

(4) The game theory rewrote microeconomics. *Theory of Games and Economic Behavior*, co-authored by John von Neumann and Oskar

价格的产生、产业资源的最优配置、市场机制的失灵及政府干预等，就成了微观经济学的主要研究内容。

微观经济学的历史渊源可追溯到亚当·斯密的《国富论》和阿尔弗雷德·马歇尔的《经济学原理》。20 世纪 30 年代以后，英国的罗宾逊和美国的张伯伦在马歇尔的均衡价格理论基础上，又提出了厂商均衡理论。而均衡价格理论、消费者行为理论、生产者行为理论、厂商均衡理论和福利经济学等的提出，则标志着微观经济学体系的最终确立。（见图 1）

微观经济学的发展迄今为止大体经历了四个阶段：第一阶段是 17 世纪中期到 19 世纪中期，这是早期微观经济学阶段，或者说微观经济学萌芽阶段。第二阶段是 19 世纪晚期到 20 世纪初叶，这是新古典经济学阶段，也是微观经济学的奠基阶段。第三阶段是 20 世纪 30 年代到 60 年代，这是微观经济学的建立阶段。第四阶段是 20 世纪 60 年代至今，这是微观经济学进一步发展、扩充和演变的阶段。

值得一提的是微观经济学近年的新发展，主要包括：

第一，新消费理论，包括显示偏好、风险条件下的选择问题、"消费也是家庭生产"理论等。

第二，新厂商理论，包括企业的性质问题、最大化模型与委托—代理问题、内部组织效率与非最大化厂商理论等。

第三，非均衡理论。该理论通过对现实社会经济的研究，特别是对发展中国家经济的研究揭示出，在某一特定时期内，大多数发展中国家甚至是一些发达国家的经济多呈现非均衡发展状态，这是对均衡理论的重要质疑、补充和发展。

第四，博弈论对微观经济学的改写。1944 年冯·诺依曼和摩根

Production Theory

Cost Theory

Enterprises' Product Supply

Theory of the Firm (Production)

Enterprises' Demand of Production Factors

Price Theory

Product Market Theory (Exchange)

Theory of Welfare Economics

General Equilibrium Theory

Perfect Monopoly Market

Oligopoly Market

Monopolistic Competitive Market

Perfectly Competitive Market

Factor Market Theory (Distribution)

Profit Theory

Interest Theory

Land Rent Theory

Wage Theory

Information Economics, Game Theory, Market Failure, Government Failure, etc.

Supply and Demand Theory

Consumers' Product Demand

Consumption Theory (Consumption)

Consumers' Supply of Production Factors

Cardinal Utility Theory

Ordinal Utility Theory

Revealed Preference Theory (Consumer Choice Under Risks)

Consumer Choice Under Certainty

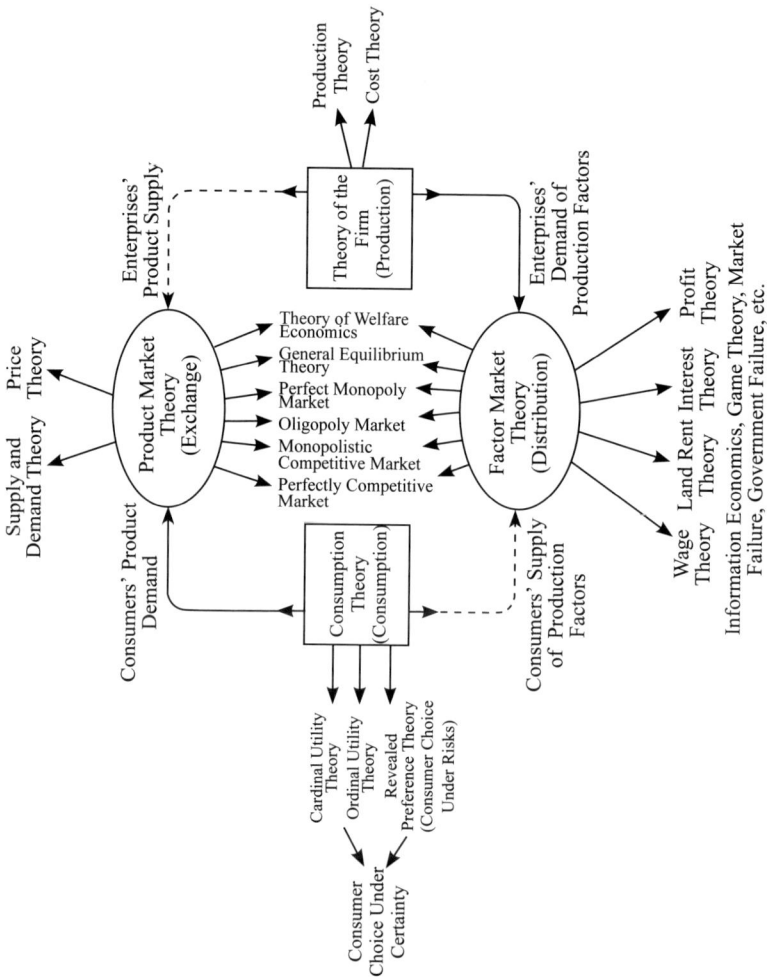

Figure 1   Microeconomics Theory System

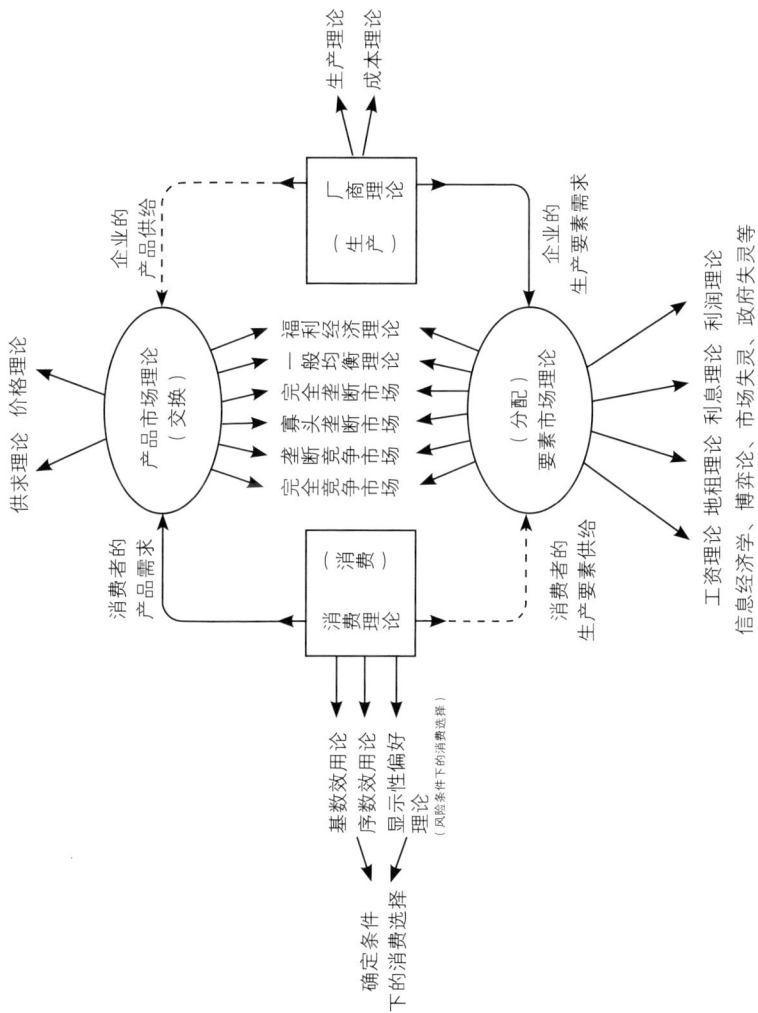

图 1 微观经济学理论体系

255

Morgenstern in 1944, signified the formal establishment of the economic game theory. After half a century, by 1994, when John Forbes Nash Jr., Reinhard Selten and John Harsanyi, the three major game theorists, shared the 1994 Bank of Sweden Prize in Economic Sciences in Memory of Alfred Nobel, the game theory had been substantially enriched and developed, and reshaped the exclusive theory of microeconomics. From Antoine Augustin Cournot, Joseph Bertrand to Edward Hastings Chamberlin, economists have come to realize that market competition in reality needs, in most cases, to be explained by the oligopoly theory, and that key empirical research on oligopoly market should be conducted under the framework of "structure-behavior-performance". Developed along this line, the theory of sunk cost, the incomplete information model, the theory of individual and collective rationality, the folk theorem and other analytical techniques, have raised market analysis in modern economics to a completely new level.

(5) The public choice theory: The public choice school, represented by James M. Buchanan, Jr., Gordon Tullock and others, pioneered the application of microeconomic principles to the analysis of the demand and supply of public goods.

(6) The new institutional economics (with the property rights theory as its main content): Since the 1970s, the new institutional economics established by John Kenneth Galbraith, Karl Gunnar Myrdal, Ronald Coase, and others, has further developed microeconomic theories by incorporating such concepts as institution, rules, property rights, social behaviors and human consciousness into research. For example, theories of property rights and firms as represented by Coase, pushed neoclassical economics forward. Subsequent to the 1980s, Douglass North pioneered the use of property rights theory to investigate the history of economics, which developed microeconomics to a new stage of institutional innovation and transformation.

(7) Information economics, which studies the individual's optimal

decision under circumstances of asymmetric information, including economic analysis under imperfect information with "information cost", optimized information search and economic analysis under asymmetric information as the core: Since the 1960s, the development of information economics, for example, the view that the value of information is basically expressed via non-convexity, has overturned not only some of Marshall's established theories, but also the existence of basic equilibrium in the

斯顿合作出版的《博弈论与经济行为》，标志着经济博弈论的正式创立。到 1994 年，纳什、泽尔滕和豪尔沙尼三位博弈论巨匠同获诺贝尔经济学奖，其间经历了整整半个世纪，博弈论得到很大的丰富和发展。它重塑了微观经济学的独占理论。从古诺、贝特朗到张伯伦，经济学家逐步认识到，现实中绝大多数市场竞争需要用寡占理论解释，应在"结构—行为—绩效"的框架中对寡占市场做重点实证研究。由此发展的沉没成本、不完全信息模型、个体理性与集体理性、佚名定理等多种分析技术，使现代经济学的市场分析跃升到一个新的境界。

第五，公共选择理论。以布坎南、塔洛克等为代表的公共选择学派，将微观经济学原理用于分析公共物品的需求与供给，开创了先河。

第六，新制度经济学（以产权理论为主体）。20 世纪 70 年代以来，由加尔布雷思、默达尔、科斯等人建立的新制度经济学将制度、规则、产权、社会行为与人的意识纳入研究范畴，发展了微观经济理论。例如，以科斯为代表的产权理论和企业理论推动了新古典经济学。20 世纪 80 年代以后，道格拉斯·诺思开创了运用产权理论研究经济史的先河，将微观经济学发展到制度创新与制度变革的阶段。

第七，信息经济学，即研究非对称信息下行为个体的最优决策问题，包括不完全信息下的经济分析——核心是"信息成本"和最优信息搜寻，以及非对称信息下的经济分析。20 世纪 60 年代以来，信息经济学的发展，如认为信息的价值基本上表现为非凸性等观点，既推翻了马歇尔的某些权威理论，又推翻了竞争市场存在基

competition market and other related theorems. Information economics has identified the limitations of traditional microeconomic theories, and further actively promoted the development of microeconomics in the late 20th century.

It should be said that as a branch of economics, microeconomics has reached relative maturity in terms of definitions, initiation of research, research contents, methodologies, analytic tools, development trends and internal configurations.

2. Mezzoeconomics

Mezzoeconomics is a branch of modern economics that mainly studies regional economic units and regional economic development[1]; hence, to a certain extent, it possesses connotations of regional economics and urban economics.

The subject of research in mezzoeconomics is regional government. Regional government behavior assumes the dual attributes of "quasi-macro" (compared with a nation, its focus is on "coordination") and "quasi-micro" (pursuing maximized regional interests, possessing certain corporate characteristics). It is precisely the dual attributes or dual roles of regional governments that remedy the defects in the traditional economics system or traditional market theory, and redefine the modern economics system and modern market theory. Modern market theory states that enterprises are subjects in market competitions, and so are regional governments. The modern economics system has also demonstrated that not only are there microeconomics which studies enterprises, and macroeconomics which studies nations (or the world), but there is also mezzoeconomics which studies regional governments.

The focus of mezzoeconomics is the allocation of urban resources. Governmental administration of regional economic activities is mainly manifested in the three main functions of economic development, urban construction, and social livelihood. Corresponding to economic development are industrial resources, which are operational resources; corresponding to urban construction are urban resources, which are quasi-operational resources (with both public welfare and commercial attributes); corresponding to social livelihood are public goods and public welfare resources, which are non-operational resources. Whether urban resources should be developed as public welfare goods or operated as commercial goods depends on the financial revenues and expenditures,

本均衡等相关定理。信息经济学认识到传统微观经济理论存在局限性，进而积极推动了 20 世纪后期微观经济学的发展。

应该说，作为经济学的一脉分支，从定义、研究起点、研究内容到研究方法、分析工具，再到发展趋势及其内在体系，微观经济学都已发展得相对成熟。

二、中观经济学

中观经济学是现代经济学的一个分支，是一门主要以区域经济单位和区域经济发展[1]作为研究对象的学科，因此它在一定意义上也具有区域经济学、城市经济学的内涵。

中观经济学研究的主体是区域政府。区域政府行为呈现准宏观（相对国家来说，强调的是"协调"）和准微观（追求区域利益最大化，存在一定的企业行为特征）的双重属性。正是区域政府的这种双重属性或双重角色，修正了传统经济学体系或传统市场理论的缺陷，书写了新的现代经济学体系和现代市场理论。现代市场理论告诉我们：不仅企业是市场竞争主体，区域政府也是市场竞争主体之一。现代经济学体系也已展示：不仅有以企业为研究主体的微观经济学和以国家（或全球）为研究主体的宏观经济学，还以区域政府为研究主体的中观经济学。

中观经济学研究的重点是城市资源配置。政府对区域经济活动的管理主要体现在经济发展、城市建设、社会民生三大职能上。与经济发展相对应的是产业资源即可经营性资源；与城市建设相对应的是城市资源即准经营性资源（其既有公益性一面，又有商业性一面）；与社会民生相对应的是公共物品、公益资源即非经营性资源。城市资源是按公益性产品来开发还是按商品性产品来经营，取决于

market demand, and affordability of the public of regional governments, and whether they are scientifically allocated also determines the competitiveness of the government in the regional market.

Mezzoeconomics thus studies regional governments' definition of the above three types of resources and their supporting policies, of which there are three key points: (1) Industrial, trade, and human resources policies correspond to operational resources (i.e., industrial resources), whose allocation principles should be "planning, guidance; support, coordination; supervision, management". Fiscal, financial, and investment policies correspond to quasi-operational resources (i.e., urban resources), whose allocation principles should be "abiding by market rules; maintaining economic order; participating in regional competition". Income, employment, and security policies correspond to non-operational resources (i.e., public welfare resources), whose allocation principles should be "general underpinning; fairness and justice; effective promotion". (2) Governments should lead foresightedly in resource allocation, that is, governments are to let enterprises do what they should do, and leave what they are unable to do or unable to do well to governments. Neither enterprises nor governments should be absent in the market. The foresighted leading by governments is to abide by market rules and rely on market to guide, coordinate and forewarn the industrial economy; to allocate, participate in and maintain the order of the urban economy; and to guarantee, underpin and promote the livelihood economy. Foresighted leading requires governments to use policies on planning, investment, consumption, pricing, taxation, interest rates, exchange rates, legislation, and others, and value, institutional, organizational, technological innovations and other measures, to effectively push forward structural reforms on the supply side or the demand side, forming a leading edge in economic growth and facilitating scientific and sustainable development of the region. (3) Value innovation plays a substantial role in driving the allocation of regional resources during the factor-driven stage; organizational innovation has multiplier effects on the allocation of regional resources during the investment-driven stage; institutional and technological innovations play decisive roles in the allocation of regional resources during the innovation-driven stage. Continuous all-round innovations in all factors throughout the process shall then promote the scientific and sustainable developments of resource allocations across all stages of regional development.

At the core of mezzoeconomics research is regional government competition, including competitions among regional governments in

各区域政府的财政收支、市场需求和社会民众的可承受程度，其配置的科学与否也决定了政府在区域市场中的竞争力大小。

中观经济学研究的内容是政府对三类资源的界定及政策配套，要点有三：第一，与可经营性资源即产业资源相配套的产业政策、贸易政策、人力政策等，配置原则应该是"规划、引导，扶持、调节，监督、管理"。与准经营性资源即城市资源相配套的财政政策、金融政策、投资政策等，配置原则应该是"遵循市场规则，维护经济秩序，参与区域竞争"。与非经营性资源即公益资源相配套的收入政策、就业政策、保障政策等，配置原则应该是"基本托底，公平公正，有效提升"。第二，政府对资源配置行为应"超前引领"，即让企业做企业该做的事，让政府做企业做不了或做不好的事，二者不能空位、虚位。政府的超前引领就是遵循市场规则，依靠市场力量，发挥对产业经济的导向、调节、预警作用，对城市经济的调配、参与、维序作用，对民生经济的保障、托底、提升作用。超前引领需要政府运用规划、投资、消费、价格、税收、利率、汇率、法律等政策和理念、组织、制度、技术创新等手段，有效推动供给侧或需求侧的结构性改革，形成经济增长领先优势，促进区域科学、可持续发展。第三，理念创新在要素驱动阶段对区域资源配置具有实质推动作用；组织创新在投资驱动阶段对区域资源配置具有乘数效应；制度与技术创新在创新驱动阶段对区域资源配置具有关键制胜作用；全方位、全过程、全要素的不断创新则在区域发展的各阶段均能促进资源配置科学、可持续发展。

中观经济学研究的核心是区域政府竞争，包括区域政府间的项

projects, supporting industrial chain, talents, science and technology, treasury and finance, infrastructure, import and export, environmental system, policy system, management efficiency, and others.

The basic assumptions and methods in mezzoeconomics research include: efficiency growth is the main goal of regional governments; improving total factor productivity is the main means by which regional governments compete; improving the supply-side structural reform is the basic direction for regional governments; optimizing the allocation of regional resources through planning to promote the sustainable development of regional social economy is the competition mode for regional governments. (See Figure 2)

Research in mezzoeconomics started rather late. In the mid-1970s, Dr. Hans-Rudolf Peters, German professor of national economics, first proposed the concept of "mezzoeconomy". In the mid-1980s, Chinese scholar Wang Shenzhi published *Mezzoeconomics* (Shanghai People's Press, 1988), which elaborated upon Peters' mezzoeconomy, and classified research subjects of mezzoeconomics into sector economy, regional economy and group economy. In 2011, I published *Foresighted Leading: Theoretical Thinking and Practice of China's Regional Economic Development*. In 2013, I co-published with Qiu Jianwei *Government Foresighted Leading: Theory and Practice of the World's Regional Economic Development*. In 2015, I co-published with Gu Wenjing *Mezzoeconomics: Innovations and Developments in Theoretical Configuration of Economics*. In 2017, I co-published with Gu Wenjing *On Regional Government Competition*. These publications have provided systematic expositions of foresighted leading by regional governments, the dual roles of regional governments, and the dual subjects in market competition, emphasizing that a mature market economy lies with the "strong effective government and strong efficient market". These theories have established the theoretical system of mezzoeconomics and clarified its prospects. The rational core in its theoretical system paves the way for economic development across the world and the construction of a new global economic governance system.

3. Macroeconomics

Being an independent theoretical system of economics, macroeconomics regards the activities in the overall process of national economy as its

目竞争，产业链配套竞争，人才、科技竞争，财政、金融竞争，基础设施竞争，进出口竞争，环境体系竞争，政策体系竞争和管理效率竞争等。

中观经济学研究的基本假设与方法包括：效率型增长是区域政府的主要目标；提高全要素生产率是区域政府竞争的主要手段；优化供给侧结构性改革是区域政府的基本导向；通过规划推动区域资源的最优配置，从而实现区域社会经济的可持续发展，是区域政府的竞争模式。（见图 2）

中观经济学的研究起步较晚。20 世纪 70 年代中叶，德国的国民经济学教授汉斯－鲁道夫·彼得斯博士首次提出"中观经济"的概念。80 年代中期，中国学者王慎之出版了《中观经济学》（上海人民出版社，1988 年）一书，阐述了彼得斯的中观经济理念，并把中观经济的研究对象概括为部门经济、地区经济和集团经济。2011 年，我出版了《超前引领——对中国区域经济发展的实践与思考》；2013 年，我与邱建伟出版了《论政府超前引领——对世界区域经济发展的理论与探索》；2015 年，我与顾文静出版了《中观经济学——对经济学理论体系的创新与发展》；2017 年，我与顾文静出版了《区域政府竞争》。这些著作系统地阐述了区域政府超前引领理论、区域政府双重角色理论、市场竞争双重主体理论、成熟市场经济是"强式有为政府＋强式有效市场"双强机制理论，确立了中观经济学的理论体系，阐述了它的发展前景。中观经济学理论体系中的合理内核，为促进各国经济发展、构建全球经济治理新体系探索了路径、指出了方向。

三、宏观经济学

作为经济学中的一个独立理论体系，宏观经济学以国民经济总过程的活动为研究对象，主要考察就业水平、国民收入等经济总量，

264

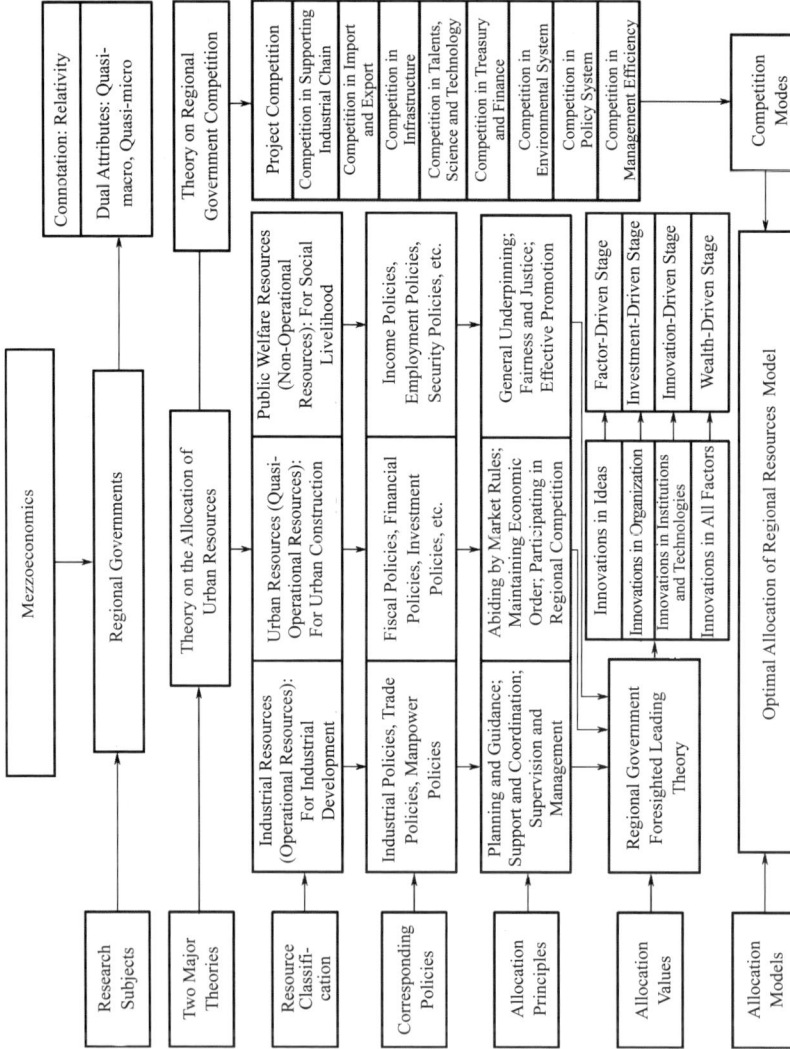

Figure 2 Mezzoeconomics Theory System

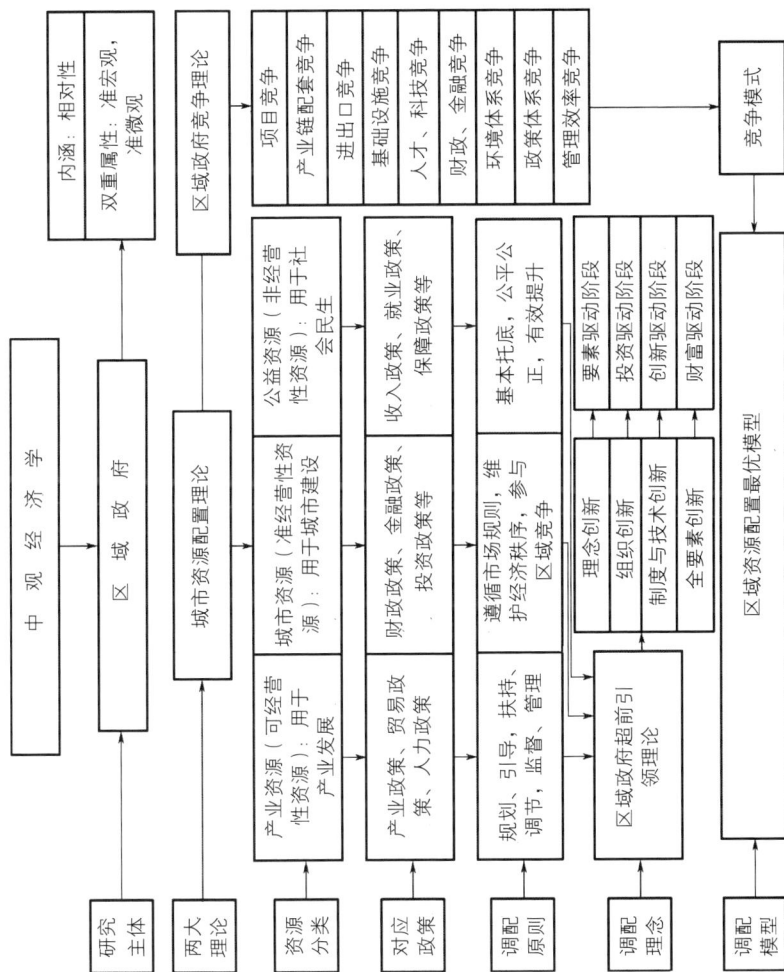

図 = 图2 中观经济学理论体系

研究主体：中观经济学 → 区域政府

内涵：相对性
双重属性：准宏观，准微观

两大理论：
- 区域政府竞争理论
- 城市资源配置理论

区域政府竞争理论：
- 项目竞争
- 产业链配套竞争
- 进出口竞争
- 基础设施竞争
- 人才、科技竞争
- 财政、金融竞争
- 环境体系竞争
- 政策体系竞争
- 管理效率竞争
→ 竞争模式

资源分类（城市资源配置理论）：
- 产业资源（可经营性资源）：用于产业发展
- 城市资源（准经营性资源）：用于城市建设
- 公益资源（非经营性资源）：用于社会民生

对应政策：
- 产业政策、贸易政策
- 财政政策、金融政策、投资政策等
- 收入政策、就业政策、保障政策等

调配原则：
- 规划、引导、扶持、管理
- 遵循市场规则，维护经济秩序，参与区域竞争
- 基本托底，公平公正，有效提升

调配理念（区域政府超前引领理论）：
- 理念创新
- 组织创新
- 制度与技术创新
- 全要素创新

调配模型（区域资源配置最优模型）：
- 要素驱动阶段
- 投资驱动阶段
- 创新驱动阶段
- 财富驱动阶段

图 2 中观经济学理论体系

research subject. It mainly examines economic aggregates such as the employment level, national income and others, and investigates the utilization of economic resources. Modern macroeconomics includes macroeconomic theories, macroeconomic policies and macro-econometric models. Macroeconomic theories mainly include theories of national income accounting and national income determination, which encompass theories on employment, inflation, economic cycles, economic growth and others.

Macroeconomics mainly studies economic growth, economic cycle, unemployment, inflation, national finance, international trade, etc. Research indicators are mainly national income, ratio of aggregate social consumption, savings and investment to national income, the amount and speed of currency circulation, price level, interest rates, population size and its growth rate, employment and unemployment rates, national budget and deficit, import and export trade, and balance of payment, etc. (See Figure 3)

Macroeconomics originated from the French economist François Quesnay's *Tableau Économique* and the British economist Thomas Robert Malthus' Theory of Population. In 1933, the Norwegian economist Ragnar Anton Kittil Frisch first put forward the concept of "macroeconomics". The subject grew rapidly after the publication of Keynes' *General Theory of Employment, Interest, and Money* in 1936, and was widely adopted across Western nations, serving the policy of state intervention in economy. Keynesian macroeconomic policies promoted economic growth to a great extent; however, state intervention in economy also caused problems.

Since its inception, macroeconomics has roughly evolved over four stages: The first stage was from the mid-17th century to the mid-19th century, which is the early or the classical macroeconomics stage. The second stage was from the late 19th century to the 1930s, which is the foundation stage of modern macroeconomics. The third stage was from the 1930s to the 1960s, which is the founding stage of modern macroeconomics. The fourth stage was from the 1960s onwards, which is the stage of further development and evolution.

The main views of modern macroeconomics include: (1) The acceleration principle suggests that to a certain extent, changes in investment are the causes and effects of changes in national income, from which the theory of interaction between "accelerator" and "multiplier" is derived. (2) The price problem discussed in macroeconomics is the

研究经济资源的利用问题。现代宏观经济学包括宏观经济理论、宏观经济政策和宏观经济计量模型。宏观经济理论主要包括国民收入核算理论和国民收入决定理论，其中内嵌了就业理论、通货膨胀理论、经济周期理论、经济增长理论等。

宏观经济学研究的主要内容包括经济增长、经济周期、失业、通货膨胀、国家财政、国际贸易等。研究指标主要是国民收入，社会总的消费、储蓄、投资占国民收入的比率，货币流通量和流通速度，物价水平，利率，人口数量及增长率，就业率和失业率，国家预算和赤字，进出口贸易和国际收支差额，等等。（见图 3）

宏观经济学来源于法国魁奈的《经济表》和英国马尔萨斯的"马尔萨斯人口论"。1933 年，挪威经济学家弗里施提出"宏观经济学"的概念。这一学科在 1936 年凯恩斯的《就业、利息和货币通论》出版后迅速发展起来，在西方各国得到广泛运用，为国家干预经济的政策服务。凯恩斯主义宏观经济政策相当大程度上促进了经济发展，但是，国家对经济的干预也引起了各种问题。

迄今为止，宏观经济学大体经历了四个发展阶段：第一阶段是 17 世纪中期到 19 世纪中期，这是早期或古典宏观经济学阶段。第二阶段是 19 世纪后期到 20 世纪 30 年代，这是现代宏观经济学的奠基阶段。第三阶段是 20 世纪 30 年代到 60 年代，这是现代宏观经济学的建立阶段。第四阶段是 20 世纪 60 年代以后，这是宏观经济学进一步发展和演变的阶段。

现代宏观经济学的重要观点包括：第一，加速原理，即在相当程度上，投资变动既是国民收入变动的原因，也是其结果，并由此衍生了"加速数"和"乘数"相互作用的学说。第二，宏观经济学讨论的

268

Macroeconomics

Theory of National Income Accounting → Understanding GDP and Its Concept → Nominal GDP Real GDP

Methods on Quantifying GDP → Expenditure Method / Income Method → Two Sectors: $Y = C + I$ / Three Sectors: $Y = C + I + G$ / Four Sectors: $Y = C + I + G + NX$

Income Identity: After Event $I =$ After Event S

Equilibrium Condition: Plan $I =$ Plan S

National Income Determination Theory

Short Run Analysis → Aggregate Demand → Product Market / Money Market / International Market

Aggregate Supply → Labor Market and Macro Production Function

45-Degree Line Model, IS-LM Model, Mundell-Fleming Model, AD-AS Model

Demand Management: Fiscal Policies, Monetary Policies

Supply Management: Income Policies, Manpower Policies, Employment Policies

Foreign Economy: Exchange Rate Policies, Trade Policies

Long Run Analysis → Economic Growth → GDP Growth → C, I, G, NX

Economic Cycle → Multiplier-Accelerator Model → Economic Fluctuation

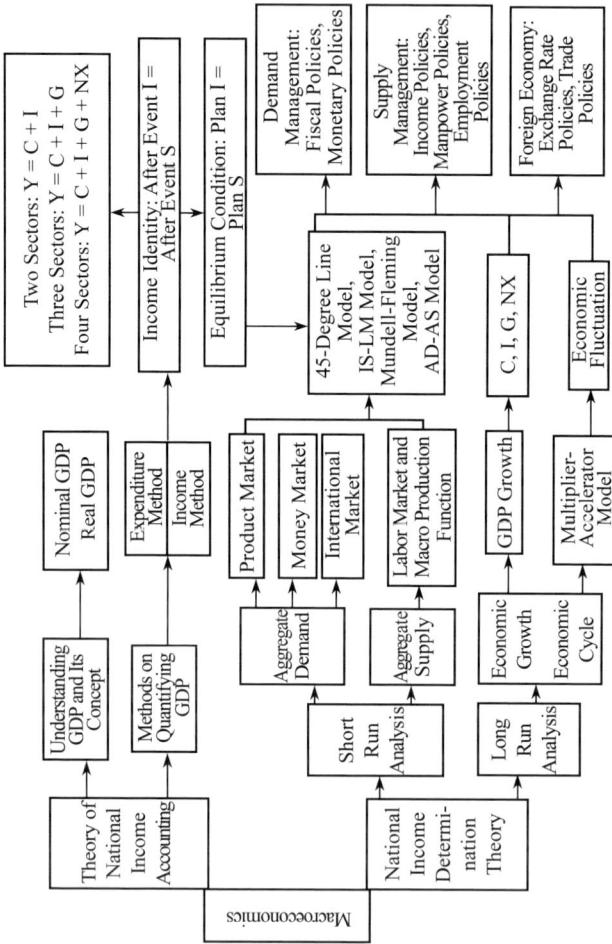

Figure 3 Macroeconomics Theory System

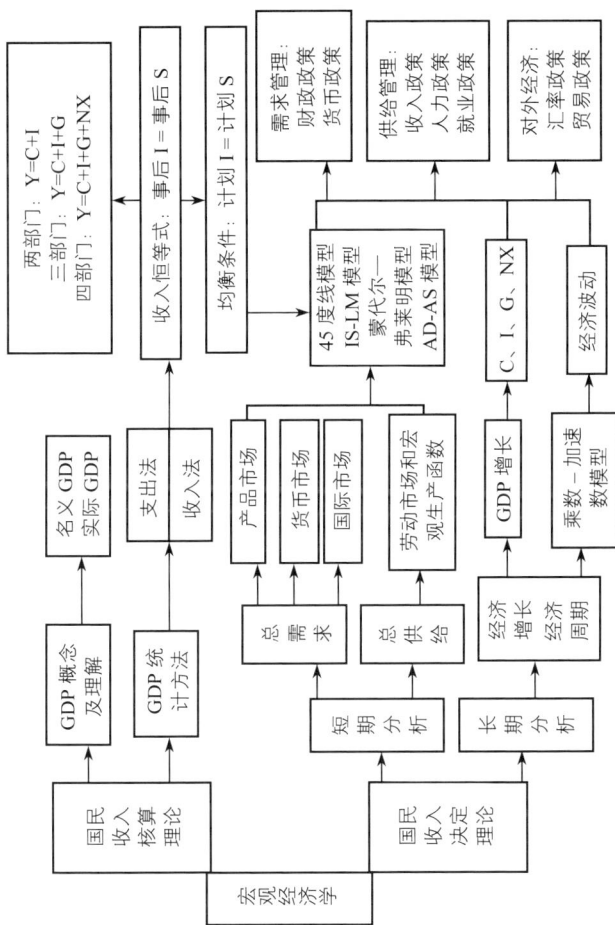

图 3 宏观经济学理论体系

宏观经济学

国民收入核算理论
国民收入决定理论

GDP概念及理解 → 名义GDP 实际GDP
GDP统计方法 → 支出法 收入法

短期分析
长期分析

总需求 → 产品市场 货币市场 国际市场
总供给 → 劳动市场和宏观生产函数

经济增长 → GDP增长 → C、I、G、NX
经济周期 → 乘数－加速数模型 → 经济波动

45度线模型
IS-LM模型
蒙代尔—弗莱明模型
AD-AS模型

两部门：Y=C+I
三部门：Y=C+I+G
四部门：Y=C+I+G+NX

收入恒等式：事后 I = 事后 S

均衡条件：计划 I = 计划 S

需求管理：财政政策 货币政策
供给管理：收入政策 人力政策 就业政策
对外经济：汇率政策 贸易政策

general price level. In the national income determination theory, the general price level depends mainly on the aggregate demand level, whilst changes in the aggregate demand level affect and are greatly affected by monetary supply and demand. Changes in monetary supply and total price level are closely related, hence monetary analysis plays an important role in macroeconomics. (3) It is believed in macroeconomics that governments should and in fact could adjust the aggregate demand through fiscal policies, monetary policies, and other measures so as to ease the periodical economic fluctuations and attain full employment without inflation.

There are still numerous defects in macroeconomics currently, which include mainly:

(1) Macroeconomics as it is currently, has not completely grasped the modern market system. Horizontally, the modern market system should include three levels of market—global, national, and state or provincial; vertically, it should include six subsystems: market factor system, market organization system, market legal system, market supervision system, market environment system, and market infrastructure. The modern market economy is a large and complete market system, and any theory attempting to explain this system without considering market segmentation is deemed to be short on vision and lacking in clarity on thoughts.

(2) Macroeconomics as it is currently, has a relatively narrow concept of "macro", which should include two levels: for provinces and cities, the nation is the macro level; for nations, the globe is the macro level. Wherein today, when the modern economic system has spread all over the "global village", to discuss a nation's macroeconomy regardless of its relations to and the impacts of the global economic system would clearly have too many defects.

(3) Macroeconomics as it is currently, needs a deeper understanding of the government and market combination modes. A mature market

economy should be an economy of "strong effective government plus strong efficient market". Effective government can be classified into three types: weak, semi-strong and strong; efficient market can also be classified into three types: weak, semi-strong and strong. The combination of effective governments and efficient markets can theoretically generate at least nine modes, but only "strong effective government plus strong efficient market" is the best mode for government and market combination. It is the goal for nations across the world in theory and

价格问题，是一般价格水平。在国民收入决定理论中，一般价格水平主要取决于总需求水平，而总需求水平的变动一方面影响货币的供求，另一方面也受货币供求变动的巨大影响。货币供给变动与总物价水平密切相关，因此，货币分析在宏观经济学中具有重要地位。第三，宏观经济学认为，政府应该而且也能够运用财政政策和货币政策等手段，调节总需求，既平抑周期性经济波动，又实现没有通货膨胀的充分就业。

现有的宏观经济学仍存在不少缺陷，主要包括：

第一，现有的宏观经济学对现代市场体系的把握还不够完整。从横向来看，现代市场体系应包括全球、国家、州市三个层次的市场；从纵向来看，应包括市场要素体系、市场组织体系、市场法制体系、市场监管体系、市场环境体系和市场基础设施六个子系统。现代市场经济是一个大而完整的市场体系，缺乏市场细分的学说会出现视野浅短、思辨不清的问题。

第二，现有的宏观经济学的"宏观"概念相对狭窄，它应包括两个层面：相对于各省市，国家属于宏观层面；相对于各国家，全球属于宏观层面。在现代经济体系已经遍及整个"地球村"的今天，脱离全球经济体系的联系与影响来谈一国经济的宏观性，显然有太多缺陷。

第三，现有的宏观经济学对政府与市场的组合模式的认识有待深化。成熟市场经济应该是"强式有为政府＋强式有效市场"经济。有为政府存在"弱式""半强式""强式"三种类型，有效市场也存在"弱式""半强式""强式"三种状况，二者的组合在理论上至少存在九种模式，只有"强式有为政府＋强式有效市场"，才是

practice, and should be explored profoundly in macroeconomics.

As such, it is increasingly urgent to reform and innovate macroeconomics. I think we can start with the following:

(1) Establishing the notion of a modern market system: Microeconomics mainly studies enterprises and focuses on the allocation of industrial resources, these being the first level of market economic activities. Mezzoeconomics mainly studies regional governments and focuses on the allocation of urban resources, these being the second level of market economic activities. Macroeconomics mainly studies (established) individual national subjects and (established and to-be-established intergovernmental) international economic institutions and focuses on the allocation, coordination and standardization of industrial, urban and public welfare resources, these being the third level of market economic activities. Macroeconomics should be based on the first and second levels of market economic activities, so as to formulate and improve the rules for market economic activities at the third level, which is the highest level.

Furthermore, at the national level, macroeconomics should focus on national income accounting and distribution theory, which includes a nation's macroeconomic fiscal policies, monetary policies, exchange rate policies and supervision policies. The national income generation and determination theory, and its corresponding policies on industries, trade, human resources, income, employment, social security, and others, should be placed into mezzoeconomics research.

(2) Establishing the path towards a mature market economy: A mature market economy combines strong effective government with strong efficient market. Regional governments have dual codes of conduct: pursing the maximized regional interests on the one hand, which requires them to participate in market competition, and coordinating super-regional interests on the other hand. Regional governments must also abide by market rules and maintain market order

whilst competing with each other in the market economic system. On the national front, macroeconomics must face and solve such problems as coordinating and standardizing regional government competition, establishing and improving legal and supervision systems and social credit system, in order to encourage them to compete fully in the market economy system, and achieve fairness, justice and win-win cooperation.

政府与市场组合的最佳、最高级模式。它是世界各国实践探索和理论突破的目标，也是宏观经济学必须认真面对、深化研究的课题。

因此，改革、创新宏观经济学的需要正日益迫切。我认为可以由下面几点入手：

第一，确立现代市场体系理念，即：微观经济学以企业为研究主体，研究重点在于产业资源配置，这是第一层面的市场经济活动。中观经济学以区域政府为研究主体，研究重点在于城市资源配置，这是第二层面的市场经济活动。宏观经济学以（既有的）单个国家主体与（既有及将有的政府间）国际经济机构为研究主体，研究重点在于产业资源、城市资源、公益资源的配置、协调与规范，这是第三层面的市场经济活动。宏观经济学应以第一层面和第二层面的市场经济活动为基础，建立健全第三层面即最高层面的市场经济活动规则。

进一步说，在国家层面，宏观经济学应侧重于国民收入的核算与分配理论，这包括一国的宏观财政政策、货币政策、汇率政策和监管政策等。而国民收入的产生和决定理论，以及与之相对应的产业政策、贸易政策、人力政策、收入政策、就业政策、保障政策等，应放到中观经济学研究的范畴中。

第二，建立成熟的市场经济路径。成熟市场经济是强式有为政府与强式有效市场相结合的经济。区域政府有双重行为准则：一方面追求区域利益最大化，需要参与市场竞争，另一方面需要协调超区域利益。区域政府在市场经济体系内相互竞争，也必须遵循市场规则、维护市场秩序。从国家的角度，宏观经济学必须面对和解决如何协调、规范区域政府竞争，如何建立健全法制监管体系、社会信用体系等问题，以鼓励各主体在市场经济体系内充分竞争，实现公平公正、合作共赢。

(3) Strengthening the importance of macroeconomic coordination in the international economy: Macroeconomics should focus on the macroeconomies at the international level, such as restructuring international economic governance institutions, innovating tools for international economic development, improving international economic regulatory standards and norms, and building up new engines at the global level for investment, innovation and regulation. This is where the significance of contemporary macroeconomics lies.

(4) Forging a new international economic order: That is, formulating corresponding international economic norms on competitions for the allocation of industrial resources across the world, based on the principles of fairness and efficiency; formulating corresponding intergovernmental governance rules on competitions for the allocation of urban resources across the world, based on the principles of win-win cooperation; formulating corresponding rules on international security order for the supply system of global public goods, based on the principles of peace and stability. In any case, to establish the global economic governance system of the "Four I's"—Innovation, Invigoration, Interconnection and Inclusiveness—in the global economy, a sound matching macroeconomics system is needed.

第三，强化国际经济宏观协调的重要性。宏观经济学应着重于国际层面的宏观经济，如改组国际经济治理机构，创新国际经济发展工具，健全国际经济监管标准与规范，构建全球层面的投资、创新和规则新引擎。这是宏观经济学在当代的意义所在。

第四，构建国际经济新秩序，即：遵循"公平与效率"原则，制定与各国产业资源配置竞争相对应的国际经济准则；遵循"合作与共赢"原则，制定与各国城市资源配置竞争相对应的政府间治理规则；遵循"和平与稳定"原则，制定与世界公共物品供给体系相对应的国际安全秩序规则。总之，要在世界经济中构建创新、活力、联动、包容的"四I"全球经济治理体系，需要与之相配合的完善的宏观经济学体系。

EPILOGUE

The book, *New Economic Engine—Effective Government and Efficient Market*, was finished in about three months, but my thoughts and explorations had lasted for more than ten years. It can be said that it is not only the result of my years of hard work, but also the fruit of our common wisdom.

In 2005, I served as Secretary of the Shunde District Committee of the CPC in Foshan City, Guangdong Province, which ranked first among more than 2,800 county economies in the country. Based on my experience accumulated whilst pursuing a Ph.D. in economics at Peking University, I took time off my busy schedule to explore the ideologies behind the mainstream schools of economics led by Adam Smith, John Maynard Keynes, and others, and proposed the idea of "Government Foresighted Leading (GFL)". In 2011, I published the monograph *Foresighted Leading* (later published in English by Springer, Germany). In 2013, I co-authored with Qiu Jianwei and published *Government Foresighted Leading: Theory and Practice of the World's Regional Economic Development* (later published in English by Routledge, UK). In 2015, I co-authored with Gu Wenjing to publish the monograph *Mezzoeconomics: Innovations and Developments in Theoretical Configuration of Economics* (later published in English by American Academic Press). And in 2017, I co-authored with Gu Wenjing again to publish the monograph *On Regional Government Competition* (later published in English by Routledge).

On the completion of this book, I would like to thank Qiu Jianwei and Gu Wenjing for our original cooperation, which has provided a solid foundation for this work. I would also like to thank the translator, Ethan Chung, for his efforts in translating this book, and thank Wu Hao from Beijing Foreign Studies University, and Yi Lu, Zhao Yaru and Shi Linan from Foreign Language Teaching and Research Press for their hard work in editing and publishing this book, whose meticulousness, rigorousness, willingness to discuss, and persistence have left an indelible impression on me. Special gratitude goes to my wife, Zhang Biying, for without her silent yet enduring companionship, encouragement, dedication and support, I could not have completed this research with my heavy work schedule.

后 记

《经济新引擎——兼论有为政府与有效市场》这本书，我用了三个月左右来撰写，但背后的思索、探讨过程则有十多年。可以说，它既是我多年辛劳的成果，又是大家共同智慧的结晶。

2005 年，我在广东省佛山市顺德区（在全国 2800 多个县域经济体中排名第一）任区委书记，因为在北京大学攻读经济学博士的积累，我在忙碌之余思索着亚当·斯密、凯恩斯等主导的主流经济学派的思想脉络，提出了"政府超前引领"理念。2011 年，我出版了专著《超前引领——对中国区域经济发展的实践与思考》（后在德国施普林格出版集团出版英文版）；2013 年，我与邱建伟合作出版了专著《论政府超前引领——对世界区域经济发展的理论与探索》（后在英国劳特利奇出版社出版英文版）；2015 年，我与顾文静合作出版了专著《中观经济学——对经济学理论体系的创新与发展》（后在美国学术出版社出版英文版）；2017 年，我再次与顾文静合作出版了专著《区域政府竞争》（后在英国劳特利奇出版社出版英文版）。

在《经济新引擎——兼论有为政府与有效市场》完成之际，我要感谢邱建伟、顾文静，我们原有的合作为这一著作提供了坚实的基础。感谢译者钟礼荣在本书翻译过程中付出的努力。感谢北京外国语大学吴浩和外语教学与研究出版社易璐、赵雅茹、石丽楠在本书编辑出版过程中付出的辛劳，他们一丝不苟、严谨认真、善于讨论、敢于坚持的工作作风让我印象深刻。更要感谢我的爱妻张碧莹，没有她长时间的陪伴、鼓励和默默无声的付出与支撑，我是不可能在繁重的工作之余完成这一研究的。

Many thanks to this great nation! Many thanks to this great era! This book is dedicated to the 40th anniversary of China's Reform and Opening Up.

Chen Yunxian

Guangzhou

May 19, 2018

感谢伟大的国家！感谢伟大的时代！谨以此书献给中国改革开放 40 周年。

陈云贤

羊城广州

2018 年 5 月 19 日

NOTES 注释

壹 CHAPTER 1

1 1 英里≈1.61 千米。

2 [英] 伊安·罗斯:《亚当·斯密传》(张亚萍译), 浙江大学出版社, 2013 年, 第 363, 384, 491 页。

Ian Simpson Ross. *The Life of Adam Smith*. New York: Oxford University Press Inc., 2010, pp. 240, 254, 333.

3 [英] 亚当·斯密:《国富论》(孙善春、李春长译), 作家出版社, 2017 年, 第 375—390 页。

Adam Smith. *An Inquiry into the Nature and Causes of the Wealth of Nations*. Chicago: University of Chicago Press, 1977, pp. 590, 593-594.

4 同上书, 第 608 页。

Ibid. pp. 963-964.

5 Robert L. Heilbroner. "Adam Smith", Encyclopedia Britannica, Jun. 13, 2019, https://www.britannica.com/biography/Adam-Smith.

贰 CHAPTER 2

1 John Maynard Keynes. *The Economic Consequences of the Peace*. New York: Skyhorse Publishing, Inc., 2016, p. 136.

2 John Wasik. "Keynes Answers His Critics", Forbes, May 30, 2013, https://www.forbes.com/sites/johnwasik/2013/05/30/keynes-answers-his-critics/#318b414e2a6b.

3 1 英亩≈4046.86 平方米。

4 转引自《日本专家:特朗普经济政策类似"罗斯福新政"》, 中国新闻网, http://www.chinanews.com/gj/2017/04-01/8189095.shtml, 2017 年 4 月 1 日。

See "Japanese Experts: Trump's Economic Policies Are like Roosevelt's 'New Deal'", China News, April 1, 2017, http://www.chinanews.com/gj/2017/04-01/8189095.shtml.

叁 CHAPTER 3

1 [美] 保罗·萨缪尔森、[美] 威廉·诺德豪斯:《经济学》(萧琛主译), 商务印书馆, 2013 年, 第 4 页。

Paul A. Samuelson and William D. Nordhaus. *Economics*. New York: McGraw-Hill/Irwin, 2010, p. 4.

肆 CHAPTER 4

1　陈云贤：《超前引领——对中国区域经济发展的实践与思考》，北京大学出版社，2011 年，第 15—32 页。

　　Chen Yunxian. *Foresighted Leading*. Beijing: Peking University Press, 2011, pp. 15-32.

2　陈云贤、邱建伟：《论政府超前引领——对世界区域经济发展的理论与探索》，北京大学出版社，2013 年，第 114—116 页。

　　Chen Yunxian and Qiu Jianwei. *Government Foresighted Leading: Theory and Practice of the World's Regional Economic Development*. Beijing: Peking University Press, 2013, pp. 114-116.

3　IMI 是一种产学研合作伙伴关系，由美国联邦或者地方政府支持成立。每个 IMI 组织都聚焦于特定的领域，重点是将公私资源结合在一起，营造更加有活力的国家创新生态系统，目标是更快地把发明转化成产品，同时加速中小企业的发展。

　　IMI is an industry-university-research partnership, which was set up under the support of the American federal government or state governments. Each IMI focuses on a certain area, combining public and private resources to create a more vigorous national innovative ecosystem. The aim is to accelerate the transformation of innovations into products and the development of medium-sized and small enterprises.

4　1 亩≈666.7 平方米。

5　陈云贤：《超前引领——对中国区域经济发展的实践与思考》，北京大学出版社，2011 年，第 128—131 页；《珠三角 辞三旧》，《人民日报》，2016 年 5 月 23 日。

　　Chen Yunxian. *Foresighted Leading*. Beijing: Peking University Press, 2011, pp. 128-131; "Pearl River Delta, Waving Goodbye to Outmoded Towns, Outmoded Factory Buildings, Outmoded Villages", *People's Daily*, May 23, 2016.

6　陈云贤：《超前引领——对中国区域经济发展的实践与思考》，北京大学出版社，2011 年，第 47—56 页。

　　Chen Yunxian. *Foresighted Leading*. Beijing: Peking University Press, 2011, pp. 47-56.

7　《广东省政府工作报告》，2016 年 1 月 25 日。

　　Report on the Work of the Guangdong Provincial Government, Jan. 25, 2016.

8　发达区域与欠发达区域的比较：在财政收入结构中，一般来说，欠发达区域的非税收入占比较高，稳定性较差，而土地出让收入和政府负债较高，发生急性财政风险的可能较大；在财政支出结构中，一般来说，欠发达区域用于经济发展的支出比重大，用于社会福利的支出比重小。发达区域与之相反。

Comparison between developed and underdeveloped regions: In the financial revenue structure, generally speaking, underdeveloped regions' non-tax revenue accounts for a large proportion, and is not stable, while land sale revenue and government debt are high, therefore there is a high chance of acute financial risk. In the financial expenditure structure, generally speaking, underdeveloped regions' expense on economic development accounts for a large proportion, while that on social welfare accounts for a relatively small proportion. With developed regions the opposite is the case.

[9] Henry Cabot Lodge, ed. *The Works of Alexander Hamilton*, Vol. 9. New York: G. P. Putnam's Sons, 1971, p. 224.

[10] ［美］埃里克·罗威：《货币大师——罗斯福和凯恩斯如何结束大萧条，打败法西斯，实现持久的和平？》（余潇译），中信出版社，2016 年，第 253—274 页。

Eric Rauchway. *The Money Makers: How Roosevelt and Keynes Ended the Depression, Defeated Fascism, and Secured a Prosperous Peace.* New York: Basic Books, 2015, pp. 183-202.

[11] 邵华铭、侯臣：《人民币国际化：现状与路径选择——以美元国际化历程为借鉴》，《财经科学》，2015 年第 11 期，第 23—33 页。

Shao Huaming and Hou Chen. "Internationalization of RMB: Status Quo and Path Choice—Taking the Internationalization of USD as an Example", *Finance & Economics*, No. 11 (2015): 23-33.

伍 CHAPTER 5

[1] Charles M. Tiebout. "A Pure Theory of Local Expenditures", *The Journal of Political Economy*, Vol. 64, No. 5 (1956): 416-424.

陆 CHAPTER 6

[1] 《是时候把航天当一门大生意来做了》，《南方日报》，2016 年 10 月 31 日。

"It Is an Opportune Time Now to Conduct 'Aerospace' as a Big Business", *Nanfang Daily,* Oct. 31, 2016.

[2] 顾昕：《重新认识市场失灵：诺奖得主斯蒂格利茨论产业政策》，澎湃，https://www.thepaper.cn/newsDetail_forward_1594001，2017 年 1 月 5 日。

Gu Xin. "Rediscover Market Failure: Stiglitz, the Nobel Laureate, Talks About

Industrial Policy", The Paper, Jan. 5, 2017, https://www.thepaper.cn/newsDetail_
forward_1594001.

3   同上。

Ibid.

柒 CHAPTER 7

1   "463"计划指从 2008 年开始，4 年内至少推动佛山 100 家企业实施股份制改造或
     正式启动上市程序，推动其中 60 家企业在境内外成功上市，融资总额力争达到
     300 亿元。

The "463" Plan: from 2008 on, to promote the shareholding system transformation
or launch of public listing of at least 100 enterprises within four years, and the
successful listing of 60 home or abroad, and to reach a gross financing of RMB 30
billion yuan.

2   《补充协议六》于 2009 年 5 月 9 日签署，并于当年 10 月 1 日正式启动，旨在进一
     步提高内地与香港的经贸交流与合作水平。根据协议，内地在法律、建筑、医疗、
     研究和开发、房地产、人员提供与安排、印刷、会展、公用事业、电信、视听、
     分销、银行、证券、旅游、文娱、海运、航空运输、铁路运输、个体工商户等 20
     个领域进一步放宽市场准入的条件。其中有很多具体措施在广东省"先试先行"。

The Supplement VI to CEPA, signed on May 9, 2009 and effective on Oct. 1 of
the same year, aims to further enhance the level of economic and trade exchanges
and cooperation between the mainland and the Hong Kong SAR. According to the
supplement, the mainland shall further relax the market access conditions in 20 areas,
namely, legal, construction, medical, research and development services, real estate,
placement and supply services of personnel, printing, convention and exhibition,
public utility, telecommunications, audiovisual, distribution, banking, securities,
tourism, cultural, maritime transport, air transport, rail transport and individually
owned stores. Many of the specific polices were piloted in Guangdong Province.

3   宋菁：《智慧佛山：分权逻辑下的转型路径》，《中国民营科技与经济》，2011 年第 7
     期，第 50—55 页。

Song Jing. "Intelligent Foshan: Path of Transformation Under the Logic of Power
Division", *China Nongovernmental Science Technology and Economy*, Vol. 7 (2011): 50-
55.

玖 CHAPTER 9

1   Joseph S. Nye. "The Kindleberger Trap", Project Syndicate, Jan. 9, 2017, https://www.

project-syndicate.org/commentary/trump-china-kindleberger-trap-by-joseph-s--nye-2017-01?barrier=accesspaylog.

2 李建平等主编:《二十国集团（G20）经济热点分析报告（2016—2017）》，经济科学出版社，2016 年，第 39—42 页。

Li Jianping, et al. eds. *Research Report on Economic Focuses of G20 (2016-2017)*. Beijing: Economic Science Press, 2016, pp. 39-42.

附录 APPENDIX

1 当然，区域是个相对概念，对全球而言国家是个区域，对国家而言省 / 市是个区域。因此，用中观经济学的视角去审视国家在全球经济中的竞争行为，也有助于深化新形势下的经济学研究。

The concept of "region" is of course a relative one: globally a nation is a region, while nationally a province or a city is a region. Therefore, to examine a nation's competition in global economy from a mezzoeconomics perspective would also deepen the economic research under new circumstances.